THE EPP METHOD

3 SUPER SIMPLE STEPS TO BUILD & RETAIN
ESSENTIAL VOCABULARY

MICHAEL CAVALLARO MA, AC

CONTENTS

Sign up for my email list to receive your FREE copy of **Vocabulary Building: Is It For Me? An E-Consultation Guide**. This free guide will explore...

- The sheer importance of building and developing your vocabulary for both natives and English language learners.
- Expert advice on developing vocabulary alongside other skills.
- How to find out your level of proficiency and practical strategies for quick and effective improvement.

"The limits of my language are the limits of my universe."

GOETHE

INTRODUCTION

Words have fascinated me for as far back as I can remember. There is something deeply enchanting about articulating your ideas through the perfect words that encapsulate what you intend to communicate.

Upgrading your vocabulary initiates you into a world of higher ideas and ideals. As your vocabulary grows, your thought processes become more refined and sophisticated. Knowing the right words helps you think and express yourself with great clarity.

As fascinated with words as I am, I had difficulty remembering new words in high school. Even though I was a reasonably decent student during those years, my vocabulary was nothing short of dismal.

Rote learning was my strategy of choice during that era of life. It would be no exaggeration to say that I was constantly let down by this method. My school offered extra help to students like me. We were handed these lists of seemingly unrelated words that were to be practiced with exercises that can only be described as shallow and disconnected.

I realized all too quickly that isolated, fragmented bouts of memorization attempts were the worst possible method you could employ for expanding your vocabulary. This disenchantment with the conventional methods of vocabulary building became my motivation for finding an efficient system that could help familiarize myself and others with new words and support long-term retention. After all, what is the point of learning about new words if you can't remember them or use them in your writing and conversations?

In the last 15 years, I have helped thousands of business professionals, aspiring ESL teachers, both ESL and native-born English students, and company employees in many different sectors build stronger vocabularies through the EPP method. Through this method, ANYONE can develop a more substantial vocabulary. If you aren't convinced right now, I promise you that you will be by the end of this book (provided you put in the effort and do the exercises, of course).

Those who plan to take tests like the SAT, TOEFL, GRE, or anything similar will benefit tremendously from this book. However, this book is for everyone interested in having a solid vocabulary. Maybe your goal is to advance in your career by becoming more articulate and expressive. Perhaps you want to expand your knowledge of words to comprehend them better when you are reading. Whatever your goal, this book is a trustworthy and invaluable companion for you.

We are going to use a method that is efficient and embedded in themes. There are 3 steps in the EPP method – Exposure, Practice, and Perfect.

Each chapter comprises words surrounding a central theme. There are 3 sections in each chapter.

The first one provides Exposure – new vocabulary words are presented meaningfully within a brief passage that begins every chapter, followed by definitions and sample sentences. Exposure is the most natural way of learning new terms: reading them. The Practice section requires you to recall the words you studied in section one. The Perfect section tests how well you understand the new words and your overall vocabulary retention. Vocabulary from previous chapters is recycled, which further fosters retention of the words you learn. Moreover, a pronunciation guide for pronouncing each word correctly is given. At its very essence, the EPP method places a tremendous emphasis on learning important vocabulary terms and retaining these words. As most vocabulary books overstuff their pages to fit in as many words as possible, I created this book to focus more on acquiring every word, providing thorough retention of the words covered.

In addition to this, I'm also offering you access to my online learning library, where you can use highly interactive tools and fun games to develop your vocabulary further.

If you are willing to do the work, you'll get the results. That's my guarantee to you!

Now, without wasting any time, let's get started!

Phonetic Pronunciation Table

	Consonants			Vowels
b	bag, barn, cob		a	can, apple, cat
d	does, ladder, wed		ey	day, hate, pray
f	frog, offer, fun		ah	arm, father
g	grow, bigger, log		air	air, care, wear
h	hair, hug, ahead		aw	all, talk, saw
j	jump, age, budget		e	get, ever, ahead
k	care, stick, spoke		ee	need, eat, bee
l	love, follow, real		eer	beer, hero, ear
m	move, summer, team		er	teacher, after, murder
n	no, thin, dinner		i	it, big, finish
ng	sing, think, wrong		ahy	ice, deny, hide
p	apple, puppy, pin		o	odd, hot, waffle
r	ring, marry, grip		oh	road, below, toad
s	city, purse, sale		oo	soop, food, ooze
sh	push, station, ship		oo	put, good, book
t	cat, tip, better		oi	toy, choice, oil
ch	nature, watch, witch		ou	now, out, loud
th	math, thirst, nothing		uh	up, mud, mother
th	mother, breathe, this		*uh*	about, animal, problem
v	seven, very, dove		ur	early, bird, stir
w	wear, away			
hw	where, somewhat			
y	yes, onion			
z	buzz, zoo, easy			
zh	beige, measure, television			

1

THE COMPLEXITY OF GENDER

Exposure Section 1: Words in Context

I REMEMBER IT CLEARLY. It was June of 2000.

Clinton was in the White House (about to embark on an epic pardoning spree), the Twin Towers still proudly marked the New York skyline, and the tin foil hat society of America emerged from their Y2K shelters, inundating a grassroots site called eBay with a decade's worth of Spam and distilled water.

I sat down in my living room with my basic cable connection on my 26-inch tube-style TV, surrounded by bags of cheese puffs my conspiracy theorist neighbor had brought over by the box. I guess she had deemed them artificial enough to survive the Apocalypse.

I agreed with her on that point.

I now flipped through the cable channels and settled on Must See TV. Alanis Morrisette, one of the iconic music stars of the past decade, would appear in one of the edgier, more sophisticated shows of the time, *Sex and the City*. I liked Alanis well enough, but I mainly just wanted to make fun of pop stars who thought they could act or properly use the word "ironic." (She couldn't do either, by the way).

In any event, Alanis played a character in a social group that we would now refer to as **pansexual**. There, lit up on my concave glass screen, were people who shrugged sexual identification off as irrelevant. Girls, boys, who cared? It didn't matter. Sex was sex, and people were people. The characters embarked on a retro game of Spin the Bottle, and there, on HBO, Sarah Jessica Parker kissed Alanis Morrisette.

Mainstream America was introduced to the long and winding road of gender complexity.

It is a long road that still has many shades of gray, is still being debated by doctors and pundits the world over, and is far from settled. But, in the process, this debate has filled our cultural lexicon with new words to describe these concepts.

Traditionally, gender has been regarded the same as one's sex – a binary system of categorizing humans as male or female. Being or exhibiting characteristics that were not fully male or female attracted a great degree of social stigma. Boys played with trucks, girls played with dolls, and that was the way the world worked.

Within the last decade, however, there has been a significant shift in society. People are now asked to embrace a more complex and dynamic nature of gender identity. Individuals that don't feel they fit these traditional models now have the language to express who they are, outside of a binary system of gender identity.

Gender is being redefined not as static or fixed but as fluid. It is being redrawn as a construct, created through one's interaction with the world, that can shift with time, circumstance, and language. Now, people can decide where they want to belong on the gender spectrum based on their own ideas of personal identity. Those that feel their identity does not match their reproductive anatomy can be described as **gender fluid**.

For instance, a **cisgender** person is someone whose gender identity is aligned with the sex they were attributed with at birth. On the contrary, a person with **gender dysphoria** is someone whose gender identity is not aligned with the sex they were assigned at birth.

To add to the complexity of being human, **bigender** is a term that permits the expression of an integrative combination of two gender identities (male and female).

Wherever one falls on the great debate over gender, it is now considered socially appropriate to understand the language and concepts of gender fluidity.

Exposure Section 2: Definitions & Example Sentences

Cisgender

(**sis-jen**-der) – (adj.) related to a person whose gender identity aligns with their assigned gender at birth.

A **cisgender** person (informally abbreviated cis) is, for example, someone who identifies as a woman and was assigned female at birth. The word cisgender is the antonym of transgender, used to describe someone who feels that they are the same gender (= sex) as the physical body they were born with.[1,2]

- Transgender individuals experience greater incidences of ridicule and discrimination than **cisgender** or gay men.
- "In a very real and measurable way, **cisgender** identity is no longer unmarked, universal, or assumed. It is denoted, limited, and in conversation with trans identities—or at least we're moving in that direction." -Hugh Ryan[3]

Gender dysphoria

(**jen**-der dis-fawr-ee-*uh*) – (n) psychological distress resulting from a sense of gender incongruence, i.e. being transgender.

Gender dysphoria is a condition that causes distress and discomfort when the gender you identify with conflicts with the gender that you were assigned at birth. You may have been assigned male at birth but feel that you're female, or vice versa—or you may believe yourself to be neither sex (nonbinary), something in between, or gender fluid.[4] In essence, the suffering associated with **gender dysphoria** is alleviated when an individual transitions.

- A person with **gender dysphoria** may choose to undergo hormone replacement therapy or gender confirmation surgery (formerly known as sex reassignment surgery).
- "People who don't have **gender dysphoria** aren't going to catch it by watching me dance on television." -Chaz Bono[5]

Gender fluidity

(**jen**-der floo-**id**-i-tee) – (n) a gender identity that is not fixed.

Someone who is **genderfluid** (also gender fluid, or, simply, fluid) is someone whose gender identity (the gender they identify with most) is not fixed. It can change over time or from day to day. **Genderfluid** is a form of gender identity or gender expression rather than a sexual orientation. **Gender fluidity** relates to how a person identifies themselves internally and presents themselves to the world. A person who is **genderfluid** may identify as male one day, female the next, both male and female, or neither. It affects their gender expression—the way a person presents themself to society (masculine, feminine, both, or neither).[6]

- Understanding **gender fluidity** helps us appreciate the complex nature of being human.
- "Do you prefer him or her? Either one's cool—I'm **gender fluid**." — Mvxx. Amillivn, Sappho Intl.[7]

Bigender

(bahy-**jen**-der) – (adj.) relating to a person who has two or more gender identities.

Bigender refers to a person who has two gender identities or a combination of two gender identities, e.g., identifying as both male and female or identifying as agender and female. It's not to be confused with bisexuality, where a person experiences romantic, emotional, or sexual attraction to two or more genders.[8]

- Being **bigender**, I can identify with gender specific roles either concurrently or with varying degrees at different times.
- "I am a queer, **bigender** immigrant from Eastern Europe to the US. My pronouns are they/them/theirs." -R.B. Lemberg, writer[9]

Pansexual

(pan-**sek**-shoo-*uh*l) – (adj.) a sexual orientation describing an attraction to individuals of all gender identities or in spite of gender identity.

Pansexuality is the attraction to people regardless of their gender. **Pansexual** people are sexually attracted to people of every gender identity and may sometimes refer to their romantic or sexual preferences as "gender blind." People of any gender identity can and do identify as **pansexual**. Some people use the terms "bisexual" and "**pansexual**" interchangeably, but there are distinctions between the two.[10]

- Most people find it hard to fathom how **pansexual** people can be sexually attracted to people of any gender or gender identity.
- "Who I'm with has nothing to do with sex—I'm super open, **pansexual**, that's just me." -Miley Cyrus[11]

Asexual

(ey-**sek**-shoo-*uh*l)– (adj.) lacking sexual attraction to others; (n.) a sexual orientation describing a lack of sexual attraction to others.

Some people consider asexuality to be their sexual orientation, and others describe it as an absence of sexual orientation. Asexual can also be an umbrella term that includes a broad spectrum of asexual sub-identities, such as demisexual, grey-A, queerplatonic, and many others. Asexual people may identify as cisgender, non-binary, transgender, or any other gender. [12]

- According to researchers, about 1% of the total human population is *asexual*.
- "Asexual people are not the same as heterosexual people who aren't having sex, which is what some misunderstand them as. There is a difference between an abstinent heterosexual person and an asexual person: abstinence is a practice (a choice), while asexuality is an orientation (not a choice—a familiar distinction for LGBTQ folks)." -Julie Sondra Decker[13]

Intersex

(**in**-ter-seks) – (adj.) relating to a person, animal, or plant having chromosomal patterns and/or sex characteristics that do not fit neatly within definitions of male and female.

Intersex is a general term used for various situations in which a person is born with reproductive or sexual anatomy that doesn't fit the boxes of "female" or "male." Sometimes doctors do surgeries on **intersex** babies and children to make their bodies fit binary ideas of "male" or "female." Doctors always assign **intersex** babies a legal sex (male or female, in most states), but, just like with non-**intersex** people, that doesn't mean that's the gender identity they'll grow up to have.[14]

- **Intersex** people face a lot of stigma and discrimination even in today's society.
- "While there is no shame in being gay, lesbian, bisexual, transgender or **intersex**—or even straight (but not narrow)—there is most certainly shame and dishonor in being a homophobe, a transphobe and a bigot." -Christina Engela, Blachart[15]

Aromantic

(ey-roh-**man**-tik) – (adj.) a romantic orientation describing a person who does not experience romantic attraction.

Aromantic people have little or no romantic attraction to others. They may or may not feel sexual attraction. An aromantic person can fall into one of two groups: **aromantic** sexual people or **aromantic** *asexual* people.[16] People who are **aromantic**, also known as "aro," don't develop romantic attractions for other people, but that doesn't mean they don't have feelings. **Aromantic** people do form strong bonds and have loving relationships that have nothing to do with romance.[17]

- Just because someone is **aromantic** doesn't mean that they don't have any feelings at all.
- An **aromantic** person may or may not feel sexual attraction toward others.

Practice Section 3: Fill-in-the-Blank

Fill in the blank with the correct word.

1. It's easy for [blank] Sarah to enjoy sexual relationships with men but she doesn't feel any romantic attraction toward anyone.

2. Since Matt is [blank], he dresses in a polo shirt and khakis when he's out with his friends, but he still speaks and acts in an effeminate manner.

3. Since Edward is suffering from [blank], he is taking the help of hormone replacement therapy to get his physical anatomy to better match how he feels inside.

4. I think we can safely assume the vast majority of people even in today's society are [blank].

5. [blank] has gained acceptance in mainstream society. People are no longer compelled to identify solely as male or female.

6. [blank] people possess a complex sexual anatomy with manifestations of both male and female sex characteristcs.

7. Sometimes I wonder if I am [blank] since I don't feel much excitement even when an extremely attractive woman shows interest in me.

8. [blank] people have a lot of options to choose from since they don't have strict preferences for any gender or gender identity.

Practice Section 4: Matching

Match each word with its correct definition.

1. Intersex   a. Interested in people of all genders

2. Cisgender   b. Gender identity shifting over time

3. Aromantic   c. When one's assigned gender at birth doesn't match the
                              gender with which they identify

4. Gender fluidity   d. No interest in sex

5. Pansexual   e. Identifying as two or more distinct genders at the same
                              time

6. Gender dysphoria   f. Gender identity matches that which was assigned at
                              birth

7. Asexual   g. Born with both male and female sex characteristics

8. Bigender   h. No interest in romance

Perfect Section 5: True or False

Test your understanding by deciding whether each of these statements is true or false.

1. Intersex people can identify as cisgender.
    ☐ True ☐ False

2. It's possible to be pansexual and bigender at the same time.
    ☐ True ☐ False

3. Gender fluid people can't suffer from gender dysphoria.
    ☐ True ☐ False

4. You can't be asexual and aromantic at the same time.
    ☐ True ☐ False

5. An aromantic person is completely incapable of getting into an intimate relationship.
    ☐ True ☐ False

6. Being intersex is entirely a biological condition.
    ☐ True ☐ False

7. An asexual person is physically incapable of performing the sexual act.
    ☐ True ☐ False

8. A cisgender man or woman is definitely not suffering from gender dysphoria.
    ☐ True ☐ False

Perfect Section 6: Drawing Conclusions

1. You read in the newspaper that a child was born with both male and female reproductive organs.
   That's an ▩▩▩▩▩ child.

2. You went on a date and realized that the person you are meeting is interested in both men and women.
   You have met a ▩▩▩▩▩ person.

3. Your friend tells you that she has never had a sexual thought in her entire life.
   She is ▩▩▩▩▩.

4. Your ex had absolutely no interest in romance or any of the typical relationship stuff.
   They are ▩▩▩▩▩.

5. You identify your gender as being the same as the sex you were born with.
   You are ▩▩▩▩▩.

6. Your favorite celebrity has started wearing gender-neutral clothing.
   They are promoting ▩▩▩▩▩.

7. You recently heard about a 39-year-old man who has started saying that he is a woman inside a man's body.
   That person is suffering from ▩▩▩▩▩.

8. You met a person at a nightclub who was interested in everyone – irrespective of their gender or gender identity.
   You can safely call that person ▩▩▩▩▩.

Section 3

1. Aromantic; 2. Bigender; 3. Gender dysmorphia; 4. Cisgender; 5. Gender Fluidity; 6. Intersex; 7. Asexual; 8. Pansexual

Section 4

1. g; 2. f; 3. h; 4. b; 5. a; 6. c; 7. d; 8. e

Section 5

1. True; 2. True; 3. False; 4. False; 5. False; 6. True; 7. False; 8. True

Section 6

1. Intersex; 2. Bigender; 3. Asexual; 4. Aromantic; 5. Cisgender; 6. Gender Fluidity; 7. Gender Dysphoria; 8. Pansexual

2

THE BESTIAL NATURE OF ANIMALS

Exposure Section 1: Words in Context

AS HUMANS, we have always been enamored with the animal king-dom. We create elaborate zoos and aquariums where we ride dolphins by hunching over their dorsal fins, and then we form near religions around anthropomorphic children's movies. If you're not sure about that, go into a parenting chat room and insult Simba and see what happens.

(On that note, who would have thought leonine family dysfunction was so much like our own? It just goes to show that if the singing lions can't get it together, the rest of us are pretty much screwed.) Then, the truly foolhardy among us attempt to tame the untamable, leading to some bizarre generational touchstones, albeit some pretty good TV. (What really happened to Carol Baskin's husband?)

All in all, animals fascinate us. They always have.

Sun Tzu wrote, "Only that which is the other, gives us fully unto ourselves." I quote that often and find it applies to many situations in life. It means we don't truly understand who or what we are until we understand who or what we aren't. Maybe that's where our fascination with animals comes from. It helps us to understand what we are.

We do, however, have a lot of similarities with animals. Many humans are probably even more **bestial** than animals themselves. (That's for you, my downstairs neighbors. Put the broom down!)

Here's, in a nutshell, what we know about animals.

We classify all living creatures using the eight-point taxonomic system of Kingdom, **Phylum**, Class, Order, Group, Species. This can be remembered with the acronym King Philip Came Over for Good Soup.

Animals are multicellular organisms inhabiting the kingdom known as Animalia. While there are a few exceptions, most animals feed on organic material, breathe atmospheric oxygen, and are capable of sexual reproduction. However, some can be *intersex* and have unique ways of reproducing.

Researchers have been able to identify and categorize more than 1.5 million animal species that are currently alive. Out of these, at least 1 million animals are insects. Researchers believe that in total, there are at least 7 million animal species now living on the planet.

The length of these animals ranges from 8.5 micrometers to 33.6 meters. Through their complex interactions with each other, animals help maintain the ecological balance of nature. They form an intricate food chain that directly impacts the well-being of our planet.

According to scientists, animal **husbandry** started somewhere around 13,000 BC when humans first began cultivating and domesti-cating animals, which predates the farming of the first crops. They learned to build **granaries** so that they could easily feed these animals.

It's not uncommon for animals in captivity to be **castrated** for steril-ity, less so for humans in modern times. It is worth noting that a castrated individual is not necessarily an *asexual* or *aromantic* one (just a depressed one).

Zoology is the field that deals exclusively with the scientific study of animals. Zoologists have developed classification systems that list organisms possessing similar traits and/or coming from a common ancestor under a particular category. For instance, an **anthropoid** is any animal that resembles humans or apes. (Again, my downstairs neighbors).

We also have specific words to describe qualities that belong to a particular animal species. For instance, the word **equine** describes anything related to horses or other members belonging to the horse family. This is where we get the word equestrian, and one of my cornier long-standing jokes, "Are you asking me an equestrian?"

Look at me—I'm not even a dad, and I've already got the dad jokes down.

Exposure Section 2: Definitions & Example Sentences

Anthropoid

(**an-**thr*uh*-poid) – (adj.) resembling humans; resembling an ape; apelike; of or relating to the suborder Anthropoidea.[18]

Anthropoid is formed from the Greek word for "human," anthrōpos, and the ending -oid, meaning "resembling." **Anthropoid** can describe fictional animals that look like humans, like the three bears in the Goldilocks story, standing upright and wearing their Sunday best. The word can also describe objects decorated to have human features, such as an **anthropoid** mask with a painted-on face--now there's a good insult for your great-aunt who wears too much make-up. Next time you require a subtle insult that will ultimately go over your oafish brother's head, accuse him of being barely **anthropoid**, or somewhat resembling a human.19

17

- Chimpanzees and gorillas are **anthropoid** apes possessing long arms, highly developed brains, and no tails.
- "No existing form of **anthropoid** ape is even remotely related to the stock which has given rise to man." -Henry Fairfield Osborn[20]

Bestial

(**bes**-ch*uh*l, **bees**-ch*uh*l) – (adj.) brutal or savage; sexually depraved; carnal; lacking in refinement; brutish; of or relating to a beast; like a beast in qualities or behavior; brutish or savage; brutal, coarse, vile, etc.; without reason or intelligence; brutal; inhuman.[22]

If you describe a behavior or situation as **bestial**, you mean that it is very unpleasant or disgusting.[21] **Bestial** sounds like "beast," and that is precisely what it means, beast-like. When a human acts like an animal, their behavior may be called **bestial**.[22]

- I'm disgusted by his **bestial** actions.
- "Art, like Nature, has her monsters, things of **bestial** shape and with hideous voices." -Oscar Wilde[23]

Castrate

(**kas**-treyt) – (v.) to remove the testicles of; to emasculate or geld; to deprive of vigour or masculinity; to spay; to render impotent, literally or metaphorically, esp. by threatening a person's masculinity or femininity; to deprive of strength, power, or efficiency; to weaken.[24]

People often choose to **castrate** pets or farm animals to keep them from reproducing. **Castrate** is one of several words used to refer to this process. However, most pet owners prefer terms such as neuter or fix.[25] **Castration** can also refer to humans, as we are, after all, animals ourselves; Italian classical singers, known as castrati, were once **castrated** as children to maintain their high angelic voices when otherwise puberty would have lowered them.

- Chemical **castration** employs drugs to lower the production of hormones in the testicles.
- "The elimination of the will altogether and the switching off of the emotions all and sundry, is tantamount to the elimination of reason: intellectual **castration**." -Friedrich Nietzsche[26]

Dorsal

(**dawr**-s*uh*l) – (adj.) on or relating to the upper side or back of an animal, plant, or organ.

Dorsal comes from Late Middle English, from late Latin dorsalis, originating from the Latin dorsum, meaning "back."[27] **Dorsal** commonly describes a body part situated on or toward the posterior plane in humans or the upper plane in quadrupeds.[28]

- After a day of strenuous physical activity, Tim needed a deep tissue massage to soothe his aching **dorsal** muscles.
- "Nereus spun and expanded, turning into a killer whale, but I grabbed his **dorsal** fin as he burst out of the water. A whole bunch of tourists went, 'Whoa!' I managed to wave at the crowd. 'Yeah, we do this every day here in San Francisco.'" -Rick Riordan[29]

Equine

(**ee**-kwahyn, **ek**-wahyn) – (adj.) of, relating to, or resembling a horse or the horse family.[30]

Many preteen girls go through what is chidingly referred to as a "horse girl" phase, wherein they develop an obsessive interest in all things **equine**—collecting books, dolls, posters, and more, sometimes partaking in actual horseback riding.[31]

- **Equine** therapy has become extremely popular these days as people are realizing the benefits of engaging in horse-related activities.
- "Sailing events are often held outside of land-locked host cities, and **equestrian** competitions were held in Stockholm in 1956 and Hong Kong in 2008 to avoid quarantine and other **equine** travel issues." -Jon Herskovitz[30]

Fodder

(**fod**-er) – (n.) coarse food for livestock, composed of entire plants, including leaves, stalks, and grain, of such forages as corn and sorghum; (figuratively) people considered readily available and of little value.[32]

- She wakes up early every morning to give **fodder** to her animals.
- "Today is the **fodder** of tomorrow's dreams, so we'd be wise to invest in today so that we don't show up with empty hands tomorrow." -Craig D. Lounsbrough[33]

Granary

(**grey**-n*uh*-ree, **gran**-*uh*-ree) – (n.) a building or storeroom for storing threshed grain, farm feed, etc.; a region that produces a large amount of grain.[34]

One clear way to remember the meaning of **granary** is that it sounds like what it is. If I were to ask you to invent a word that means "the place where grain is stored," you'd very likely come up with **granary** —though admittedly, the spelling is a little different. In the same way that wine comes from a winery, you'll find **granaries** filled the world over with, well, grain.[35]

- From the ruins of Harappa Civilization, it is evident that ancient **granaries** used to be made out of mud bricks.
- "Recognizing a problem may help us to understand and solve a problem. Rather than lying down and selling our sound judgment short, let us appeal to the opulent **granary** of our memory and explore the green pastures lingering in our mind." -Erik Pevernagie[36]

Husbandry

(**huhz**-b*uh*n-dree) – (n.) the cultivation and production of edible crops or of animals for food; agriculture; farming; the science of raising crops or food animals.[37]

Husbandry has nothing to do with being a husband and a lot to do with being a farmer. If you cultivate the land or breed animals, you are practicing **husbandry**.[38]

- The ranch employs a large number of animal **husbandry** staff to care for all the cows that are raised there.

- "There is, as yet, no sense of pride in the **husbandry** of wild plants and animals, no sense of shame in the proprietorship of a sick landscape. We tilt windmills on behalf of conservation in convention halls and editorial offices, but on the back forty we disclaim even owning a lance." -Aldo Leopold[39]

Leonine

(**lee**-*uh*-nahyn) – (adj.) of or pertaining to the lion; resembling or suggestive of a lion.[40]

Leonine means "like a lion" and is used primarily to describe men with a lot of hair on their heads or with big beards.[40] Its origin is Late Middle English from the name Leo, from Latin Leo for lion.[41]

- With his **leonine** face and plush mane of dark hair, Alex is nothing less than the epitome of courage and strength.
- "Be concentrated and **leonine** in the hunt for what is your true nourishment. Don't be distracted by blandishment-noises, of any sort." -Rumi[42]

Phylum

(**fahy**-l*uh*m) – (n.) a major taxonomic division of living organisms that contain one or more classes.[43]

An example is the phylum *Arthropoda*, which includes insects, crustaceans, arachnids, myriapods, and more.[43] In linguistics, the word **phylum** is used to refer to a group of closely related languages.[44] If someone asks you what you have in common with the Antarctic icefish, you can say that you both belong to the same **phylum**, meaning the same taxonomic group: you are both vertebrates.[45]

- Cows belong to a **phylum** known as *Chordata*.
- "For the smallest fry these are often rotifers, a **phylum** of tiny animals discovered in the late 17th century by early microscopists." -*The Economist*[46]

Ursine

(**ur**-sahyn) – (adj.) of, relating to, or resembling a bear or bears.[47]

Ursine means to have bear-like qualities: big, furry, muscular, and lumbering. If you're using the word to describe a big, hulking football player, it might be perceived as a compliment. You can also use this word to refer to actual bears. You might, for instance, study the **ursine** diet in biology class. **Ursine** originates back in the 16th century, coming from the Latin word for—you guessed it—bear.[48]

- Charlie told us about this **ursine** mythological creature that possesses the body of a bear and face of a man.
- "Barrett is a bigger guy, not fat (not yet) but **ursine**, crimson of eye and lip; ginger-furred, possessed (he likes to think) of an enchanted sensual slyness, the prince transformed into wolf or lion, all slumbering large-pawed docility, awaiting, with avid yellow eyes, love's first kiss." -Michael Cunningham[49]

Practice Section 3: Fill-in-the-Blank

Fill in the blank with the correct word.

1. All soft-bodied animals that don't possess a backbone are classified under _____ mollusc.

2. _____ are buildings specially designed for the long-term storage of food grains.

3. He has been engaged in animal _____ for more than a decade.

4. A man's testosterone levels go down significantly after undergoing _____

5. Late into the night, we heard a bone-chilling _____ roar.

6. A _____ dictator like him doesn't deserve any respect.

7. They needed someone with experience in _____ care to work at the horse stable.

8. Tom decided to opt for an _____ Halloween costume since he has always been fascinated with bears.

9. In the case of dolphins, their _____ fins are located on their slippery backs.

10. _____ are highly intelligent creatures that often also know how to use stones and sticks as tools.

11. She bought a large bag of _____ to feed her cows.

Practice Section 4: Matching

Match each word with its correct definition.

1. Equine	a. Back side of an animal
2. Bestial	b. Human-like
3. Husbandry	c. Storehouse for grains
4. Leonine	d. Food for animals
5. Castrate	e. Bear-like
6. Ursine	f. Taxonomic classification of animals in groups
7. Anthropoid	g. Lion-like
8. Phylum	h. Cultivating animals
9. Fodder	i. Horse related
10. Granary	j. Cruel and depraved
11. Dorsal	k. To remove testicles

Perfect Section 5: True or False

Test your understanding by deciding whether each of these statements is true or false.

1. An organism's phylum is strongly correlated with its physiological and anatomical characteristics.
   ▢ True ▢ False

2. Cooked food can also be stored inside a granary.
   ▢ True ▢ False

3. Humans can also eat fodder.
   ▢ True ▢ False

4. There is nothing ursine about Winnie the Pooh.
   ▢ True ▢ False

5. Breeding of farm animals (including dogs, cattle, sheep, and horses) can be classified as animal husbandry.
   ▢ True ▢ False

6. Castrated men can't get an erection and engage in sexual activity.
   ▢ True ▢ False

7. No human being is capable of bestial actions.
   ▢ True ▢ False

8. An equine saddle is something you would use to ride a horse.
   ▢ True ▢ False

9. Thanks to their dorsal shells, turtles can protect themselves from predators and other environmental threats.
   ▢ True ▢ False

10. The three bears of the Goldilocks story that stand upright and wear their Sunday best can be described as Anthropoids.
    ▢ True ▢ False

11. If someone calls you leonine, it means you resemble a tiger in some way.
    ▢ True ▢ False

Perfect Section 6: Pronunciation

Match each word with its correct phonetic pronunciation.

1. Dorsal	a. **ee**-kwahyn
2. Husbandry	b. **fahy**-l*uh*m
3. Leonine	c. **an**-thr*uh*-poid
4. Ursine	d. **kas**-treyt
5. Equine	e. **huhz**-*buh*n-dree
6. Fodder	f. **bees**-ch*uh*l
7. Castrate	g. **dawr**-s*uh*l
8. Bestial	h. **lee**-*uh*-nahyn
9. Anthropoid	i. **ur**-sahyn
10. Phylum	j. **grey**-n*uh*-ree
11. Granary	k. **fod**-er

Section 3

1. Phylum; 2. Granary; 3. Husbandry; 4. Castrate; 5. Leonine; 6. Bestial; 7. Equine; 8. Ursine; 9. Dorsal; 10. Anthropoid; 11. Fodder

Section 4

1. i; 2. j; 3. h; 4. g; 5. k; 6. e; 7. b; 8. f; 9. d; 10. c; 11. a

Section 5

1. True; 2. False; 3. False; 4. False; 5. True; 6. False; 7. False; 8. True; 9. True; 10. True; 11. False

Section 6

1. g; 2. e; 3. h; 4. i; 5. a; 6. k; 7. d; 8. f; 9. c; 10. b; 11. j

3

THE PHENOMENON OF SLEEP

Exposure Section 1: Words in Context

ANDY WARHOL WAS one of the more intriguing characters in the modern era. In case art history class found you **somnolent** (or otherwise **comatose**, particularly by way of self-prescribed **soporifics**), Warhol was the one that did the Campbell's Soup paintings and the pieces of Marilyn Monroe in reverse color. (As such, he was the original inventor of the filter, so it seems. Eat that, Instagram). He is also credited for creating the cliche "fifteen minutes of fame" by stating, "In the future, everyone will be world-famous for fifteen minutes."

It's unfortunate that he never lived to see the rise of reality TV and YouTube stars. (It's also unfortunate that the rest of us did). Warhol's other cultural contributions included the advent of the art film. One of the more famous (or infamous depending on your view) was the 1964 film *Sleep*. It's five hours of his boyfriend sleeping. He called it art. His generation called it hippie-dippie granola bovine excrement.

We call it Facebook Live.

In any event, *Sleep* was an attempt to understand the mystery that happens during those unconscious hours. (At least that's my interpretation of it, and according to my art teachers, that's all that matters because I'm a special little snowflake).

In studying the brain and chemical reactions, sleep is one of nature's more curious phenomena, and scientists don't fully understand it.

Scientifically, sleep is a state of physical and mental restfulness in which humans, animals, anthropoids, and even insects regularly engage. It's interesting to note that various creatures experience sleep differently. For instance, equine sleep patterns are significantly different from what humans are used to. Horses can function perfectly even with only three hours of sleep every day, and ursine sleep habits include extended periods of hibernation.

During sleep, sensory and muscular activities are inhibited to a large extent. While experiencing REM (Rapid Eye Movement) or deep sleep, almost all voluntary muscular activity is suspended.

The distinction between sleep and wakefulness lies in a person's ability to react to stimuli. During the waking hours, a person is highly responsive to stimuli, while the ability to respond to stimuli reduces significantly when a person is sleeping. However, while sleeping, one remains more reactive than a **comatose** person.

Sleep occurs in regular cycles wherein the body alternates between two different stages: REM and non-REM sleep. We enter REM sleep around 90 minutes after falling asleep. The first REM cycle lasts for about 10 minutes. Each REM cycle gets progressively longer—the final one might last up to one hour. Most of our dreams occur during REM sleep. So, if you **dozed** off for just half an hour, then you likely didn't experience REM sleep, which is not to say that getting our share of **forty winks** isn't essential!

While we are asleep, most of our body systems enter an anabolic state which helps restore the nervous, immune, muscular, and skeletal systems. Our internal circadian rhythm helps in retaining a regular sleep schedule. Any disturbance caused to the body clock results in disrupted sleep or **insomnia** wherein you find it difficult to fall or stay asleep.

This is, of course, the primary purpose of certain politicians appearing on 24-hour news channels, to cure the nation's insomniacs. (Who says Rupert Murdoch doesn't give back?!)

Exposure Section 2: Definitions & Example Sentences

Comatose

(**kom**-*uh*-tohs) – (adj.) of, resembling, a coma or a coma-like state; characterized by lethargic inertness and torpidity; (informally) very tired or in a deep sleep because of extreme tiredness, hard work, or too much alcohol.[50, 51]

The word **comatose** originates from the Greek kōma meaning "deep sleep." When you're in a deep sleep, your body is still, and you don't respond to things around you. Being **comatose** means being in that sleepy, unresponsive state and not able to get out of it. Less serious use of this adjective is as a description for getting really tired while doing or watching something, like when you feel **comatose** after a chemistry lecture—assuming chemistry's not your thing—or after overindulging in a holiday turkey dinner.[52]

- The rescue officers found some victims in a disoriented state while others were **comatose**.
- "Having a perilous adventure is always better than **comatose** safety. Always, always, always, always, always." - James Alan Gardner[53]

Doze

(dohz) – (n.) a short sleep, especially during the day; (v.) to have a short period of sleep, especially during the day.[54]

- She **dozed** off right after lunch.
- "An ant on the move does more than a **dozing** ox." -Laozi[55]

Forty winks

(**fawr**-tee wingks) – (n.) informally, a short sleep or nap; a short sleep during the day.[56, 57]

- After an exhausting morning, she needed her share of **forty winks** to feel energetic and functional again.
- "A **forty winks** nap in a horizontal posture, is the best preparative for any extraordinary exertion of either." -Dr. William Kitchiner[58]

Insomnia

(in-**som**-nia) – (n.) a sleep disorder in which one has difficulty falling and/or staying asleep.

Insomnia as a condition can be short-term (acute) or can last a long time (chronic). It may also come and go. Acute **insomnia** lasts from one night to a few weeks. Insomnia is chronic when it happens at least three nights a week for three months or more.[59]

- His guilty conscience was making his **insomnia** worse every day.

- "That's the advantage of **insomnia**. People who go to bed early always complain that the night is too short, but for those of us who stay up all night, it can feel as long as a lifetime. You get a lot done." -Banana Yoshimoto[60]

Reverie

(**rev**-*uh*-ree) – (n.) a state of imagining or thinking about pleasant things, as if you are dreaming.[61]

A **reverie** is an absentminded dream while awake. For example, if you're relaxing on the beach, dreaming of how you will never have to get up and go back to work, you're engaged in a **reverie**, a pleasant daydream.[62]

- She was lost in **reverie** while watching the sunset.
- "**Reverie** is when ideas float in our mind without reflection or regard of the understanding." -John Locke[63]

Somnambulist

(som-**nam**-by*uh*-lizt) – (n.) a person who suffers from somnambulism (= a condition in which a person walks around while they are sleeping).[64]

Somnambulism comes to us from the Latin *somnus* ("sleep") + *ambulō* ("to walk").[65]

- Apparently, it's very dangerous to try to wake up a **somnambulist**.

- "It gave me no hope to see him doing these simple things with the sluggishness of a **somnambulist**. It proved nothing more than that he could go like this forever, our silent accomplice, little more than a resuscitated corpse." -Anne Rice, *The Vampire Lestat*[66]

Somnolent

(**som**-n*uh*-l*uh*nt) – (adj.) inclined to or marked by drowsiness.[67]

If you're **somnolent**, you're feeling sleepy or drowsy, from the Latin word somnolentia, meaning sleepiness, which in turn is from the Latin root somnus, for sleep.67 It's best to avoid operating speed boats or motorcycles in such a state. An adjective describing an object, **somnolent** applies to something likely to induce sleep, like a boring movie in an overheated theater or the low, **somnolent** lighting in a museum exhibit of fragile, old illuminated manuscripts.[67]

- Christine gently placed the **somnolent** baby in her crib.
- "Nevertheless, there can be but few of us who had never known one of these rare moments of awakening when we see, hear, understand so much everything in a flash before we fall back again into our agreeable **somnolence**." -Joseph Conrad[68]

Soporific

(sop-*uh*-**rif**-ik, soh-p*uh*-**rif**-ik) – (n.) a drug that induces sleep; (adj.) sleep inducing; inducing mental lethargy.[69]

Something **soporific** is sleep-inducing. Certain medicines, but also extreme coziness, can have a soporific effect. In the 1680s, **soporific,** which doubles as both adjective and noun, was formed from the French soporifique. That word, in turn, came from the Latin sopor or "deep sleep." Beloved Peter Rabbit author Beatrix Potter once noted, "It is said that the effect of eating too much lettuce is **soporific.**"[69]

- No one seemed to be interested in the professor's **soporific** lecture.
- "Most people use music as a couch; they want to be pillowed on it, relaxed and consoled for the stress of daily living. But serious music was never meant to be **soporific**." -Aaron Copland[70]

Hebetudinous

(heb-i-**tood**-uh-nuhs, heb-i-**tyood**-uh-nuhs) – (adj.) lacking mental and physical alertness and activity.[71]

- The teacher was growing weary of the **hebetudinous** student's lack of curiosity and interest in his studies.
- "The leaden weight of an irremediable idleness descended upon General Feraud, who having no resources within himself sank into a state of awe-inspiring **hebetude**." -Ruth Walker, *The Christian Science Monitor*[72]

Practice Section 3: Fill-in-the-Blank

Fill in the blank with the correct word.

1. For someone with ▒▒▒▒▒▒, it is not unusual to get only a few hours of sleep every night.

2. Feeling extremely ▒▒▒▒▒▒, it was impossible for the artist to get out of bed and finish his artwork.

3. Many poets and writers have gotten their greatest ideas while lost in a state of ▒▒▒▒▒▒.

4. The heavy lunch had a ▒▒▒▒▒▒ effect on all the guests.

5. My neighbor has to keep their doors locked at night to prevent their ▒▒▒▒▒▒ grandmother from venturing out in her sleep.

6. After a busy morning, the captain handed over the boat to his first mate and went down for his ▒▒▒▒▒▒.

7. The movie was so boring that most people ▒▒▒▒▒▒ off.

8. Most people are ▒▒▒▒▒▒ as they have no sense of higher purpose in life.

9. The relaxing atmosphere on the beach made her ▒▒▒▒▒▒.

Practice Section 4: Matching

Match each word with its correct definition.

1. Forty winks	a. Pleasant daydream
2. Reverie	b. Inability to sleep
3. Somnambulist	c. Light sleep
4. Somnolent	d. A sleep walker
5. Comatose	e. Sleep inducing
6. Doze	f. Dull and lethargic
7. Soporific	g. Short nap
8. Insomnia	h. In a coma-like state
9. Hebetudinous	i. Almost asleep

Perfect Section 5: True or Fale

Test your understanding by deciding whether each of these statements is true or false.

1. A medically comatose person can respond to painful stimuli.
   ☐ True ☐ False

2. A somnambulist walks around in his sleep.
   ☐ True ☐ False

3. Deep sleep can also be classified as dozing off.
   ☐ True ☐ False

4. Being hebetudinous implies a good habit that you have.
   ☐ True ☐ False

5. Forty winks refers to a short nap, taken especially during the day.
   ☐ True ☐ False

6. A soporific lecture is stimulating and interesting.
   ☐ True ☐ False

7. An insomniac struggles with falling asleep.
   ☐ True ☐ False

8. You are fast asleep when you are somnolent.
   ☐ True ☐ False

9. You can have scary experiences while you are lost in a reverie.
   ☐ True ☐ False

Perfect Section 6: Drawing Conclusions

1. For 2 nights in a row, you have been struggling to close your eyes even for a brief moment.
   You're afraid you are turning into an ⬚⬚⬚⬚.

2. You look out your window at midnight and find Aunt Margarent wandering the neighbourhood in her nightgown like a zombie.
   Aunt Margaret has started ⬚⬚⬚⬚.

3. The poem was so beautiful that while listening to it, you lost all sense of space and time. It's like you were transported into a different reality.
   You slipped into a ⬚⬚⬚⬚.

4. Every day around 2 pm, you start feeling a slump in energy. You need to take a short nap to revitalize yourself.
   You have a ⬚⬚⬚⬚ off ritual reserved for each afternoon.

5. Tom speaks in such a monotonous tone that you can't prevent yourself from yawning.
   Tom has a ⬚⬚⬚⬚ tone and style of speaking.

6. After a tiring journey, you are half asleep on your way back home.
   You are ⬚⬚⬚⬚.

7. Most people live life like zombies—they just eat, sleep, drink, and take the path of least resistance.
   Most people are living life in a ⬚⬚⬚⬚ state.

8. You feel refreshed after taking a short nap.
   ⬚⬚⬚⬚ is a refreshing therapy.

9. You are feeling enraged by the mental dullness and lack of curiosity that some of your peers display.
   You are finding it hard to tolerate your ⬚⬚⬚⬚ peers.

Section 3

1. Insomnia; 2. Hebetudinous; 3. Reverie; 4. Soporific; 5. Somnambulist; 6. Forty winks; 7. Doze; 8. Comatose; 9. Somnolent

Section 4

1. g; 2. a; 3. d; 4. i; 5. h; 6. c; 7. e; 8. b; 9. f

Section 5

1. False; 2. True; 3. False; 4. False; 5. True; 6. False; 7. True; 8. False; 9. False

Section 6

1. Insomniac; 2. Somnambulating; 3. Reverie; 4. Dozing; 5. Soporific; 6. Somnolent; 7. Comatose; 8. Forty winks; 9. Hebetudinous

4

HEALTHY EATING, EXERCISE, AND HYPOCHONDRIACS

Exposure Section 1: Words in Context

SOME YEARS BACK, I had a friend going through a nasty divorce. She had a newborn baby, and he left her high and dry, with nothing. She and the baby ended up living with her parents while she tried to **resuscitate** her marriage. It was no use. He was done.

One night, she was home alone with the baby and began experiencing severe abdominal pain. Within minutes, she was doubled over on the living room floor, with pain so intense she couldn't even crawl to the phone. She stayed like that all evening, until some hours later, her parents returned home. They found her curled up on the floor, with the baby left screaming in the crib. They rushed this young mother to the emergency room, and she was diagnosed with kidney gallstones. The doctors told her she needed an expensive surgery that she could not afford.

Over the next several months, she worked up some **pell-mell** strategy to pay for the surgery. The strategy didn't work, and she still had regular pain flare-ups. It wasn't long before I began to notice a pattern to these flare-ups. They always came when she was thinking about, discussing, or dealing with her ex-husband. I suggested this to her, and she was shocked to realize that it was true.

I began to research and found a book from Louise Hay called *You Can Heal Your Life*. She explains that our bodies respond to our emotional life. Often, when people have health problems, they can be traced back to unresolved emotional turmoil or trauma. If the emotional component can be dealt with, then the physical manifestation of it often heals.

I explained this to the young mother. Since she didn't have money for the surgery, she gave the theory a chance. She began instituting boundaries with her ex-husband both in her actual life and her mental life. Within weeks, the gallstone flare-ups disappeared. Seven years later, they still have not returned. It was the beginning of my journey into the study of holistic health.

In holistic health, sickness or disease is a state of unease. Medicine is used to bring the body and mind back in balance. This is the yin and yang theory from Taoist philosophy. There is no sickness or health, only balance or imbalance of the body's energies.

Western medicine often uses **palliative** drugs, providing only so much relief as they lack curative power. Eating healthy, exercising regularly, and simply spending time in a **salubrious** (health-promoting) atmosphere are the most powerful measures one can employ to restore health.

Sickness and disease can be fully prevented by developing a thorough understanding of how the human body works. The body's needs are simple but should be met with regularity and care.

Cardiovascular health is a crucial component of staying healthy. Ignoring this can lead to myriad health problems. Some consequences of ignoring heart health include diabetes, heart attack, or stroke. While people can recover from a stroke, they are sometimes impaired with conditions like **aphasia**, in which they have a hard time speaking or comprehending meaning. Keeping a regular cardiovascular fitness routine throughout your life will help you to avoid these conditions.

Apart from maintaining a healthy diet and a regular exercise regime, following a regular sleep schedule is absolutely critical. If you must pull off an all-nighter, then don't forget to catch your *forty winks* in the daytime. But don't make a habit out of this. Staying awake late into the night isn't good for your health. Benjamin Franklin is credited as saying, "Early to bed and early to rise, makes a man healthy, wealthy, and wise."

Coffee and wine have become cultural staples, but these can have adverse effects on the body. The effects of too much alcohol are well-documented, but excessive amounts of caffeine are also known to cause **vertigo**. There are fewer things scarier than the entire room moving, yet you are sitting still. (Or are you? Hmmm...)

Fitness and positive attitudes are also vital to a healthy life. **Hypochondriacs** neither truly enjoy life nor good health because they are perpetually worried about falling sick. They keep obsessing over the idea of falling sick until their fears transform into self-fulfilling prophecies.

Whenever you find yourself getting worried about diseases, remind yourself that the body is an incredible machine that knows how to heal itself. Isn't it amazing how even the deepest **lacerations** and biggest wounds heal on their own over a certain span of time?

Exposure Section 2: Definitions & Example Sentences

Aphasia

(*uh*-**fey**-zh*uh*) – (n.) a communication disorder that makes it difficult to use words.[73]

Aphasia can affect your speech, writing, and ability to understand language. **Aphasia** results from damage or injury to language parts of the brain. It's more common in older adults, particularly those who have had a stroke. **Aphasia** gets in the way of a person's ability to communicate, but it doesn't impair intelligence. People who have **aphasia** may have difficulty speaking and finding the "right" words to complete their thoughts.[73]

- Doug developed **aphasia** right after getting a stroke last year.
- "Since so much of our identity is constructed through our social relationships, which rely so heavily on language, **aphasia** can obliterate that feeling of belonging." -Debra Meyerson[74]

Hypochondria

(hahy-p*uh*-**kon**-dree-*uh*) – (n.) a state in which a person continuously worries about their health without having any reason to do so; excessive concern about one's health especially when accompanied by imagined physical ailments.[75, 76]

- Mary turned into a **hypochondriac** after her mother's death.
- "After obsessively Googling symptoms for four hours, I discovered 'obsessively Googling symptoms' is a symptom of **hypochondria**." -Stephen Colbert[77]

Laceration

(las-*uh*-**rey**-sh*uh*n) – (n.) a kind of tear-like wound or cut within the skin or flesh that is open and may be deep, caused by a blunt impact to soft tissue; an injury in the form of a cut owing to separation of connective tissues; the act of lacerating; the result of lacerating; jagged tear or wound.[78, 79]

- It will take a while for the **laceration** to heal completely.
- "Most self-**laceration** is more noisy than painful." -Mason Cooley[80]

Palliate

(**pal**-ee-eyt) – (v.) to lessen the severity, especially that of pain or disease, without curing or removing; alleviate; mitigate; to make appear less serious or offensive; excuse; extenuate.[81]

Palliate is the word to use when you want to make something feel or seem better. **Palliate** doesn't mean "cure" or "solve." Instead, something that **palliates** relieves the symptoms or consequences of something without addressing the underlying cause. Your dentist might give you pain-killing drugs to **palliate** the discomfort caused by an impacted molar, but that molar is still there, waiting to cause more trouble.[82]

- Allopathy is great at **palliative** care.
- "I **palliate** the sufferings of others. Yes I see myself as softening the blows, dissolving acids, neutralizing poisons, every moment of the day. I try to fulfill the wishes of others, to perform miracles. I exert myself performing miracles." -Anaïs Nin[83]

Pell-mell

(**pel**-mel) – (adv.) in a jumbled, confused mass or manner; without order or method; in wild, disorderly haste; headlong; (n.) a jumble; confusion; disorder; (adj.) with undue hurry and confusion.[84, 85]

When things are messy, wacky, crazy, and all over the place, they are **pell-mell**—chaotic. If your room is a mess, with clothes everywhere, it's **pell-mell**. If people are running in every direction and yelling, that's a pell-mell situation. Whenever things are out of hand, off the hook, and chaotic, that's, well... **pell-mell**.[85]

- As soon as the bell went off, the students ran **pell-mell** toward the doors.
- "Let us to't **pell-mell**. If not to Heaven, then hand in hand to Hell." -William Shakespeare[86]

Prophylactic

(proh-f*uh*-**lak**-tik, prof-*uh*-**lak**-tik) – (adj.) protecting from or preventing disease; protective or preventive, (n.) a prophylactic drug or device, esp. a condom; a remedy that prevents or slows the course of an illness or disease.[87, 88]

- **Prophylactic** treatments often lead to the growth of resistant bacteria.
- "The study of error is not only in the highest degree **prophylactic**, but it serves as a stimulating introduction to the study of truth." -Walter Lippmann[89]

Resuscitate

(ri-**suhs**-i-teyt) – (v.) to bring someone who is dying back to life, wake someone who is unconscious, or bring something back into use or existence.[90]

If you **resuscitate** someone who has stopped breathing, you cause them to start breathing again. If you **resuscitate** some*thing*, like a failing marriage, you cause it to become active again.[91]

- Despite their best attempts, they couldn't **resuscitate** the dog that got hit by a car.
- "Two people making love, she once said, are like one drowned person **resuscitating** the other." -Anatole Broyard, *Kafka Was the Rage: A Greenwich Village Memoir*[92]

Salubrious

(suh-**loo**-bree-uhs) – (adj.) conducive or favourable to health; wholesome; (of a place) pleasant to live in; clean and healthy.[93, 94]

- The fresh mountain air of rural Switzerland felt extremely **salubrious** and uplifting.
- "There is a comfortable feeling in small towns. It is **salubrious**." -Andie MacDowell[95]

Unguent

(**uhng**-gwuhnt) – (n.) semisolid preparation (usually containing a medicine) applied externally as a remedy or for soothing an irritation; a soothing or healing salve; ointment.[96, 97]

- The nurse gently applied a thick **unguent** to the patient's wounds.
- "Each night when she prepared for bed she smeared her face with some new **unguent** which she hoped illogically would give back the glow and freshness to her vanishing beauty." -F. Scott Fitzgerald[98]

Vertigo

(**vur**-ti-goh) – (n.) a feeling of spinning around and being unable to balance, often caused by looking down from a height; a feeling that everything is spinning around, causing you to be unable to balance and therefore to fall.[99]

If you get **vertigo** when you look down from a high place, you feel unsteady and sick.[100]

- Sarah's **vertigo** made it impossible for her to continue the trip any further.
- "In a VR setting, you tilt your head up, and you really have the **vertigo** and the sense that it goes up to infinity, and it's like you're in New York City or Dubai, and you're looking up at a giant skyscraper. You have a sense of awe." -Ramez Naam[101]

Practice Section 3: Unscramble the Words

1. YCORIAPTLHCP

2. UEAESTCTSIR

3. LLPEEMLL

4. RNTLIAOAEC

5. TNNGUEU

6. IAALTLEP

7. APHHNDRIOOYC

8. AAIPHS

9. TVEORGI

10. URBIOUASSL

Practice Section 4: Recall

Fill in the blank with the correct word.

1. Deep cut in skin tissue:
2. Reduce disease symptoms:
3. Revive someone or something:
4. Illness anxiety disorder:
5. Reeling and whirling sensation:
6. In a hasty and confusing manner:
7. Medical inability to communicate:
8. Conducive to health:
9. Contraceptive device:
10. Healing salve:

Perfect Section 5: Test Your Knowledge

Has the word been used correctly?

1. Aphasia is just a phase.
   ☐ Yes ☐ No

2. As a hypochondriac she is perpetually scared of heights.
   ☐ Yes ☐ No

3. His hand and face were badly lacerated during the fall.
   ☐ Yes ☐ No

4. As a great leader, he was seeking to palliate crime and violence.
   ☐ Yes ☐ No

5. When the fire broke out, there was a pell-mell rush for the exit door.
   ☐ Yes ☐ No

6. Prophylactic treatments are curative.
   ☐ Yes ☐ No

7. Even though the paramedics arrived in time, all resuscitation attempts failed.
   ☐ Yes ☐ No

8. The dark dingy cockroach-infested room felt salubrious.
   ☐ Yes ☐ No

9. An unguent is a thin runny liquid that can be applied on wounds.
   ☐ Yes ☐ No

10. Vertigo is a condition in which a person's superficial veins become twisted and enlarged.
    ☐ Yes ☐ No

Perfect Section 6: Pronunciation

Match each word with its correct phonetic pronunciation.

1. Hypochondria	a. **uhng**-gw*uh*nt
2. Pell-mell	b. *uh*-**fey**-zh*uh*
3. Resuscitate	c. **pal**-ee-eyt
4. Salubrious	d. proh-f*uh*-**lak**-tik
5. Unguent	e. las-*uh*-**rey**-sh*uh*n
6. Palliate	f. **vur**-ti-goh
7. Vertigo	g. s*uh*-**loo**-bree-*uh*s
8. Aphasia	h. hahy-p*uh*-**kon**-dree-*uh*
9. Prophylactic	i. ri-**suhs**-i-teyt
10. Laceration	j. **pel-mel**

Section 3

1. Prophylactic; 2. Resuscitate; 3. Pell-mell; 4. Laceration; 5. unguent; 6. Palliate; 7. Hypochondria; 8. Aphasia; 9. Vertigo; 10. Salubrious

Section 4

1. laceration; 2. palliate; 3. Resuscitate; 4. hypochondria; 5. vertigo; 6. pell-mell; 7. aphasia; 8. Salubrious; 9. prophylactic; 10. unguent

Section 5

1. No; 2. No; 3. Yes; 4. Yes; 5. Yes; 6. No; 7. Yes; 8. No; 9. No; 10. No

Section 6

1. h; 2. j; 3. i; 4. g; 5. a; 6. c; 7. f; 8. b; 9. d; 10. e

5

AN EXPLORATION OF DEATH

Exposure Section 1: Words in Context

EDGAR ALLEN POE was known for being one of the more **macabre** authors in classical literature. He wrote stories like *The Tell-Tale Heart,* in which the character murders an older man, dismembers the body, and **inters** the beating heart under the floorboard. *The Pit and the Pendulum* is a **lurid** suspense story that features a man sentenced to death, **martyred** during the Spanish Inquisition.

Both stories are indicative of a theme in Poe's life, the fear of being buried alive. In his time, medical science was rudimentary, and there were stories of unconscious or *comatose* victims that were perceived to be dead and therefore buried alive. It has been said that this happened so often that as science advanced, graves were dug up, and there were found to be nail marks in coffins as the victims regained consciousness and struggled to break free from a darkened box.

Urban legend has it that Poe was so terrified of the prospect that he designed his own coffin, leaving an exit mechanism should he need to escape. It is clear that this fear, along with a ripe imagination, inspired many of his works.

Life and death are two sides of the same coin. All that exists must meet its demise eventually. The dead can't be *resuscitated*, but their memories can live in our hearts forever.

Hence, it is not surprising that almost all cultures around the world have some kind of rituals associated with **interring**, cremating the dead, or enshrining them in elaborate **sepulchers**. Most of it is meant to help the grieving family gain closure, and a lot of rituals are also performed with the belief that they will help the deceased move on to higher dimensions.

Losing our near and dear ones is never easy. We try to keep them alive by writing **epitaphs** on their graves that commemorate their lives. Sometimes we channel our grief through beautiful music by composing and singing a heart-touching **dirge**.

Those who have a hard time coping with death might even resort to something as extreme and ethically questionable as **necromancy**. They can't be blamed for this as we have all felt this powerful urge to communicate with our departed loved ones.

Exposure Section 2: Definitions & Example Sentences

Decimate

(**des**-*uh*-meyt) – (v.) to destroy large numbers of people, animals, or other creatures, or to harm something severely.[102]

The verb **decimate** referred originally to a form of capital punishment for Roman troops. If there was a rebellion, one out of every ten men (thus the "dec-" in decimate) was put to death. So the word's first expanded usage meant a ten percent reduction or a ten percent tax. Modern usage gives the word **decimate** a "drastically reduced" meaning, but the verb can also be used to mean "to wipe out" or "to eliminate."[103]

- Famine and war eventually **decimated** the entire city.
- "What to do with a leading business that's challenged by a new technology wave without hurting an existing profit stream? The single greatest example of recent memory is Apple's willingness to **decimate** iPod sales by incorporating all the category-defining product's features into a new gizmo, the iPhone." -Adam Lashinsky[104]

Dirge

(**durj**) – (n.) a song or hymn of grief or lamentation; a slow, solemn, and mournful piece of music; something (such as a poem) that has the qualities of a dirge; (informal, disapproving) any song or piece of music that is too slow and sad.[105, 106]

- Everyone at the church wept when Charles sang a **dirge** honoring his deceased father.
- "Glory falls around us as we sob a **dirge** of desolation on the Cross" -Maya Angelou, *Letter to My Daughter*[107]

Epitaph

(**ep**-i-taf, **ep**-i-tahf) – (n.) a short piece of writing about someone who is dead, often carved on a person's gravestone.[108]

Some **epitaphs** are specified by people before their death, while others are chosen by those responsible for the burial. An **epitaph** may be written in prose or poem verse. Poets have been known to compose their own **epitaphs** prior to their death, as did William Shakespeare.[109]

- His **epitaph** reads: 'A man who truly loved his family and country.'
- "'Would you like me to [kill you] now?' asked Snape, his voice heavy with irony. 'Or would you like a few moments to compose an **epitaph**?'" -J. K. Rowling, *Harry Potter and the Deathly Hallows*[110]

Lurid

(**loor**-id) – (adj.) shocking due to violence, sex, or immoral activity; glaringly vivid and graphic; marked by sensationalism; horrible in fierceness or savagery; shining with an unnatural red glow as of fire seen through smoke; ghastly pale.[111, 112]

An expression used to avoid hearing or seeing disturbing things is "spare me the **lurid** details," and people say that so they won't have shocking or ugly images put into their imaginations.[112]

- The film has an R-rating because of its **lurid** depiction of war-time violence.
- "Vanity plays **lurid** tricks with our memory, and the truth of every passion wants some pretence to make it live." -Joseph Conrad, *Lord Jim*[113]

Macabre

(m*uh*-**kah**-br*uh*, m*uh*-**kahb**) – (adj.) used to describe something that is very strange and unpleasant because it is connected with death or violence; causing shock and fear due to a connection with death, esp. strange or cruel death.[114]

If a story involves lots of blood and gore, you can call it **macabre**.[115] A simple way to remember the word's meaning is to associate the **macabre** with the famous poet Edgar Allen Poe.

- Her dark sense of humor is nothing short of **macabre**.
- "He couldn't believe Jude's mute, **macabre** roommate had saved his life. He wondered if he'd have to get her a small taxidermied spider or something for her efforts." -Mary H.K. Choi, *Emergency Contact*[116]

Martyr

(**mahr**-ter) – (n.) a person who voluntarily suffers death as penalty for witnessing and refusing to renounce a religion; a person who sacrifices something of great value and especially life itself for the sake of principle; (usually disapproving) a person who tries to get sympathy from other people by telling them how much he or she is suffering; martyr to something (informal) a person who suffers very much because of an illness, problem or situation; (v.) to kill someone because of their religious or political beliefs.[117, 118, 119]

- Christina became a **martyr** while fighting for her country's freedom.
- "Let us all be brave enough to die the death of a **martyr**, but let no one lust for martyrdom." -Mahatma Gandhi[120]

Sepulcher

(**sep**-*uhl*-ker) – (n.) a small room or monument, cut in rock or built of stone, in which a dead person is laid or buried.[121]

A **sepulcher** (or if you're British, **sepulchre**) is basically a stone room with a stone coffin where your body lies.[122]

- Everyone who loved the Queen came out to place flowers and gifts near her **sepulcher.**
- "After the Sabbath, at dawn on the first day of the week, Mary Magdalene and the other Mary went to look at the tomb. There was a violent earthquake, for an angel of the Lord came down from heaven and, going to the tomb, rolled back the stone and sat on it. On the first day of the week came Mary Magdalene early, when it was yet dark, unto the sepulcher and saw the stone taken away from the **sepulcher.**" - Matthew 28:1-2

Necromancy

(**nek**-*ruh*-man-see) – (n.) the act of communicating with the dead in order to discover what is going to happen in the future, or black magic (magic used for bad purposes).[123]

Necromancy is the art of raising the spirits of the dead, either for their predictions about the future, or their ghostly help in making something happen.[124]

- Alice has been going to a psychic who allegedly uses **necromancy** to help her communicate with her deceased husband.

- "'If you do this, Nedra, if you choose **necromancy**... I cannot follow you into that darkness.' 'Oh, Grey,' I said, shifting my bag onto my shoulder. 'What do you know of darkness?'" -Beth Revis, *Give the Dark My Love*[125]

Inter

(in-**tur**) – (v.) to bury a dead body.[126]

Inter means to bury, usually in a tomb or grave. If you loved your cat a lot, you might want to **inter** her remains in the backyard and make a nice little memorial.[127] Not to be confused with "intern."

- Since there was a war going on, soldiers had to be hastily **interred** in mass graves.
- "The evil that men do lives after them; the good is oft **interred** with their bones." -William Shakespeare[86]

Regicide

(**rej**-*uh*-sahyd) – (n.) the killing of a king or queen.

The word **regicide** derives from the Latin *regis*, meaning "king," and the ancient French *cide*, meaning "killer." Today, the word **regicide** can also be applied to politicians who topple a president or prime minister; someone who commits **regicide**; the killer of a king.[128]

- My brother committed **regicide** by killing my king in a game of chess.

- "We live through the belief of children . . . **Regicide** is suicide, citizens. Inscribe that in your hearts. The Great Pretend is a fragile construct." -Bill Willingham, *Fables, Vol. 18: Cubs in Toyland*[129]

Practice Section 3: Fill-in-the-Blank

Fill in the blanks with the correct words. Most of the words are from this chapter, but you might have to recall a word you learned in the previous chapter.

1. When we visited Sam's father's ▓▓▓▓▓, Sam told us with a heavy heart how his father had suffered from ▓▓▓▓▓ after having a stroke. He had lost his ability to understand language and never regained it until his death.

2. I think the very idea of using ▓▓▓▓▓ to communicate with the dead is quite ▓▓▓▓▓.

3. We were all deeply moved by the ▓▓▓▓▓ the church choir sang in order to honor the war's ▓▓▓▓▓.

4. The ▓▓▓▓▓ on her father's grave has become so hard to read. I think someone has deliberately ▓▓▓▓▓ her father's ▓▓▓▓▓.

5. After committing ▓▓▓▓▓, the king's servants ▓▓▓▓▓ his body in an unmarked grave.

Practice Section 4: Matching

Match each word with its correct definition.

1. Dirge   a. Kill; destroy

2. Martyr   b. Tombstone inscription

3. Necromancy   c. Connected to death and violence

4. Inter   d. Tomb

5. Regicide   e. Funeral song

6. Decimate   f. Killing the king

7. Lurid   g. Burying the dead

8. Macabre   h. Communicating with dead people

9. Sepulcher   i. Killed because of one's beliefs or convictions

10. Epitaph   j. Immoral and shocking

Perfect Section 5: True or False

Test your understanding by deciding whether each of these statements is true or false.

1. A heinous crime can be described as macabre.
   True   False

2. A sepulcher is a burial chamber.
   True   False

3. Necromancy and necrophilia are the same thing.
   True   False

4. To inter means taking an interval.
   True   False

5. Any piece of slow and mournful music can be called a dirge.
   True   False

6. Someone who sacrifices their life for their principles can be called a martyr.
   True   False

7. An epitaph is a type of hieroglyph.
   True   False

8. Historically, to decimate implied killing 5 out of every 10 people in a group.
   True   False

9. The killing of a queen can also be described as an act of regicide.
   True   False

10. We call something lurid when it lures us in some way.
    True   False

Perfect Section 6: Drawing Conclusions

1. Your brother takes you to a concert where the band is playing extremely slow, boring, and miserable sounding songs.
   You can't tolerate listening to the _____ .

2. You are selfless to an extent but you can't sacrifice yourself beyond a point.
   You are not willing to become a _____ .

3. You hear in the news how the king has been brutally murdered by his ministers.
   The king's ministers have committed _____ .

4. The tour guide told you how the dead king's body was anointed and then placed inside a tomb.
   The dead king's body was placed inside the royal _____ .

5. You go to a monument and want to read what is written on the king's grave.
   You want to read what the _____ says.

6. Your soldier friend starts telling you about all the violence he witnessed during the Vietnam war in graphic detail.
   You can't bear listening to his _____ accounts of violence and war.

7. Your son's pet bird died and you have both decided to bury the bird's body in the backyard.
   You both will be _____ the bird's body in the backyard.

8. You are horrified reading about an inhuman murder that took place in the neighborhood.
   You are horrified by the _____ nature of the murder.

9. You have been wondering if there is a way you can speak with your deceased Aunt Ruth.
   You are curious if _____ will really work for you.

10. Your farmer friend tells you how locusts have destroyed his crops.
    His crops have been _____ by locusts.

Section 3

1. Sepulcher, Aphasia; 2. Necromancy, Macabre; 3. Dirge, Martyrs; 4. Epitaph, Decimated, Epitaph; 5. Regicide, Interred

Section 4

1. e; 2. i; 3. h; 4. g; 5. f; 6. a; 7. j; 8. c; 9. d; 10. b

Section 5

1. True; 2. True; 3. False; 4. False; 5. True; 6. True; 7. False; 8. False; 9. True; 10. False

Section 6

1. Dirge; 2. Martyr; 3. Regicide; 4. Sepulcher; 5. Epitaph; 6. Lurid; 7. Interring; 8. Macabre; 9. Necromancy; 10. Decimated

CHAPTERS 1-5 REVIEW

Review Section 1: Synonyms

Match the synonym with the given word on the left.

1. Dorsal	a. Rip
2. Inter	b. Hasty
3. Martyr	c. Bury
4. Pell-mell	d. Rear
5. Laceration	e. Penny-pinching
6. Forty winks	f. Attack
7. Salubrious	g. Disorder
8. Husbandry	h. Healthy
9. Hypochondria	i. Obituary
10. Epitaph	j. Cat nap

Match the antonym with the given word on the left.

1. Decimate	a. Kill
2. Soporific	b. Cultivated
3. Bestial	c. Lively
4. Macabre	d. Science
5. Palliate	e. Construct
6. Comatose	f. Stimulant
7. Resuscitate	g. Gendered
8. Necromancy	h. Aggravate
9. Dirge	i. Enticing
10. Asexual	j. Eulogy

Review Section 3: Crossword Puzzle

Complete the crossword puzzle based on your acquired knowledge of the vocabulary terms.

Across
2. Pleasant daydreaming
4. Tiger-like
9. A sound of mourning
11. Varying male and female anatomy
14. Inability to be romantic
15. Suffering death in the name of religion
16. Gender identity disorder
20. State of being dull
22. Substance applied to a wound
23. Relating to a bear
24. Ghastly; horrible

Down
1. Storehouse for food
3. Dizziness
5. Removal of testicles
6. An alignment of gender and anatomy
7. A burial place; a tomb
8. Varying manifestations of gender
10. Ape/human-like
12. Preventive against disease
13. A sleepwalker
17. To sleep lightly
18. Revolting
19. Category based on body type
21. Resembling a horse

Chapters 1-5 Review Answer Key

Section 1

1. d, 2. c, 3. f, 4. g, 5. a, 6. j, 7. e, 8. h, 9. g, 10. i

Section 2

1. e, 2. i, 3. b, 4. j, 5. f, 6. c, 7. a, 8. d, 9. h, 10. g

Section 3

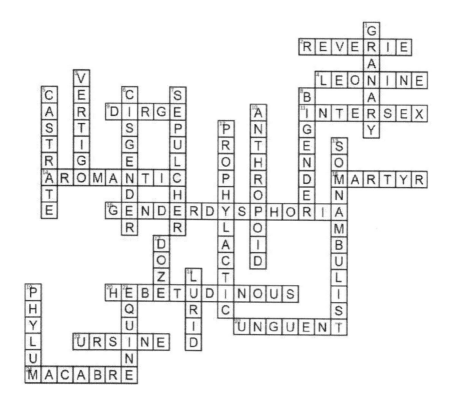

6
___

THE MACABRE NATURE OF MURDER

EARLY ON IN MY CAREER, I worked as a writer for a national news site. It was one of those news sites that was openly biased from the name on down and served as a gathering point for a particular point of view. I didn't particularly share their point of view, but I was young and broke, and they were paying well. I had done theater in high school, and I figured it was the same concept. I wasn't being eaten alive with red hot political outrage any more than I was one of Charles Dickens' ghosts. I had managed to pull them off pretty well, so why not?

It ended up being a horrible job. I should have stuck with Dickens.

In the beginning, I had a difficult time getting stories past the editorial approval board. Since I was a relative outsider to the movement, it was hard for me to find good stories. They paid me well, but my salary was also correlated to the number of stories I wrote. I would spend hours each day coming up with stories I thought would work, only to be told *no, no, no.*

I was discouraged. Not only was I wasting so much time researching story leads, but I was also losing money with every denied story idea. Finally, I noticed a pattern in the few stories I could get passed. The more sensationalist and bizarre, the better. It was the very definition of yellow journalism, and I knew it, but I didn't care. I had rent to pay. I went after the worst, most violent parts of human nature and then watched the money start rolling in.

Day after day, I wrote about death and violent destruction. **Uxoricide** by a member of a violent gang, while the children cowered in a corner, helplessly watching their father **obliterate** their mother's life. Violent extremist groups with detailed accounts about how they **mutilated** their victims or did things like **asphyxiate** them in quicksand.

I wrote about a crazed mental patient so amped up on extremist ideology, he used it as an excuse for **matricide**. When the police arrived, he had **decapitated** his own mother and answered the door holding her **cruentating** head.

My last story for the site was on the plight of orphaned children, parents **slain** by political regimes working to **eradicate** other groups. I wrote about these kids trudging through the snow, frostbitten feet wrapped in rags, leaving a trail of blood spotting the white ground across international borders.

I finished the story and promptly turned in my resignation. I lasted all of eight months and learned a valuable lesson. Sometimes there's no shame in admitting that it's just not worth the money.

Exposure Section 2: Definitions & Example Sentences

Matricide

(**ma-**tri-sahyd) – (n.) murder of one's own mother; a person who kills their own mother.[130]

The suffix *-cide* is a clue that something murderous is going on with this word: it means "killer," from the Latin *-cida*, "cutter or slayer." You'll find this suffix in words like insecticide and pesticide as well. The first part of **matricide** comes from the root *mater*, or "mother."[130]

- Incidents of **matricide** are generally a lot more common in single-parent homes.
- "If a politician murders his mother, the first response of the press or of his opponents will likely be not that it was a terrible thing to do, but rather that in a statement made six years before he had gone on record as being opposed to **matricide**." - Meg Greenfield, Author[131]

Uxoricide

(uhk-**sawr**-*uh*-sahyd) – (n.) murder of a wife by her husband; a husband who murders his wife.[132]

- **Uxoricide** is the most extreme form of domestic violence that a man can commit.
- Diego couldn't possibly have committed **uxoricide** – he is such a gentle and sweet man!

Cruentation

(**kroo**-in-tey-sh*uh*n) – (n.) the oozing of blood from a corpse after incision or according to superstitious belief in the presence of the murderer.[133]

Cruentation was one of the medieval methods of finding proof against a suspected murderer. The common belief was that the victim's body would spontaneously bleed in the presence of the murderer.[134]

- **Cruentation** was used as a method of finding proof against a suspected murderer until the early seventeenth century.
- Under Germanic law, **cruentation** was used as a means of proving guilt.

Manqueller

(man-**kwel**-er) – (n.) (archaic) a killer of men; a manslayer; executioner.[135]

- It's a pity that they were treating the holy man as if he was a thief or **manqueller**.
- The **manqueller** finally died a sad and lonely death.

Obliterate

(*uh*-**blit**-*uh*-reyt) – (v.) to remove utterly from recognition or memory; to remove from existence: destroy utterly all trace, indication, or significance of; (medical) to cause (something, such as a bodily part, a scar, or a duct conveying body fluid) to disappear or collapse; to make undecipherable or imperceptible by obscuring or wearing away; to cancel.[136]

- John did his best to **obliterate** all signs of his shady past.
- "Polka dots can't stay alone. When we **obliterate** nature and our bodies with polka dots, we become part of the unity of our environments." -Yayoi Kusama[137]

Eradicate

(ih-**rad**-i-keyt) – (v.) to kill in large numbers; to destroy completely, as if down to the roots.[138]

Eradicate is from the Latin meaning "to root out." When you yank that weed up by the roots, it has been eradicated; it's not coming back. To **eradicate** often means to kill a bunch of things, like what you want the poison to do to the roach family and their extended relatives living in your house, and what we thought we did to bedbugs. You can also **eradicate** corruption, poverty, or diseases. Although there are all kinds of things to get rid of, we usually want only to **eradicate** bad things.[138]

- He has been working hard to **eradicate** poverty from his community.
- "We have to make it a personal responsibility to **eradicate** ignorance from our society." -Sunday Adelaja, *The Mountain of Ignorance*[139]

Slain

(**sleyn**) – (adj.) killed; (n.) people who have been slain (as in battle)[140]

Slain is often used formally or literarily, as in "**slain** warriors."[140]

- It's hard to forget the trials and tribulations of those who were **slain** in World War 1.
- "He that fights and runs away, May turn and fight another day; But he that is in battle **slain**, Will never rise to fight again." -Tacitus[141]

Asphyxiate

(as-**fik**-see-eyt) – (v.) to be unable to breathe, usually resulting in death, or to cause someone to be unable to breathe; suffocate.[142]

To **asphyxiate** is to keep someone from breathing—to suffocate or smother them. Choking on a piece of food can **asphyxiate** a person.[143]

- The murderer **asphyxiated** his victim by squeezing her throat with a belt.
- "Fear is an acid which is pumped into one's atmosphere. It causes mental, moral and spiritual **asphyxiation**, and sometimes death; death to energy and all growth." -Horace Fletcher[144]

Mutilate

(**myoot**-l-eyt) – (v.) to damage something severely, especially by violently removing a part; to destroy an idea or a piece of art or entertainment; to alter so as to make unrecognizable.[145, 146]

- The murder victim's body was **mutilated** beyond recognition.
- "I will no longer **mutilate** and destroy myself in order to find a secret behind the ruins." -Hermann Hesse, *Siddhartha*[147]

Decapitate

(dih-**kap**-i-teyt) – (v.) to cut off the head of a person or animal; (decapitate something) to reduce the power of a group or organization by removing its leaders.[148, 149]

- The king was **decapitated** by the men he trusted the most.
- "The results of their experiments, published Monday in Current Biology, provide evidence that Elysia marginata, and a closely related species, Elysia atroviridis, purposefully **decapitate** themselves in order to facilitate the growth of a new body." -New York Times, 8 Mar. 2021[150]

Practice Section 3: Unscramble the Words

1. RETDAMICI

2. EURXODIIC

3. NNTITOCRAEU

4. LLQMNRAEEU

5. OETBTRLAEI

6. ADITACEER

7. ASINL

8. EASHXTPAIY

9. TMETIALU

10. IEDATTCAPE

Practice Section 4: Matching

Match each word with its correct definition.

1. Uxoricide   a. Murdering one's mother

2. Slain   b. Mankiller

3. Mutilate   c. Erase from memory or recognition

4. Cruentation   d. Violently killing a person or an animal

5. Asphyxiate   e. Cut off someone's head

6. Obliterate   f. Oozing blood from a corpse

7. Matricide   g. Kill in large numbers

8. Eradicate   h. Severe injury or cutting off a limb

9. Decapitate   i. Die from lack of oxygen

10. Manqueller   j. Murdering one's own wife

Perfect Section 5: Pronunciation

Match each word with its correct phonetic pronunciation.

1. Uxoricide   a. **kroo**-in-tey-sh*uh*n

2. Decapitate   b. man-**kwel**-er

3. Slain   c. ih-**rad**-i-keyt

4. Mutilate   d. as-**fik**-see-eyt

5. Eradicate   e. dih-**kap**-i-teyt

6. Matricide   f. **myoot**-l-eyt

7. Obliterate   g. **sleyn**

8. Asphyxiate   h. *uh*-**blit**-*uh*-reyt

9. Cruentation   i. **ma**-tri-sahyd

10. Manqueller   j. uhk-**sawr**-*uh*-sahyd

Perfect Section 6: Test Your Knowledge

Has the word been used correctly?

1. Some memories just can't be obliterated.
   Yes   No

2. Cruentation implies cruel intentions.
   Yes   No

3. Asphyxiation indicates an attitude of fixation.
   Yes   No

4. Going by the original Latin word, eradicate quite literally means removing from the root.
   Yes   No

5. A manqueller is a man killer.
   Yes   No

6. Regicide can be committed through decapitation.
   Yes   No

7. The slain warrior has been immortalized in a beautiful poem.
   Yes   No

8. The jealous husband eventually ended up committing uxoricide.
   Yes   No

9. The intruders mutilated some of the greatest pieces of art.
   Yes   No

10. He killed his daughter—he's guilty of matricide!
    Yes   No

Section 3

1. Matricide; 2. Uxoricide; 3. Cruentation; 4. Manqueller; 5. Obliterate; 6. Eradicate; 7. Slain; 8. Asphyxiate; 9. Mutilate; 10. Decapitate

Section 4

1. j; 2. d; 3. h; 4. f; 5. i; 6. c; 7. a; 8. g; 9. e; 10. b

Section 5

1. j; 2. e; 3. g; 4. f; 5. c; 6. i; 7. h; 8. d; 9. a; 10. b

Section 6

1. Yes; 2. No; 3. No; 4. Yes; 5. Yes; 6. Yes; 7. Yes; 8. Yes; 9. Yes; 10. No

7

THE GIFT OF TIME

Exposure Section 1: Words in Context

I REMEMBER the day I finally understood Captain Hook—the villain in the Peter Pan tale. I was 28, and with just two short years left of what was supposed to be the best decade of my life, I somehow felt I'd come up short.

I didn't have any reason to feel that way. I had an excellent education, was in a great relationship, and had enough professional accomplishments under my belt that I didn't even have to pad my resume. I drove a nice car and had a smashingly gorgeous apartment in a four-story building with a concierge and a valet.

On top of that, I had even got to have those "circus years." You know, those **ephemeral** years in your twenties, where you travel the country in a fifteen-passenger van and do God only knows what, and later use it as material to pretend you're F. Scott Fitzgerald and write your generation's version of *The Great Gatsby*? Yeah, those years.

To any outsider looking in, my life was a success. But I didn't think so. My own insecurities **superseded** the joy de Vivre I should have had.

I would often wake in the middle of the night, in a panic attack, feeling like thirty, and the inevitable end of my sacred youth was just around the corner.

That was when I started hating clocks.

Each tick of the clock signified a second of my life, my youth, that I could never regain. I began to **prognosticate** about what the future held. From here on out, my life would be filled with responsibility and the expectations people placed on me. Never again would I be able to walk in a room and be the up-and-coming prodigious "young thing" or "the hot new rising talent." I was old news, and where I was, only what I had earned and what I had gained.

Somewhere between yet another mortarboard, and **biennial** cross-country road trips, I had left the island of the Lost Boys and crossed over into the real world. And suddenly, the **perennial** tale of a **hoary** old man, haunted by clocks, battling his **preternaturally** forever-young archnemesis, made sense. In fact, it made a lot of sense.

It took some time to get over this sort-of-quarter-age crisis, but I made it out the other side just fine. Gone are the days of **yore**, and I am firmly rooted in the present, not marred by time, but embracing the gift of life for what it truly is—a gift.

Exposure Section 2: Definitions & Example Sentences

Yore

(**yohr**) – (n.) time past and especially long past—commonly used in the phrase "days of yore."[151]

Yore, meaning "a time long ago," is used in the same manner as yesteryear, days gone by, and olden times. Yore has a sentimental or nostalgic tone to it, implying that the olden times being described are in some way superior to the present day. You might hear someone say, "This tragedy wouldn't have happened in days of **yore**," or "The car designs of **yore** were more imaginative than anything being built today."[152]

- I love listening to stories of fair maidens and gallant knights from the days of **yore**.
- "At a time when the titans of tech and their overreach are viewed by the public as being on par with the robber barons of **yore**, not everyone will be surprised by the wholesale southern migration." -Horacio Silva, *Town & Country*[153]

Ephemeral

(ih-**fem**-er-*uh*l) - (adj.) short-lived; fleeting.

Something fleeting or short-lived is **ephemeral**, like a fly that lives for one day, a beautiful sunset, text messages flitting from cellphone to cellphone, or "the **ephemeral** joys of childhood."[154]

- Their **ephemeral** romance ended on an unpleasant note.
- "I like the **ephemeral** thing about theater, every performance is like a ghost—it's there and then it's gone." - Maggie Smith[155]

Supersede

(soo-per-**seed**) – (v.) to replace something, especially something older or more old-fashioned.[156]

If a law, rule, agreement, process, system, or product **supersedes** another, it replaces it. Often something is **superseded** because it is outdated and losing its popularity.[156]

- Robots are rapidly **superseding** humans in many areas of work.
- "No method nor discipline can supersede the necessity of being forever on the alert. What is a course of history, or philosophy, or poetry, or the most admirable routine of life, compared with the discipline of looking always at what is to be seen? Will you be a reader, a student merely, or a seer?" - Henry David Thoreau[157]

Prognosticate

(prog-**nos**-ti-keyt) – (v.) to make a prediction about; tell in advance; indicate by signs.

To prognosticate means to predict something or at least hint at what will happen in the future.[158]

- Astrology is an ancient discipline of study that seeks to **prognosticate** the future by studying the placement of various planets and stars.
- "I think if you look back at my projections and my **prognostications**, they turn out to be very, very accurate." -Donald Trump[159]

Preternatural

(pree-ter-**nach**-er-*uhl*, pree-ter-**nach**-ruhl) – (adj.) existing outside of or not in accordance with nature; surpassing the ordinary or normal.[160]

Note that **preternatural** contains the word "natural." Preter comes from the Latin word praeter, which means "beyond," so something **preternatural** is beyond nature. It is a less commonly used word these days than unnatural or supernatural, but it means essentially the same thing. If you lift a truck off the ground and hold it above your head, people will marvel at you and say you have **preternatural** strength.[160]

- In a moment of desperation, Charlie acquired **preternatural** strength and someone managed to break open the locked door.
- "She protected me. We had the souls of each other. We loved in some realm where the natural and the **preternatural** meant nothing." - Anne Rice, *Prince Lestat*[161]

Perennial

(p*uh*-**ren**-ee-*uh*l) – (adj.) lasting an indefinitely long time; suggesting self-renewal; recurring again and again; lasting three seasons or more; (n.) (botany) a plant lasting for three seasons or more.[162]

- Martha's mother is a **perennial** beauty—she just doesn't seem to age!
- "The problem . . . is inherent and **perennial** in any democracy, but it has been more severe in ours during the past quarter-century because of the near universal denigration of government, politics, and politicians." -Michael Kinsley, *Time Magazine*[163]

Marred

(**mahrd**) – (adj.) damaged or spoiled to a certain extent; made less perfect, attractive, useful, etc.; disfigured or defaced, as by scratches, nicks, scars, or discoloration.[164]

If something is **marred**, it's damaged due to a flaw. If the big football game on Sunday ends with a fight among fans of the opposing teams, commentators will say that the game was **marred** by violence.[165]

- The event was **marred** by many untoward incidents.
- "The credit belongs to the man who is actually in the arena, whose face is **marred** by dust and sweat and blood; who strives valiantly; who errs, who comes short again and again, because there is no effort without error and shortcoming; but who does actually strive to do the deeds; who knows great enthusiasms, the great devotions; who spends himself in a worthy cause; who at the best knows in the end the triumph of high achievement, and who at the worst, if he fails, at least fails while daring greatly, so that his place shall never be with those cold and timid souls who neither know victory nor defeat." -Theodore Roosevelt[166]

Hoary

(**hohr**-ee) – (adj.) showing characteristics of age, especially having gray or white hair; ancient; covered with fine whitish hairs or down.[167]

Use the adjective **hoary** to describe something old and worn out—like the hoary jokes your great uncle Albert clings to.[167]

- The wise old man nodded his **hoary** head in agreement.
- "The **hoary** joke in the literary world, based on *Dreams From My Father*, was that if things had worked out differently for Barack Obama, he could have made it as a writer." -James Fallows[168]

Epoch

(**ee**-pok, **ep**-*uh*k) – (n.) a point in time beginning a new or distinctive period; a long period of time marked by some predominant or typical characteristic; era; (astronomy) a precise date to which information, such as coordinates, relating to a celestial body is referred; (geology) a unit of geological time within a period during which a series of rocks is formed.[169]

- The decapitation of the king marked the beginning of a new **epoch**.
- "Architecture is the will of an **epoch** translated into space." - Ludwig Mies van der Rohe[170]

Biennial

(bahy-**en**-ee-*uh*l) – (adj.) occurring every second year; having a life cycle lasting two seasons; (n.) (botany) a plant having a life cycle that normally takes two seasons from germination to death to complete.[171]

Flowering **biennials** usually bloom and fruit in the second season.[171] Careful not to confuse the words **biennial** and biannual, the latter of which means "occurring twice per year."

- Since the city's carnival is a **biennial** event, you'll have to wait for two years to attend the next one.
- As members of the committee, we have to attend both the annual and the **biennial** meetings.

Antediluvian

(an-tee-di-**loo**-vee-*uh*n) – (adj.) of or relating to the period before the flood described in the Bible; made, evolved, or developed a long time ago; extremely primitive or outmoded.[172]

The word is used—often humorously—to describe something really, really old, or even a very old person.[173]

- It's one thing to be old-fashioned, and another to be completely **antediluvian**.
- "The problem is that those dates going back before 9600 BC take us deep into the last Ice Age, when Indonesia was not a series of islands as it is today but was part of a vast **antediluvian** Southeast Asian continent dubbed 'Sundaland' by geologists. Sea level was 122 meters (400 feet) lower then. Huge ice caps 3.2 kilometers (2 miles) deep covered most of Europe and North America until the ice caps began to melt. Then all the water stored in them returned to the oceans and sea-level rose, submerging many parts of the world where humans had previously lived." -Graham Hancock, *Magicians of the Gods: The Forgotten Wisdom of Earth's Lost Civilization*[174]

Practice Section 3: Fill-in-the-Blank

Fill in the blanks with the right words.

1. This moment in history marks the end of an _____ and the beginning of a new one.

2. We are really excited to attend the _____ film festival.

3. _____ has been derived from the Greek word *prognōstikos* which translates as foretelling.

4. The king will be _____ by his son.

5. The story's hero was a _____ old man who lived alone in the woods.

6. No matter how bad things get, she manages to remain a _____ optimist.

7. He is so out of the ordinary—there is something really _____ about him.

8. The _____ frown _____ his handsome face.

9. The eccentric artist prefers to wear _____ clothes that look terribly out of place.

10. With a pang in his heart, he recalled the glorious days of _____.

11. Fashion trends are _____.

Practice Section 4: Matching

Match each word with its correct definition.

1. Epoch	a. Take the place of another person or thing
2. Preternatural	b. Happening every two years
3. Perennial	c. An era prior to the Biblical flood
4. Hoary	d. Injured or disfigured
5. Yore	e. An era or age
6. Prognosticate	f. Ancient
7. Antediluvian	g. Short-lived
8. Marred	h. Of a long gone past
9. Biennial	i. Lasting for an infinitely long time
10. Supersede	j. Foretell the future
11. Ephemeral	k. Beyond what is natural

Perfect Section 5: True or False

Test your understanding by deciding whether each of these statements is true or false.

1. Marred implies something has been destroyed or damaged.
   ▢ True ▢ False

2. Preternatural is anything that's beyond what's natural or normal.
   ▢ True ▢ False

3. Prognostication involves prolonging a particular situation.
   ▢ True ▢ False

4. Supersede implies coming before something or someone.
   ▢ True ▢ False

5. Hoary implies a connection with grey hair.
   ▢ True ▢ False

6. An epoch always implies the duration of one year.
   ▢ True ▢ False

7. Perennial plants keep re-growing each spring season while annuals survive only one season.
   ▢ True ▢ False

8. A biennial event occurs twice a year.
   ▢ True ▢ False

9. Anything that is ephemeral lasts eternally.
   ▢ True ▢ False

10. Yore is an alternate archaic spelling of your.
    ▢ True ▢ False

11. Antediluvian refers to something that's not relevant to the current times anymore.
    ▢ True ▢ False

Perfect Section 6: Drawing Conclusions

1. The heroine of the story was so beautiful that he hardly seemed human.
   The heroine possessed _____ beauty.

2. You are waiting with bated breath to know who will win the race.
   You wish someone could _____ the future.

3. Your sister tells you about this religious festival that happens every two years.
   You are considering going to the _____ religious festival.

4. Your family loves the special chocolate mousse recipe you make at get-togethers.
   Your chocolate mousse recipe is a _____ crowd-pleaser.

5. You read in the newspapers how violent individuals infiltrated a peaceful protest.
   The peaceful protest was _____ by violent troublemakers.

6. You still remember all the celebrations you had when you turned 18—it was like the beginning of a new life.
   A new _____ began in your life when you turned 18.

7. You are a bit frustrated with your Aunt Ruth's outdated advice on dating and gender roles.
   You don't like Aunt Ruth's _____ ideas about dating and gender roles.

8. Your boss informs you that your colleague Rachel will be taking your place in the company.
   You are going to be _____ by Rachel.

9. You decide to visit the ancient ruins of a sun temple.
   You visit the _____ ruins of the sun temple.

10. You notice a dead bee in your garden and you ponder how short its life was.
    You're thinking about the _____ nature of a bee's life.

11. Your grandfather keeps telling you how in his time people used to believe in socializing face-to-face instead of merely commenting on one another's profiles on social media.
    In the days of _____, social media wasn't a thing.

Section 3

1. Epoch; 2. Biennial; 3. Prognosticate; 4. Superseded; 5. Hoary; 6. Perennial; 7. Preternatural; 8. Perennial, marred; 9. Antediluvian; 10. Yore; 11. Ephemeral

Section 4

1. e; 2. k; 3. i; 4. f; 5. h; 6. j; 7. c; 8. d; 9. b; 10. A, 11. g

Section 5

1. True; 2. True; 3. False; 4. False; 5. True; 6. False; 7. True; 8. False; 9. False 10. False; 11. True

Section 6

1. Preternatural; 2. Prognosticate; 3. Biennial; 4. Perennial; 5. Marred; 6. Epoch; 7. Antediluvian; 8. Superseded; 9. Hoary; 10. Ephemeral; 11. Yore

8

THE FEARLESS GIRL STATUE

Exposure Section 1: Words in Context

ONCE, as I was waiting to catch an early morning flight, I sat in the terminal and scrolled my Facebook news feed. I ran across a photo of *The Fearless Girl* statue.

For those that don't know, *The Fearless Girl* was a sculpture that stood for a little over a year as a compliment to Wall Street's iconic *Charging Bull*. It's a bronze statue of a young girl, in a skirt and swishing ponytail, with her hands on hips, placed to stare down *The Charging Bull* unflinchingly. The girl is meant to be a statement on the future of female empowerment and the future of American finance and culture.

It was a great statue, and there was a lot of powerful meaning to be gleaned from the placement of the two figures. For the year and a half that it stood, tourists flocked to take photos of it, particularly mothers and their young daughters.

However, Arturo Di Modica, the bull's original sculptor, didn't take kindly to this. He argued that, no offense to feminism, the girl took away from the integrity of the bull statue. *The Charging Bull*, set against the girl statue, was now reduced to an impotent **bugaboo**, rather than a symbol of the raging strength and power of the American financial district. His argument gained momentum, and one of his supporters, fellow sculptor Alex Gardega, hastily threw together another statue of a dog urinating. He called it *The Pissing Pug* and installed it next to the girl's left leg. Supporters of *The Fearless Girl* Statue were offended and were known to kick the dog, calling it and its sculptor misogynistic.

In November 2018, the case for *The Charging Bull* won, and *The Fearless Girl* was moved to another location. *The Charging Bull* now stands alone, also without *The Pissing Pug*.

Despite the controversy, *The Fearless Girl* against *The Charging Bull* is still an excellent symbol of empowerment, in any way you want to cut it. On this day, when I scrolled Facebook, someone had captioned it, "What is standing in your way right now?"

I loved the question so much that I pulled out a notebook. I made a list of things that were holding me back in life. As I read them over, I realized they all went back to fear. Fear of failure. Fear of success. Fear of rejection. My problem in life wasn't opportunity, or talent, or luck, or anything else. It was all fear. If I could confront the fear in my life, I could reach a potential I had only dreamed of.

I chewed on this as I boarded the plane and strapped myself in. My seatmate was an elderly woman, clearly nervous, and kept to her dime store novel. As we took off, I noticed every muscle in her body tense with **trepidation**. She squeezed her eyes shut and gripped the armrest so tight her knuckles were actually white.

"First time flying?" I yelled as my ears popped in and out from the changing air pressure. She nodded vigorously and emitted a nervous **titter**.

"Have you ever heard of *The Fearless Girl* statue?" I asked.

Fear.

We fear so many things in life, some of them consequential, some not so much. Some fear high places, and we call that **acrophobia**. (Not to be confused with *arachnophobia*, fear of spiders). **Acrophobia** often makes people feel dizzy and nauseated as they peer down from high buildings or other structures.

Others fear water, and we call them **hydrophobic**. This fear can range from the simple avoiding of pools to tortured individuals that have difficulty with basic hygiene. Some fear other types of people, and we call that **xenophobia**. Xenophobia has become a new buzzword, as American culture has become more openly diverse, causing some people to be more **timorous** of stepping out of their own circles.

Some fear being assertive and stating what they need and want. We call them **timid**, and some are so unreasonably beyond timid that we call them **pusillanimous**. Although, we can all be **pusillanimous** in certain situations, and that's not always bad. It's like the cliche, "Fools rush in, where angels fear to tread."

There are times that fear is sometimes just plain good sense. The universal conundrum in life is knowing the difference.

Exposure Section 2: Definitions & Example Sentences

Acrophobia

(ak-r*uh*-**foh**-bee-*uh*) – (n.) abnormal fear or dread of great heights.[175]

You can see the word *phobia*, or extreme fear, in **acrophobia**. Acro comes from the Greek word *akron*, which means "summit" or "high point." When you put it all together, you have a word that means "fear of heights."[176]

- Because of her **acrophobia**, high-rise elevators make her dizzy.

- When Tim told me how much he loves skydiving, I knew he definitely doesn't suffer from **acrophobia**.

Hydrophobia

(hahy-dr*uh*-**foh**-bee-*uh*) – (n.) another name for rabies; a fear of drinking fluids, esp. that of a person with rabies because of painful spasms when trying to swallow; Compare: aquaphobia.[177]

Take hydro (meaning "water") and phobia (meaning "fear") and you have **hydrophobia**—a fear of water.[178]

- In the past, rabies used to be known as **hydrophobia** since patients often developed an extreme fear of water.
- Patients with **hydrophobia** find it impossible to swallow water.

Xenophobia

(zen-*uh*-**foh**-bee-*uh*, zee-n*uh*-**foh**-bee-*uh*) – (n.) fear and hatred of strangers or foreigners or of anything that is strange or foreign.[179]

- Racism is deeply rooted in **xenophobia**.
- "Refugees don't make our country less safe. But **xenophobia**, fear, and hate do." -Ted Lieu[180]

Trepidation

(trep-i-**dey**-sh*uh*n) – (n.) fear or anxiety about something that you are going to do or experience; a condition of quaking or palpitation, esp.

one caused by anxiety; tremulous or trembling movement; quaking; tremor; fearful uncertainty, anxiety, etc.; apprehension.[181]

- Even though he was shaking with **trepidation**, he somehow managed to ask Cynthia out on a date.
- "Every turning point in a person's life isn't reached by luck, they choose to be successful, they know what it takes to be there, they can do what is expected of them to do, they do not show **trepidation** about the requirements needed to be on top." -Michael Bassey Johnson, *Classic Quotations From The Otherworlds*[182]

Timorous

(**tim**-er-*uh*s) – (adj.) nervous and easily frightened; timid by nature or revealing timidity; showing fear and lack of confidence.[183, 184]

A timorous person is timid or shy, like your timorous friend who likes to hang out with close pals but gets nervous around big groups of new people.[184]

- The **timorous** puppy was afraid to come out of the basket he had been hiding in.
- He is so shy and **timorous** that he lacks the ability to take a stand for himself.

Pusillanimous

(pyoo-s*uh*-**lan**-*uh*-m*uh*s) – (adj.) lacking in courage, strength, and resolution; contemptibly fearful.[185]

You can describe someone who lacks courage as **pusillanimous**, such as a cowardly student who is too afraid to speak out against someone who is bullying others.[185]

- The men of the community have become so **pusillanimous** that they could not even take a stand for the old widower who was being harassed by the police.
- "Some folks hide, and some folks seek, and seeking, when it's mindless, neurotic, desperate, or **pusillanimous** can be a form of hiding." -Tom Robbins[186]

Timidity

(ti-**mid**-i-tee) – (n.) the quality of being shy and nervous; fear of the unknown or unfamiliar or fear of making decisions; fearfulness in venturing into new and unknown places or activities.[187, 188]

- **Timidity** is the enemy of greatness.
- "An hour's terror is better than a lifetime of **timidity.**" - Walter de la Mare, *The Return*[189]

Eerie

(**eer**-ee) – (adj.) inspiring a feeling of fear; strange and frightening; suggestive of the supernatural; mysterious.[190]

Eerie means spooky, creepy, or suggestively supernatural. A close friend of the *macabre*, if it's **eerie**, it's sure to make the hair on the back of your neck stand up.[190]

- There was something really **eerie** about that desolate ghost village.
- "The city had an **eerie** abandoned feeling to it. There were cars on the roads, which created a few random obstacles to avoid, but they were unoccupied. People had given up trying to escape and, for some reason, left their vehicles in a hurry, probably due to infected attackers." -Jason Medina, *The Manhattanville Incident: An Undead Novel*[191]

Titter

(**tit**-er) – (n.) a nervous laugh, often at something that you feel you should not be laughing at; (v.) to laugh in a half-suppressed way, suggestive of silliness, nervousness, etc.; giggle; to laugh in a restrained, self-conscious, or affected way, as from nervousness or in ill-suppressed amusement.[192, 193]

- The comedian's inappropriate jokes provoked an embarrassed **titter** in the audience.
- "Most importantly, I can see the candidates' body language when they're off-camera and hear the murmurs and **titters** in the crowd." -Dana Milbank[194]

Bugaboo

(**buhg**-*uh*-boo) - (n.) an imaginary object of fear; something that causes fear or distress out of proportion to its importance.[195]

- He has created a **bugaboo** out of his imaginary inadequacies.

- "Anything which is physically possible can always be made financially possible; money is a **bugaboo** of small minds." - Robert A. Heinlein[196]

Practice Section 3: Unscramble the Words

Unscramble the following words.

1. RTTITE

2. OAHBHYRIPOD

3. NTIADIROPET

4. RSMUIOTO

5. REEEI

6. LILNMSPASOUIU

7. HAXIONBEPO

8. MYIIIDTT

9. OBOBAUG

10. ICPAAOOBRH

Practice Section 4: Matching

Match each word with its correct definition.

1. Hydrophobia	a. Irrational fear of strangers
2. Titter	b. Nervous and lacking confidence
3. Trepidation	c. Someone who is timid
4. Eerie	d. Imaginary monster
5. Acrophobia	e. Extreme fear of water
6. Pusillanimous	f. Trembling due to fear
7. Timidity	g. Contemptibly fearful
8. Xenophobia	h. Nervous laughter
9. Bugaboo	i. A superstitious sense of fear
10. Timorous	j. Extreme fear of heights

Perfect Section 5: Pronunciation

Match each word with its correct phonetic pronunciation.

1. Timorous	a. hahy-dr*uh*-**foh**-bee-*uh*
2. Acrophobia	b. **tim**-er-*uh*s
3. Pusillanimous	c. ti-**mid**-i-tee
4. Titter	d. **buhg**-*uh*-boo
5. Xenophobia	e. trep-i-**dey**-shu*hn*
6. Timidity	f. **tit**-er
7. Eerie	g. pyoo-s*uh*-**lan**-*uh*-mu*hs*
8. Bugaboo	h. **eer**-ee
9. Hydrophobia	i. zee-n*uh*-**foh**-bee-*uh*
10. Trepidation	j. ak-r*uh*-**foh**-bee-*uh*

Has the word been used correctly?

1. Trepidation implies anticipating falling into a trap.
   Yes No

2. Hydrophobia is an extreme fear of water that often develops due to a rabies infection.
   Yes No

3. A brave person can be called pusillanimous.
   Yes No

4. A loud laugh can be called a titter.
   Yes No

5. Xenophobia makes us fear others for no good reason.
   Yes No

6. There is something really eerie about haunted houses.
   Yes No

7. A bugaboo is a monstrous problem that's almost impossible to solve.
   Yes No

8. A timorous person displays timidity.
   Yes No

9. Acrophobia is the fear of being confined inside a closed space.
   Yes No

10. Timidity implies lack of sanity.
    Yes No

Section 3

1. Titter; 2. Hydrophobia; 3. Trepidation; 4. Timorous; 5. Eerie; 6. Pusillanimous; 7. Xenophobia; 8. Timidity; 9. Bugaboo; 10. Acrophobia

Section 4

1. e; 2. h; 3. g; 4. i; 5. j; 6. g; 7. b; 8. a; 9. d; 10. c

Section 5

1. b; 2. j; 3. g; 4. f; 5. i; 6. c; 7. h; 8. d; 9. a; 10. e

Section 6

1. No; 2. Yes; 3. No; 4. No; 5. Yes; 6. Yes; 7. No; 8. Yes; 9. No; 10. No

9

CONCEPTS OF WAR

Exposure Section 1: Words in Context

I LOVE BRITISH TELEVISION. It's snarky, it's witty, and it reminds us that this is indeed the society that gave us Oscar Wilde and William Shakespeare. (On the latter, by the way, if you can get past the Elizabethan language, you'll find that the Bard is delightfully savage).

The series I've been watching lately is about an aristocratic family set at the onset of World War II. They go about their business with parties, social calls, and torrid love affairs, all while the shadow of Hitler looms in the not-so-distant background.

While the women talk of parties and balls, the men sit in smoky gentleman's clubs, drinking scotch and arguing about spitting hot politics. They talk of Nazi **battalions** at European borders and argue for diplomacy. From time to time, they **bellicosely** barge into politician's offices, spouting their respective position on Herr Hitler's **blitzkrieg** or Parliament's position on Jewish immigration. Because they are, in fact, aristocracy, such **belligerence** is occasionally rewarded with an

espionage mission, meeting with ranking members of the Third Reich.

Then, of course, the series cuts to the changing role of consumerism and fashion. And the scandal of scandals—*women in shorts!*

I'm just in it for the clever dialogue and the fabulous fashion. Everyone dressed so smartly during those days.

But, war—particularly the wars that fill our history texts, comes with its own set of vocabulary. Soldiers that are on leave are said to be on **furlough**, although this can also be used in religious settings to refer to a missionary taking an extended break.

Wounded soldiers are sometimes said to be **convalescent**, and there are homes and programs for them to recover. In more recent memory, England's Prince Harry worked with the Invictus Foundation to assist wounded soldiers, both American and British, coming back from Iraq and Afghanistan.

Civilians in war-torn countries will often keep **stockades** of weapons and armament to protect themselves against **insurgents** or bitter refugees that form militia **regiments**.

War is a messy business, and in the end, no one ever wins. The wounds only fester until the next one begins.

Exposure Section 2: Definitions & Example Sentences

Battalion

(buh-**tal**-yuhn) – (n.) a military unit, typically consisting of 300 to 1000 soldiers commanded by a lieutenant colonel, and subdivided into a number of companies.[197]

A **battalion** of people is a large group of them, especially a well-organized, efficient group with a particular task. Any large group joined together in some activity may be called a **battalion**, not necessarily just a large group of soldiers arrayed for battle.[198]

- The **battalion** of angry protesters marched toward the Capitol building.
- "God is not on the side of the big **battalions**, but on the side of those who shoot best." -Voltaire[199]

Convalescent

(kon-*vuh*-**les**-*uh*nt) - (adj.) (of or relating to) convalescing; being in the process or period of resting to get better after an illness or operation; (n.) someone who is getting better after a serious illness or injury.[200]

A **convalescent** home is where people stay when they need minor medical care, but they do not need a hospital stay.[200]

- As a **convalescent**, Eric felt drained, giddy, and weak.
- "For [D.H.] Lawrence, existence was one continuous **convalescence**; it was as though he were newly reborn from a mortal illness every day of his life. What these convalescent eyes saw, his most casual speech would reveal." - Aldous Huxley[201]

Coxswain

(**kok**-*suh*n) – (n.) a sailor who has charge of a ship's boat and its crew and who usually steers; a steersman of a racing shell who usually directs the rowers; the person who is in charge of a lifeboat and who controls its direction; (also cox) the person who controls the direction of a rowing boat while other people are rowing.[202, 203]

- A **coxswain** is absolutely essential on an eight person rowing boat.
- "Then the **coxswain** called out, 'Ready all!' Joe turned and faced the rear of the boat, slid his seat forward, sank the white blade of his oar into the oil-black water, tensed his muscles, and waited for the command that would propel him forward into the glimmering darkness." -Daniel James Brown, *The Boys in the Boat: Nine Americans and Their Epic Quest for Gold at the 1936 Berlin Olympics*[204]

Bivouac

(**biv**-oo-ak) – (n.) a temporary shelter or camp for sleeping in outside that is not a tent; a usually temporary encampment under little or no shelter; encampment usually for a night; a temporary or casual shelter or lodging; (v.) to camp (= sleep) in a bivouac; to take shelter often temporarily; to make a bivouac; camp.[206, 207, 208]

If you have ever built a "blanket fort" and pretended to bunk down under it (perhaps with your kid), you've made a **bivouac**—a temporary camp with little-to-no cover.[208]

- The explorers built a **bivouac** to protect themselves from the thunderstorm.
- "The new French theme park based on Napoleon is named Napoleon's **Bivouac**, and will honor Napoleon with rides, battle reenactments, and the brutal March on Moscow ride. That's a walk-in freezer you stand in for 18 months while you try to eat a dead horse." -Peter Sagal[209]

Stockade

(sto-**keyd**) – (n.) a wall of large wooden posts built around an area to keep out enemies or wild animals; an enclosure or barrier of stakes and timbers; a penal camp where political prisoners or prisoners of war are confined (usually under harsh conditions); (v.) to surround with a stockade in order to fortify.[210, 211]

- Joseph deftly erected a thick **stockade** to protect the lambs from the wild animals.
- "Anthony set sail for New Amsterdam in 1629, and before long acquired a large farm just north of the city **stockade** at Wall Street, along with a reputation as one of the most quarrelsome characters in a town full of them." -Jennifer Schuessler, *New York Times*[212]

Insurgent

(in-**sur**-juhnt) – (n.) someone who is fighting against the government in their own country; someone who opposes political authority; a person who is a member of a group that is fighting against the government of their country.[213]

- The soldiers had been sent by the government to find and capture all enemy **insurgents**.
- "The violent illiteracies of the graffiti, the clenched silence of the adolescent, the nonsense cries from the stage-happening, are resolutely strategic. The **insurgent** and the freak-out have broken off discourse with a cultural system which they despise as a cruel, antiquated fraud. They will not bandy words with it. Accept, even momentarily, the conventions of literate linguistic exchange, and you are caught in the net of

the old values, of the grammars that can condescend or enslave." -George Steiner[214]

Blitzkrieg

(**blits**-kreeg) – (n.) a fast and intense military attack that takes the enemy by surprise and is intended to achieve a very quick victory; war conducted with great speed and force; Journalists sometimes refer to a rapid and powerful attack or campaign in, for example, sport, politics, or advertising as a blitzkrieg.[215, 216, 217]

Blitzkrieg is a German word used to describe a method of offensive warfare designed to strike a swift, focused blow at an enemy using mobile, maneuverable forces, including armored tanks and air support. Such an attack ideally leads to a quick victory, limiting the loss of soldiers and artillery. Most famously, **blitzkrieg** describes the successful tactics used by Nazi Germany in the early years of World War II, as German forces swept through Poland, Norway, Belgium, Holland, and France with astonishing speed and force.[218]

- Emma knew that she could immediately boost her book sales by launching a publicity **blitzkrieg**.
- "Bird got its black-and-white scooters into a hundred cities globally during a yearlong **blitzkrieg**." -John Seabrook, *The New Yorker*[219]

Espionage

(**es**-pee-*uh*-nahzh) – (n.) the practice of spying or using spies to obtain information about the plans and activities especially of a foreign government or a competing company; the activity of secretly collecting and reporting information, especially secret political, military, business, or industrial information.[220, 221]

- Edward Snowden committed **espionage** by leaking the top secret NSA (National Security Agency) documents to the media.
- "All warfare is based on deception. There is no place where **espionage** is not used. Offer the enemy bait to lure him." - Sun Tzu[222]

Furlough

(**fur**-loh) - (n) a leave of absence granted to a governmental or institutional employee (such as a soldier or civil servant); a temporary leave from work that is not paid and is often for a set period of time; a set period of time when a prisoner is allowed to leave a prison; (v) to grant a leave of absence or furlough to (someone); to put (a worker) on furlough; to lay off (a worker) for usually a brief or temporary period.[223]

- The army sergeant was looking forward to coming home on **furlough**.
- "If you asked Neil today, he would tell you his **furlough** was in 3-D: dates, delirium, and disaster. I provided the dates, the Greenville girls provided the delirium, and Allie, well, she provided the disaster." -Ray Blackston, *A Delirious Summer*[224]

Regiment

(**rej**-*uh*-m*uh*nt, **rej**-*uh*-ment) – (n.) a large group of soldiers, or (more generally) any large number of things or people; a large group of soldiers combining several battalions;[225] a large group of soldiers that is commanded by a colonel; (v.) to manage or treat in a rigid, uniform manner; subject to strict discipline; to form into a regiment or regiments; to assign to a regiment or group; to form into an organized group, usually for the purpose of rigid or complete control.[226, 227]

- Tina has been carefully **regimenting** her diet lately.
- "My dad came from Trinidad to Jamaica when he was 19. He had to go to Jamaica to join the British **regiment**, where it was based. After Sandhurst, he returned to the Caribbean as a junior lieutenant, based in Jamaica. He met my mum and became a Jamaican citizen." -John Barnes[228]

Bellicosity

(**bel**-i-kohs-i-tee) - (n.) the behavior or manner of someone who wants to fight or start a war; the fact of having or showing the desire to argue or fight.[229, 230]

- The tenant's **bellicosity** provoked the landlord to call the police.
- "Back in George W. Bush's second term, when diplomatic realism began to overtake foolish **bellicosity**, the president developed one of his patented nicknames for the two most powerful neoconservative journalists, William Kristol and Charles Krauthammer: he called them 'the Bomber Boys.'" - Joe Klein[231]

Belligerence

(b*uh*-**lij**-er-*uh*ns) – (n.) the act of starting or fighting a war; the wish to fight or argue; an aggressive or truculent attitude, atmosphere, or disposition.[232, 233]

- The savagery and **belligerence** with which the police treated the peaceful protesters is beyond despicable.
- "Russia began its troop drawdown in anticipation of the NATO summit in June, where Moscow's neighborhood **belligerence** and global cyberattacks will be a main topic on the agenda." -Ariel Cohen, Forbes[234]

Practice Section 3: Matching

Match each word with its synonym.

1. Blitzkrieg	a. Army corps
2. Convalescent	b. Military quarters/tents
3. Espionage	c. Guerrilla
4. Stockade	d. Bellicosity
5. Regiment	e. Eavesdropping
6. Coxswain	f. Detention camp
7. Bivouac	g. Leave-of-absence
8. Insurgent	h. Sudden military attack
9. Furlough	i. Recuperating
10. Belligerence	j. Strict
11. Battalion	k. Sailor/captain

Practice Section 4: Fill-in-the-Blank

Fill in the blanks with the correct word.

1. He has been sent to a _____ home in the hopes that he will be able to recover from his illness there.

2. We camped outside cosily laying under a _____ of blankets.

3. The king's castle is surrounded by a _____ of large poles.

4. The two-day _____ was just not enough for the overworked employees to recharge themselves.

5. The soldier was asked to reveal the name of his _____ .

6. For almost a decade his father worked as a _____ on a boat.

7. No one wants to sit next to a _____ old man who wants to pick a fight with everyone.

8. The politician quickly realized that he had been a target of _____ when small cameras and microphones were found all over his house.

9. The _____ responded to the draconian government policies with dramatic and swift action.

10. His _____ gets him in trouble more often than not.

11. The commander-in-chief was welcomed by a large _____ .

12. The _____ attack had been carefully planned for months.

Perfect Section 5: True or False

Test your understanding by deciding whether each of these statements is true or false.

1. Blitzkrieg involves a blitz.
   ▢ True ▢ False

2. Insurgency often transforms into belligerency.
   ▢ True ▢ False

3. An angry and hostile person often displays bellicosity.
   ▢ True ▢ False

4. Both belligerence and bellicosity can be used to refer to someone who is constantly cantankerous.
   ▢ True ▢ False

5. Espionage can be committed only within a political setting.
   ▢ True ▢ False

6. A bivouac is a shelter built only for temporary use.
   ▢ True ▢ False

7. To be on furlough implies to go absconding from work.
   ▢ True ▢ False

8. To regiment something means you are resigning it to fate.
   ▢ True ▢ False

9. For a convalescent person, there is no hope for recovery.
   ▢ True ▢ False

10. There is no difference between a coxswain and a helmsman.
    ▢ True ▢ False

11. A stockade provides protection from intruders.
    ▢ True ▢ False

12. A battalion can be composed of 2-3 soldiers.
    ▢ True ▢ False

Perfect Section 6: Drawing Conclusions

1. Your chickens got attacked by the neighborhood dogs.
   You have resolved to build a _____ around their coop.

2. Your brother has finally started recovering from a serious illness.
   You have decided to visit your _____ brother.

3. You have officially been assigned the task of steering a rowing boat.
   Now you can call yourself a _____ .

4. Your neighbor's kid has set up a tent in his garden and he's calling it his temporary home.
   Your neighbor's kid has built a _____ for himself.

5. You hear that citizens are getting together to rebel against many of the unjust policies that the state has imposed.
   _____ are ready to challenge the state's unjust policies.

6. A rival company offers you a lot of money to reveal some of the trade secrets of the company you are working for.
   You can't imagine committing _____ .

7. The company you work for has decided to temporarily lay off 200 workers.
   200 workers are going to be _____ .

8. You find out how the media is assaulting the survivors of a gas leak tragedy with insensitive questions.
   The media is attacking the survivors with a _____ of insensitive questions.

9. You go out with your friend John to a bar. After getting a few drinks John starts trying to pick a fight with everyone.
   John's _____ behavior gets you both thrown out of the bar.

10. You don't like how strict aunt Gaby is with her kids.
    You don't like how aunt Gaby _____ her kids.

11. Jim is one of those people who are always in a bad and hostile mood.
    Jim's _____ turns people off.

12. Your friend Marie asks you if you would join the large group of dissenters she has organized together for peaceful protests in the city.
    You are ready to join Marie's _____ of dissenters.

Section 3

1. h; 2. i; 3. e; 4. f; 5. j; 6. k; 7. b; 8. c; 9. g; 10. d; 11. a

Section 4

1. Convalescent; 2. Bivouac; 3. Stockade; 4. Furlough; 5. Regiment; 6. Coxswain; 7. Belligerent; 8. Espionage; 9. Insurgents; 10. Bellicosity; 11. Battalion; 12. Blitzkrieg

Section 5

1. True; 2. True; 3. True; 4. True; 5. False; 6. True; 7. True; 8. False; 9. False; 10. False; 11. True; 12. False

Section 6

1. Stockade; 2. Convalescent; 3. Coxswain; 4. Bivouac; 5. Insurgents; 6. Espionage; 7. Furloughed; 8. Blitzkrieg; 9. Belligerent; 10. Regiments; 11. Bellicosity; 12. Battalion

10

A VERY SHORT LOVE STORY

Exposure Section 1: Words in Context

TODAY'S EXPOSURE reading is on love, and given that love is arguably the most written about subject in both film and literature, I decided to turn away from the personal essay format and give you A Very Short Love Story.

*She entered the room, her **paramour** seated on the divan where he had been when she last left him. She shot him a **fervent** glance, and her whole body longed for his touch.*

"I've missed you," she said, removing her work pumps and rubbing her foot. She moaned as her fingertips coaxed the feeling back to her feet.

"Long day?" he asked.

She rolled her eyes. "It always is. The ad world never sleeps."

"So says Don Draper."

*She laughed at his Mad Men reference, and then he smiled slowly, in that **amorous** manner that he only did with her.*

*"I've missed you too," he said, his tone **tenderhearted** and kind. "Tell me about it."*

*Her heart leapt inside her chest. He wasn't a shallow **infatuation,** like the **oversexed** men she'd dated in the past, the kind that would see her entire life as some sort of temporary **amatory.** He loved her for her, and it just made her want him even more.*

"Shall we?" she grabbed the wine bottle from the mantle and held it up.

*He laughed. "Please, My **Betrothed.**"*

*From any other lips, she would have found it nauseating, but the **endearing** way he said it, made her heart quicken. She let the table lamp catch the reflection of the diamond on her finger while she poured. Yes, they were **affianced**, and it had been an exquisite proposal.*

She grabbed the wine off the mantle, uncorked it, and slowly poured the red liquid into the glass. She took a seat next to him on the divan.

Then, she grabbed hold of him and sipped her glass of wine. Then she opened the cover and devoured the first page like a thirsty man in a desert. God, how she loved her books!

Exposure Section 2: Definitions & Example Sentences

Fervency

(**fur**-*vuhn*-see) – (n.) fervour; describing beliefs strongly and sincerely felt, or people who hold strong and sincere beliefs; an intense passion.[235, 236, 237]

- I was amazed by the **fervency** with which the football fans were showing support for their favorite team.
- "Cultivate an appreciation and passion for books. I'm using passion in the fullest sense of the word: a deep, **fervent** emotion, a state of intense desire; an enthusiastic ardor for something or someone." - Cassandra King[238]

Infatuation

(in-fach-oo-**ey**-sh*uh*n) - (n.) foolish or obsessively strong love, admiration, or interest in someone or something; strong, unreasoning attachment, or the object of such an attachment.[239, 240]

Like a schoolgirl's first crush, an **infatuation** is an extreme—but short-lived—love experienced intensely.

- Alice's **infatuation** with John compelled her to do extremely silly things that she later felt terribly embarrassed about.
- "Love sees clearly, and seeing, loves on. But **infatuation** is blind; when it gains sight, it dies." -Mary Roberts Rinehart[241]

Endearing

(en-**deer**-ing) - (adj.) arousing feelings of affection or admiration.[242]

If you describe someone's behavior as **endearing**, you mean that it causes you to feel very fond of them.[243]

- There is nothing **endearing** about his cockiness.
- "Though she has trouble deciphering other people's facial expressions, her face is an open book and no one would ever have trouble understanding hers. I've always wondered if she exaggerates them to help people understand what she's thinking, the way she wishes they would for her. I find it **endearing**." -Tracey Garvis Graves, *The Girl He Used to Know*[244]

Amorous

(**am**-er-*uhs*) - (adj.) of or expressing sexual desire or romantic love.[245]

If you describe someone's feelings or actions as **amorous**, you mean that they involve sexual desire.[246] Perhaps they are giving you "bedroom eyes."

- Olivia continued to resist the **amorous** advances of her ex-husband.
- "I can no longer think of anything but you. In spite of myself, my imagination carries me to you. I grasp you, I kiss you, I caress you, a thousand of the most **amorous** caresses take possession of me." -Honore de Balzac[247]

Tenderhearted

(**ten**-der-**hahr**-tid) - (adj.) easily moved to love, pity, or sorrow;[248] very kind and showing a lot of sympathy.[249]

- Sophia is just as **tenderhearted** as she is beautiful.
- "The greatness of our God lies in the fact that He is both tough minded and **tenderhearted**." - Martin Luther King Jr.[250]

Oversexed

(**oh**-ver-**sekst**) - (adj.) exhibiting an excessive sexual drive or interest; wanting sex more often than is considered normal.[251, 252]

If you describe someone as **oversexed**, you mean that they are more interested in sex or more involved in sexual activities than you think they should be.[253]

- The **oversexed** man can't help going to the brothel every day.
- "From any cross-section of ads, the general advertiser's attitude would seem to be: if you are a lousy, smelly, idle, underprivileged, and **oversexed** status-seeking neurotic moron, give me your money." -Kenneth Bromfield, Advertiser's Weekly[254]

Amatory

(**am**-*uh*-tawr-ee, **am**-*uh*-tohr-ee) - (adj.) of, relating to, or inciting sexual love or desire; of or pertaining to lovers or lovemaking; expressive of love.[255]

- Jim's **amatory** letters to Jen were nothing short of scandalous.
- The boss kept making **amatory** gestures toward the new intern, until HR was called in.

Affianced

(*uh*-**fahy**-*uh*nst) - (v.) engaged to be married; betrothed; promised to marry; (n.) (archaic) a pledging of faith, as a marriage contract.[256]

- The **affianced** bride was eagerly waiting her groom.
- "Alexandra Crotin, a rep for Stone, later confirmed to *USA*

Today the actress and writer are now **affianced**." -Charles Trepany, *USA Today*[257]

Betrothed

(bih-**troh*thd***) - (n.) a person that someone has promised to marry, or has been promised to as a marriage partner; (adj.) engaged to be married.[258, 259]

If you are **betrothed** to someone, you have agreed to marry them, for better or worse.[260]

- Her **betrothed** accompanies her wherever she goes.
- "'She is not my mistress,' replied the young sailor gravely, 'she is my **betrothed**.' 'Sometimes one and the same thing,' said Morrel, with a smile. 'Not with us, sir,' replied Dantes." - Alexandre Dumas, *The Count of Monte Cristo*[261]

Paramour

(**par**-*uh*-moor) - (n.) a person with whom one has a romantic or sexual relationship but to whom one is not married; an illicit or secret lover.[262, 263]

- Andrew has been meeting his **paramour** at a shady motel outside the city.
- "His Vietnamese **paramour** was a young woman of remarkable beauty." -Neil Sheehan, *A Bright Shining Lie*[263]

Practice Section 3: Unscramble the Words

Unscramble the following words.

1. DDETTRRHEEANE

2. DROEEEVXS

3. AYTARMO

4. MPRRUAAO

5. OOMRSAU

6. DAAFFNICE

7. DHBTRTEOE

8. ANNTTIIOFUA

9. RNAEEGDNI

10. VYNCEEFR

Practice Section 4: Matching

Match each word with its correct definition.

1. Amorous	a. Fervour
2. Affianced	b. Excessive sexual desire or interest
3. Infatuation	c. A person to whom one is engaged to be married
4. Tenderhearted	d. Involving or expressing sexual desire
5. Paramour	e. Arousing feelings of affection and fondness
6. Fervency	f. Illicit or secret lover
7. Oversexed	g. Inciting sexual love or desire
8. Amatory	h. Extremely kind and sympathetic
9. Endearing	i. Strong feelings of attraction that don't last long

Perfect Section 5: Pronunciation

Match each word with its correct phonetic pronunciation.

1. Amatory	a. in-fach-oo-**ey**-sh*uh*n
2. Fervency	b. **ten**-der-**hahr**-tid
3. Betrothed	c. **am**-*uh*-tawr-ee
4. Endearing	d. **oh**-ver-**sekst**
5. Paramour	e. *uh*-**fahy**-*uh*nst
6. Amorous	f. **fur**-v*uh*n-see
7. Affianced	g. **pam**-er-*uh*s
8. Oversexed	h. bih-**trohthd**
9. Infatuation	i. **par**-*uh*-moor
10. Tenderhearted	j. en-**deer**-ing

Perfect Section 6: Test Your Knowledge

Has the word been used correctly?

1. A tenderhearted person has a soft heart that melts easily.
   Yes   No

2. You can't have amorous feelings for someone if you aren't in love with them.
   Yes   No

3. There's a huge difference between infatuation and love.
   Yes   No

4. You can use the word amatory to describe platonic feelings for someone.
   Yes   No

5. You can call your fiancé your paramour.
   Yes   No

6. An oversexed person is a tad too preoccupied with sex and sexual desires.
   Yes   No

7. When you are affianced, you have a fiancé.
   Yes   No

8. You find someone endearing only when they are already dearest to you.
   Yes   No

9. When you are betrothed to someone, you are already married to them.
   Yes   No

10. Just because someone is supporting an idea with great fervency doesn't mean that they are fully committed to the cause.
    Yes   No

Section 3

1. Tenderhearted; 2. Oversexed; 3. Amatory; 4. Paramour; 5. Amorous; 6. Affianced; 7. Betrothed; 8. Infatuation; 9. Endearing; 10. Fervency

Section 4

1. d; 2. c; 3. i; 4. h; 5. f; 6. a; 7. b; 8. g; 9. e

Section 5

1. c; 2. f; 3. h; 4. j; 5. i; 6. g; 7. e; 8. d; 9. a; 10. b

Section 6

1. Yes; 2. No; 3. Yes; 4. No; 5. No; 6. Yes; 7. Yes; 8. No; 9. No; 10. Yes

CHAPTERS 6-10 REVIEW

Review Section 1: Split Up

Each word has been cut up. Recombine the word based on the correct answer to each sentence below in section 2. Of the split words, ten are used out of 20.

lough	e	affi	captiate
per	bi	surgent	swain
am	be	ennial	boo
buga	xeno	trothed	tory
in	mour	en	tter
de	dearing	ti	ennial
para	cox	ation	phobia
trepid	eer	anced	poch
orous	fer	am	ie
cade	fur	stock	vency

Review Section 2: Fill-in-the-Blank

Fill in the blanks with the correct word.

1. The patient became overtaken by _____ when he was forced to confront his stepfather's abusive past.

2. I discovered that my ex-husband had more than three _____. In retrospect, this makes sense to me now as I never could understand why he so infrequently spent nights at home.

3. It was a great _____ regardless of the fact that there were pockets of less than desirable occurrences.

4. The presentation was clearly serious and somewhat morbid; however, I could not help but _____ at what I found to be hysterical.

5. The prince is _____ to a young lady who happens to be 20 years old.

6. I was under the impression that Henry and his _____ would disappear after the wedding ceremony.

7. I strongly feel the _____'s aggressive manner hindered the ability of the rowers to continue at the fastest possible speed.

8. Every time I observe those _____ shadows that appear in my doorway at night, they make me tremble with fright.

9. I am on _____ from my job.

10. To _____ someone for a transgression may be viewed by many as a tad bit too harsh.

Review Section 3: Crossword Puzzle

Complete the crossword puzzle based on your acquired knowledge of the vocabulary terms.

Across

2. All-encompassing love-like passion

5. Murderer

12. A distinctive extended period of time

15. A long time ago

17. A military unit

18. To predict based on signs

20. To cut up

22. An aggressive attitude

23. Extreme fear of water

24. To spy on a foreign country

Down

1. A somewhat nervously fearful approach

3. Lack of courage

4. Fear of high places

6. Wife that kills a husband

7. A contemptible lack of courage

8. Recovering from sickness

9. A quick and powerfully conducted war

10. Possessing love and compassion

11. The slicing of a dead corpse

13. Excessive sexual urge and/or interest

14. Inexplicable within the parameters of nature

16. War-like temperament

19. Relating to the expression of love

20. To spoil perfection

21. A temporary encampment with minimal structure

Section 2

1. Trepidation; 2. Paramour; 3. Epoch, 4. Titter; 5. Affianced; 6. Betrothed; 7. Coxswain; 8. Eerie; 9. Furlough; 10. Decapitate

Section 3

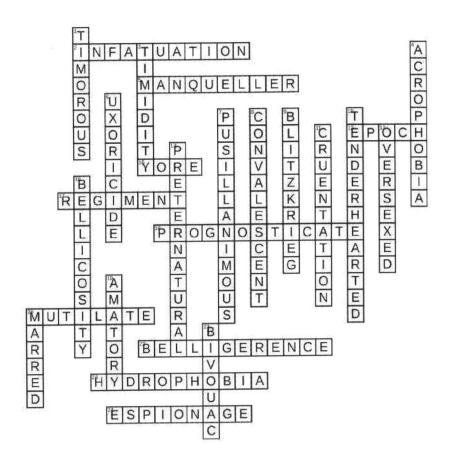

HATE IS AN INTENSE EMOTION

Exposure Section 1: Words in Context

I ONCE WORKED in a medical billing office as a processor for a claims department. It was among the more boring jobs I've had and would have been completely forgettable had it not been for one bizarre incident.

The medical billing office itself was calm enough. It was part of a swanky little business area that would love to have fancied themselves upscale European. They weren't. They were just regular American bourgie. But, as such, the office suite occupied a three-story wing right off a shopping mall. It was a lunch custom to eat at the food court or one of the many eateries the mall district had to offer.

Each day, I came to work, entering through the mall entrance near Macy's, where the security guard was posted. He was an intimidating fellow, tall and lanky, with a thick, bushy mustache, dark glasses, and never, ever, a smile.

He stood with his black windbreaker, reading in big, yellow letters, "Security." He perpetually stared out into the hall, weight evenly distributed on both feet and hands clasped behind his back. Each time I saw him, I felt sorry for whoever shoplifted on his watch.

Being not of the sort that ever had any encounters with security guards or anything of the like, I didn't think much of him and would pass him on my way to the coffee kiosk. I'd order my coffee and proceed up to my office for the day.

I did this for about six months before realizing that my little morning coffee run had been construed beyond offensive to straight-up **abhorrent**. Being in an especially upbeat mood on a particular day, I smiled at the unsmiling and made eye contact with the man behind the glasses.

"Hi!" I greeted him cheerily, with a pleasant and warm smile.

His lips snarled into an expression of pure loathing as if I were a straight-up social **abomination**. "You've worked here since Thanksgiving, and ALL THROUGH THE HOLIDAYS, and now you finally say, 'hi?'"

My stomach froze, and no words came out. I had no idea that this man felt this way. "Oh, man, I'm... I'm sorry. I didn't mean to offend you. I..."

I couldn't think of anything else to say. He snorted as if I were a **detestable** creature.

"You just look right past me," he said, every word dripping with so much **execration**, I was physically taken aback.

It was true, but it was because he appeared to be unapproachable. A fact that he was clearly proving now. I didn't know what else to say. I just laughed weakly, grabbed my coffee, and went up to my office.

Safely at my desk, I took a survey of my co-workers. Was this man just a **misanthrope**, or had I seriously been offensive?

"The security guard? You mean, Rob?" Janet, my co-worker, asked breezily as she handed me a file. "Sure, I always say 'hi' to him. Why do you ask?"

I cleared my throat and sipped my latte. "No reason."

I continued my survey. Brian in accounting swapped sports talk with him, and Betty, the receptionist, once brought him brownies.

"But to be fair," she said. "I brought everyone brownies that day."

But Natasha in customer service furrowed her brow. "He creeps me out. I use the other door."

I smiled and sighed. "Thank you!"

At lunchtime, however, I felt I should make amends with Rob, the security guard. I went downstairs and bought an extra coffee. I approached the statue of a man surveying his kingdom. "Hey, I'm sorry. I didn't mean to offend you. I sometimes have a lot on my mind."

He snorted and took the coffee.

"Yeah, you do," he spat the words out clearly, **despising** me. He cocked his head upward as if he were somehow owed the gift. Then, he turned and walked away.

I rubbed my neck. Geez. Over a 'hi'?

Over the next week, I made a particular point to greet the man. He greeted me back, with an **abhorrent** tone, spitting it back at me with condescension, as if I owed him a greeting. Finally, I got tired of his **antipathy**. If he were going to demand courtesy, in this manner, then he owed me small talk. I approached the unmoving sentry staring out over his territory.

I dug my hands into my pockets and delivered the line I had been preparing all morning. "Did you see the game last night?"

He said nothing and didn't even smile. I walked away and then took Natasha's advice. I used the other door from then on.

That was the most interesting thing that ever happened at that company.

Abominate

(*uh*-**bom**-*uh*-neyt) - (v.) to hate something very much; to dislike intensely; to loathe; to detest.[264, 265]

- Terry **abominates** loud music while his fiancé loves it.
- "There is no story that is not true, [...] The world has no end, and what is good among one people is an **abomination** with others." -Chinua Achebe[266]

Abhor

(ab-**hawr**) - (v.) to hate or loathe something or someone; to regard with extreme repugnance; to feel hatred or loathing for.[267, 268]

If you **abhor** something, you hate it very much, especially for moral reasons.[269]

- Alexander was tired of working at a job he **abhorred**.
- "The hardest chore to do, and to do right, is to think. Why do you think the common man would choose labor, partially, as a distraction from his own thoughts? It is because that level of stress, he most absolutely **abhors**." -Criss Jami, *Healology*[270]

Despise

(dih-**spahyz**) - (v.) to feel a strong dislike for; to look down on with disrespect or aversion; to regard as negligible, worthless, or distasteful.[271, 272]

If you despise something or someone, you dislike them and have a very low opinion of them.[273]

- Tom has been pretending to **despise** Mary when he's actually deeply in love with her.
- "Those that **despise** people will never get the best out of others and themselves." -Alexis de Tocqueville[274]

Detest

(dih-**test**) - (v.) to feel intense and often violent antipathy toward; to hate someone or something very much.[275, 276]

- I **detest** melodramatic soap operas.
- "Now hatred is by far the longest pleasure; men love in haste but they **detest** at leisure." -Lord Byron[277]

Execrate

(**ek**-si-kreyt) - (v.) to declare to be evil or detestable; to loathe, detest, and abhor; to denounce; to curse or damn (a person or thing).[278, 279]

- Since Jonathan is an animal lover, he **execrates** people who abuse dogs.
- "Many Democrats striving to replace Donald Trump are, while **execrating** him, paying him the sincerest form of flattery: imitation." -George Will, *The Dispatch*[280]

Loathe

(loh*th*) - (v.) to hate someone or something; to feel strong hate, dislike, or disgust for someone or something; to dislike greatly and often with disgust or intolerance.[281, 282]

- I **loathe** waiting in queues to get things done.
- "In hatred as in love, we grow like the thing we brood upon. What we **loathe**, we graft into our very soul." -Mary Renault[283]

Misandrist

(**mis**-an-drist) - (n.) someone, especially a woman, who dislikes, despises, mistrusts, or is strongly prejudiced against men; (adj.) showing feelings of hating men, or a belief that women are better than men.[284, 285, 286]

- Feminists are quite frequently accused of being **misandrists**.
- "To critics, Megalians' mirroring tactic is hateful and **misandrist**; to supporters, they are reclaiming a male-centered language that threatens and diminishes women." - Megalia[287]

Misogynist

(mi-**soj**-*uh*-nist) - (n.) a person whose views are shaped by ingrained and institutionalized prejudice against women; a sexist; a person who hates or discriminates against women; (adj.) feeling, showing, or characterized by hatred of or prejudice against women, especially by men.[288, 289]

- She is married to a **misogynist** who believes in controlling every single thing she does.
- "I'm not a **misogynist**, I respect any woman who knows her place." -Stephen Braithwaite[290]

Misanthrope

(**mis**-*uh*n-throhp) - (n.) a person who hates or distrusts humankind; the fact or quality of not liking other people.[291, 292]

- Everyone thinks that the grouchy old man is a **misanthrope** who hates people.
- "You call me a **misanthrope** because I avoid society. You err; I love society. Yet in order not to hate people, I must avoid their company." -Caspar David Friedrich[293]

Antipathy

(an-**tip**-*uh*-thee) - (n.) a natural or habitual repugnance or aversion, or an object of such an aversion; an instinctive opposition in feeling.[294]

- The pair of heated rivals share a mutual **antipathy** toward one another.
- "Green in nature is one thing, green in literature another. Nature and letters seem to have a natural **antipathy**; bring them together and they tear each other to pieces." -Virginia Woolf, *Orlando*[295]

Practice Section 3: Unscramble the Words

Unscramble the following words.

1. ETAHOL

2. RBHAO

3. EEEAXTCR

4. NTMADSRSII

5. OTYGMIINSNS

6. TTDSEE

7. EMSNTRPHOIA

8. SEEDIPS

9. EAMNTIBAO

Practice Section 4: Fill-in-the-Blank

Fill in the blanks with the right words. You may have to recall some words from the previous chapters. Some of the letters of the words have been given here as clues to help you find the most appropriate answers.

1. The **o v e r** _ _ _ _ **d** playboy eventually started **d e s** _ _ _ _ _ _ his own obsession with sex.

2. If you _ _ _ _ _ **e** her so much, then why do you accept her party invitations?

3. He is a playboy and a _ _ _ _ _ _ **n** _ _ _ who treats women like dirt.

4. The _ _ _ _ _ _ _ _ _ _ **e** avoids people at all costs.

5. Chris _ **b** _ _ _ _ working extra hours at his current job.

6. Ava is always trying to pick up a fight with Lucas. It's not surprising that Lucas **e** _ _ _ _ _ _ _ **s** Ava's **b** _ _ _ _ **c** _ _ _ attitude toward him.

7. The media has been constantly selling _ _ **s** _ _ _ _ _ _ _ propaganda to the public by portraying men as enemies of women.

8. Tina **d** _ _ _ _ _ **s** liars and manipulators.

9. He a _ _ _ _ _ _ _ _ _ the insensitive attitude of the science teacher with **f** _ _ _ _ _ _ **y**.

Perfect Section 5: True or False

Test your understanding by deciding whether each of these statements is true or false.

1. When you execrate someone, you are cursing them in some way.
   ☐ True ☐ False

2. The word detest implies that something is really testing you but it's helping you grow.
   ☐ True ☐ False

3. A man-hater can be called a misandrist.
   ☐ True ☐ False

4. You really like the things you abhor.
   ☐ True ☐ False

5. A misogynist is anyone who hates men.
   ☐ True ☐ False

6. A misanthrope hates both men and women.
   ☐ True ☐ False

7. You can say you despise someone when you have great respect for that person.
   ☐ True ☐ False

8. Abominate implies intense hatred towards someone or something.
   ☐ True ☐ False

9. Loathe is the opposite of love.
   ☐ True ☐ False

Match each word with its correct phonetic pronunciation.

1. Abhor	a. dih-**spahyz**
2. Detest	b. mi-**soj**-*uh*-nist
3. Execrate	c. **mis**-an-drist
4. Abominate	d. **mis**-*uh*n-throhp
5. Misandrist	e. *uh*-**bom**-*uh*-neyt
6. Loathe	f. dih-**test**
7. Misanthrope	g. ab-**hawr**
8. Misogynist	h. **loht***h*
9. Despite	i. **ek**-si-kreyt
10. Antipathy	j. an-**tip**-*uh*-thee

Section 3

1. Loathe; 2. Abhor; 3. Execrate; 4. Misandrist; 5. Misogynist; 6. Detest; 7. Misanthrope; 8. Despise; 9. Abominate

Section 4

1. Oversexed, despising; 2. Loathe; 3. Misogynist; 4. Misanthrope; 5. Abhors; 6. Execrate, bellicose; 7. Misandrist; 8. Detests; 9. Abominates, fervency

Section 5

1. True; 2. False; 3. True; 4. False; 5. False; 6. True; 7. False; 8. True; 9. True

Section 6

1. g; 2. f; 3. h; 4. e; 5. c; 6. h; 7. c; 8. b; 9. a; 10. j

12

THE SEXUAL WORLD IN WHICH WE LIVE

Exposure Section 1: Words in Context

I TOOK an advertising class in college. We were to pick any consumer product we wanted and come up with an ad campaign.

We were supposed to use all of our notes, marketing principles, and demographic research to develop an ad campaign. It wasn't a full campaign, mind you, but it involved several print ads.

I had a lot going on that term—like sleeping, and watching TV, so while the others labored over demographic acronyms like "DINK" (double income no kids), census figures, and median annual household incomes, I procrastinated until the last minute.

The night before, I freaked out and threw the ad campaign together. I don't remember what product I chose, but I found a **salacious** photo of a couple kissing. It was beautifully and tastefully done, but the **voluptuous** woman, and the muscular man in a **lascivious** embrace, were clearly intended to evoke **prurient** desire. I loved the photo. I put it in Photoshop, and the picture lent itself so well to emotion that it didn't take much clever wordplay to slap on a couple of slogans. After that, it was all downhill, and I finished the project before dawn.

I'm sad to say I won the gift card. Sex sells.

I felt a twinge of guilt that I had shortcut what was supposed to be a genuine education experience. But then I realized I had learned the true lesson of that assignment, the one they don't teach you in classrooms. Sometimes getting ahead doesn't mean working harder. It just means thinking differently.

I would like to say that I used that lesson to kick life's butt, but the trick to all life lessons is knowing which ones to apply to a specific situation. And that's a judgment call.

Sex sells, and that's true, but, unfortunately, it's become a universal principle. Some would say it's all people ever think about. That's sad, considering the fantastic power of the human mind and how much of it we spend on those base, primal desires. If we didn't place such an emphasis on sex in our culture, perhaps we'd be more advanced than we'd ever dreamed.

There are people, particularly religious groups, that believe that sex is meant only to be shared between a married couple. They remain **chaste** until marriage. In these groups, to violate that standard is to be **promiscuous**, which is a label of immoral behavior.

Exposure Section 2: Definitions & Example Sentences

Bawdy

(**baw**-dee) - (adj.) containing humorous remarks about sex; boisterously or humorously indecent; obscene, lewd.[296, 297]

Bawdy describes humor that is vulgar or off-color. **Bawdy** things are a little inappropriate, intended to be funny, and definitely not the kind of things you want to say in school.[298]

- Delphine certainly didn't appreciate Roger's **bawdy** jokes.
- "It's stupid, **bawdy,** low-stakes fun that knows its audience, always a virtue." -Elle Carroll, *Vulture*[299]

Chaste

(**cheyst**) - (adj.) not having had sex, or only having a sexual relationship with the person you are married to; without having any sexual activity or involvement outside of marriage; severely simple in design or execution; austere.[300, 301]

- Jim has been living a **chaste** and modest life for a very long time now.
- "Be thou as **chaste** as ice, as pure as snow, thou shalt not escape calumny." -William Shakespeare, *Hamlet*[302]

Lascivious

(luh-**siv**-ee-uhs) – (adj.) expressing a strong desire for sexual activity; feeling or expressing strong sexual desire; inclined to lustfulness; wanton; lewd; arousing sexual desire; indicating sexual interest or expressive of lust or lewdness.[303, 304]

If you describe someone as **lascivious**, you disapprove of them because they show a strong interest in sex.[305]

- His **lascivious** smirk spoke volumes about his intentions.
- "The suspect, Elon Duarte, was arrested just before 1 p.m. Sunday and will be arraigned in the West Roxbury division of Boston Municipal Court on charges of lewd and lascivious conduct and two counts of indecent assault and battery, police said." -*The Boston Globe*[306]

Promiscuous

(pruh-**mis**-kyoo-uhs) - (adj.) having or involving many sexual partners; not restricted to one class, sort, or person; indiscriminate.[307]

Commonly used as a pejorative, **promiscuous** refers to someone who has many romantic partners. The word can also be used in a general sense to mean "not limited, restrained, or restricted." If you're a **promiscuous** reader, you'll read just about anything—from nonfiction to science fiction to the back of your shampoo bottle.[208]

- The **promiscuous** footballer takes pride in the fact that he has slept with many women.
- "Tons of women would love to have sex with me. I hate the image of black men as **promiscuous** and unable to control themselves sexually. I don't like that image." -Will Smith[309]

Satyr

(**sey**-ter) - (n.) literally, a woodland creature or deity commonly depicted as having the body of a man and the legs of a goat, with pointy ears, horns, and a tendency toward lecherous merriment; figuratively, a lustful or lecherous man.[310]

- John thinks that he can really get away with living like a **satyr**.
- "Once the plot requires Percy to go on a picturesque quest to retrieve the titular lightning bolt, with Annabeth and a satyr named Grover (Jorrel Javier) in tow, the storytelling and songwriting become hectic and monotonous." -Jesse Green, *New York Times*[311]

Salacious

(*suh*-**ley**-sh*uhs*) - (adj.) arousing or appealing to sexual desire or imagination; having an excessive interest in sex; bawdy, lewd, or erotic.[312]

Something **salacious** is full of juicy details—but they're the kind of raunchy, lusty, dirty details you probably don't want to hear.[313]

- Ava has become addicted to reading **salacious** gossip columns in the Sunday newspaper.
- "In this case, despite the **salacious** and frankly racist attempts to paint Ms. Jones as undeserving and at fault for the death of her unborn child, Washington used discretion to make a call that was about preserving humanity in a moment of tragedy." -Jason Williams, Time[314]

Titillate

(**tit**-l-eyt) - (v.) to tease; to arouse; to interest, especially sexually; to excite pleasurably; to cause a tickling sensation in someone.[315]

A juicy steak may **titillate** your taste buds, or sexy images in a foreign film may titillate your desire. **Titillate** means to excite someone's imagination, especially in a sexual way.[316]

- That mystery novel is designed to **titillate** you without ever providing full satiation.
- "I can't **titillate** the audience just for the sake of doing it." -Tamannaah[317]

Voluptuous

(vuh-**luhp**-choo-uhs) - (adj.) (esp. of women) having a curvaceous and sexual desirable body; soft, pleasurable, or comfortable; lavish.[318, 319]

A voluptuous woman is full-figured and curvy, but this word can apply to more than just body types. From the Latin for "delightful," voluptuous might describe a luxuriously decorated house or a lavish bounty of delicious food.[320]

- Marilyn Monroe had an alluringly **voluptuous** figure.
- "What is erotic? The acrobatic play of the imagination. The sea of memories in which we bathe. The way we caress and worship things with our eyes. Our willingness to be stirred by the sight of the **voluptuous**. What is erotic is our passion for the liveliness of life." -Diane Ackerman[321]

Prurient

(**proor**-ee-uhnt) - (adj.) lascivious; lewd; exciting or encouraging lust; unusually or morbid interested in sex.[322]

Something is **prurient** if it focuses attention on sex not in an artistic way or to teach something, but purely to appeal to one's baser instincts. A **prurient** joke is sure to offend somebody.[323]

- The **prurient** old man was addicted to watching pornographic content online.
- "When the **prurient** and the impotent attack you, be sure you are right." -Oscar Wilde, *The Complete Letters of Oscar Wilde*[324]

Genitalia

(jen-i-**tey**-lee-*uh*, jen-i-**teyl**-y*uh*) - (plural n.) genitals; one's external sexual organs; the testicles and penis of a male or the labia, clitoris, and vagina of a female.[325]

- I could sense that she was feeling a little uncomfortable looking at impressionistic paintings portraying male **genitalia**.
- "'Captain,' I said after ten steps, without breaking stride. 'I do understand that this is the **Genitalia** Festival. But when you say **genitalia**, doesn't that usually mean **genitals** generally? Not just one kind?' For all the steps I'd taken, and as far down the corridor as I could see, the walls were hung with tiny penises. Bright green, hot pink, electric blue, and a particularly eye-searing orange." -Ann Leckie, *Ancillary Sword*[326]

Practice Section 3: Matching

Match each word with its meaning.

1. Salacious	a. A lecherous man
2. Lascivious	b. Pleasantly excite, just a little
3. Voluptuous	c. Humorously indecent
4. Promiscuous	d. A morbid interest in sex
5. Titillate	e. Reproductive organs
6. Prurient	f. Having a full and curvy shape
7. Bawdy	g. Celibate, sexually pure
8. Genitalia	h. Juicy and sexy
9. Satyr	i. Lewd behavior
10. Chaste	j. Having multiple sexual partners

Practice Section 4: Fill-in-the-Blank

Fill in the blanks with the right word.

1. Liam is addicted to **p** _ _ _ _ _ _ _ _ _ behavior—he just can't keep himself restricted to one person.

2. The _ _ _ _ _ _ _ _ **s** woman inadvertently attracted a lot of attention to herself.

3. An _ _ **t** _ _ _ _ _ person possesses various parts of both the male and the female _ **e** _ _ _ _ _ _ _.

4. Not everyone can live a pure and _ _ _ _ **t** _ life devoid of sensual pleasures.

5. The sex offender has a **p** _ _ _ _ _ _ _ interest in watching child pornography.

6. The drunk man took off his clothes and started running naked on the street. He was arrested for his indecent and _ _ **s** _ _ _ _ _ _ conduct.

7. Cooper has earned himself the label of a **s** _ _ _ _ _ _ _ womanizer.

8. Zoey was walking around the house in the sexy dress to _ _ _ _ _ _ **a** _ _ her husband.

9. The drunk man at the bar just won't stop singing _ _ **w** _ _ songs.

10. The old man is an absolute _ _ **t** _ _ ! I hate the lewd looks he gives to all women.

Perfect Section 5: True or False

Test your understanding by deciding whether each of these statements is true or false.

1. Titillate and titular mean the same thing.
   ☐ True ☐ False

2. Salacious is a pejorative term that you will never use to describe a person or thing in a positive way.
   ☐ True ☐ False

3. Prude and prurient are synonyms.
   ☐ True ☐ False

4. A promiscuous person practices monogamy.
   ☐ True ☐ False

5. Minimalistic architecture can be described as chaste.
   ☐ True ☐ False

6. The word genitalia refers to both the male and the female reproductive organs.
   ☐ True ☐ False

7. A satyr is a character in a satire.
   ☐ True ☐ False

8. A Lascivious person is full of lust.
   ☐ True ☐ False

9. Bawdy is a word that's used for describing bards.
   ☐ True ☐ False

10. You can use the word voluptuous to describe things that are very lush and luxurious.
    ☐ True ☐ False

Perfect Section 6: Drawing Conclusions

1. Your mother insists on showing you her large collection of mismatched China.
   Your mother's China collection is quite   .

2. You come across an ancient statue of a creature that is half man and half goat.
   The creature was apparently very fond of wine, women, and sex.
   You have come across the statue of a   .

3. You watched the trailer of a movie and now you are hungry to watch the entire movie.
   The trailer has managed to   you.

4. Your friend tells you that she is saving herself for the right man until marriage.
   Your friend is keeping herself   .

5. A wealthy man invites you on a house tour. You're awe-struck by how grand and luxurious the house décor is.
   You are feeling amazed by the   décor of the house.

6. Your colleague tells you how your boss has been making inappropriate advances toward the new intern.
   Your colleague informs you about your boss's   behavior toward the new intern.

7. You are feeling disgusted when pictures of a penis suddenly pop up while you are surfing the internet.
   You are feeling repulsed by unnecessary online ads featuring the male   .

8. Your friend Jim makes some remarks that are terribly inappropriate and sexual in nature. Yet, they are also quite funny so you are trying to muffle your laughter.
   You can't prevent yourself from laughing at Jim's   remarks.

9. You discover that your neighbor has been peeking inside your bathroom window while you are in the shower.
   You are feeling disturbed by your neighbor's   curiosity.

10. Your neighbor wants to share a juicy piece of gossip with you.
    You are not interested in listening to the neighbor's   gossip.

Section 3

1. h; 2. i; 3. f; 4. j; 5. b; 6. d; 7. c; 8. e; 9. a; 10. g

Section 4

1. Promiscuous; 2. Voluptuous; 3. Intersex, genitalia; 4. Chaste; 5. Prurient; 6. Lascivious; 7. Salacious; 8. Titillate; 9. Bawdy; 10. Satyr

Section 5

1. False; 2. True; 3. False; 4. False; 5. True; 6. True; 7. False; 8. True; 9. False; 10. True

Section 6

1. Promiscuous; 2. Satyr; 3. Titillate; 4. Chaste; 5. Voluptuous; 6. Lascivious; 7. Genitalia; 8. Bawdy; 9. Prurient; 10. Salacious

13

EVERYTHING IS CONNECTED

Exposure Section 1: Words in Context

I LOVE THAT MOVIE, *About a Boy*. It's a Hugh Grant movie from the early 2000s about a 38-year-old British bachelor stuck in a Peter Pan complex. He plays Will, a trust fund kid sitting around his house all day, watching TV, getting drunk, and scamming women for sex. But, when a tortured young boy runs across his path, Will has to grow up.

But, in the beginning, in the voice-over, he explains his view of the world. He defies John Donne's famed quote, "No man is an island," by saying, "All men are islands." He compares himself to a tourist beach paradise, in which visitors, particularly beautiful women, can come and go, but he is the only constant. He has the entire system worked out where he lives utterly unfettered by the world around him, in drama-free, carefree bliss.

But he is alone.

Life doesn't work that way. We all need others in our lives. Everything and everyone is **interconnected** in our world. What happens with or to one person affects all living beings on the planet in some way. We are a product of our **consanguine**, or blood relatives, and our place in the world is created by the **ancestry** before us. As we live and move through this world, we are constantly impacted by the others around us.

Some love us. Some hate us. Some befriend us. Some break our hearts. Some break our spirits. Some point us to our destinies. Some lead us astray. Some stand there and snap the photos.

All of us are part of the collective whole. We can't extricate ourselves from our responsibilities toward our fellow humans. Every time we do something that negatively impacts another person, we are also attacking ourselves.

While we are impacted by society at large, the people who remain near us daily affect us the most. Therefore, we need to be very careful when picking our friends and **acquaintances**.

Don't surround yourself with people who are inauthentic or phony in any way. There is a **disjunction** between who they say they are and who they actually are. These people would stab you in the back whenever they get the chance. Instead, build friendships and **alliances** with those who truly care about you. At work, make **liaisons** with people and companies that you can trust, and join **affiliations** that will further your career.

Exposure Section 2: Definitions & Example Sentences

Nexus

(**nek**-*suhs*) - (n.) an important link or connection point between the parts of a system or a group of things.[327]

If you happen to be at the **nexus** of something, you are right in the middle of it, like standing in the middle of an intersection.[328]

- There is a **nexus** between growing depression and suicide.

- "What we are seeking is the **nexus** of all possible worlds and states of mind, which is within us. The source of yin and yang is within you." -Frederick Lenz[329]

Conjunction

(k*uh*n-**juhngk**-sh*uh*n) - (n.) an occurrence of two or more things at the same time or place; a state of being conjoined; in grammar, a word or group of words that joins together words, groups, or clauses; in astrology, a situation in which two planets appear to be in the same part of the sky as seen from earth.[330, 331, 332]

- By a strange **conjunction** of extraordinary circumstances, she ended up meeting the stranger she had fallen in love with once again at the same spot.
- "In politics a capable ruler must be guided by circumstances, conjectures, and **conjunctions**." -Catherine the Great[333]

Coupling

(**kuhp**-ling) - (n.) the act of coming together, esp. as a pair; sexual union; a means of electric connection of two electric circuits by having a part common to both.[334]

- Jason decided to recheck the **coupling** before driving the trailer van.
- "Very few people realise that sex is a psychic and not a physical act. The clumsy **coupling** of human beings is simply a biological paraphrase of this truth—a primitive method of introducing minds to each other, engaging them. But most people are stuck in the physical aspect, unaware of

the poetic rapport which it so clumsily tries to teach." -
Lawrence Durrell[335]

Liaison

(lee-ey-**zawn**) - (n.) communication between people or groups who
work with each other; communication between groups and the useful
relationship that this creates, or a person who does the communicating
between the groups; an illicit sexual relationship: affair; a close bond or
connection.[336]

You can refer to a sexual or romantic relationship between two people
as a **liaison**.[337]

- The **liaison** officer did his best to placate the situation.
- "The advertising man is a **liaison** between the products of
  business and the mind of the nation. He must know both
  before he can serve either." -Glenn Frank[338]

Interconnection

(in-ter-k*uh*-**nekt**-zh*uh*n) - (n.) a mutual connection between two or
more things; (computer science) the act of interconnecting (wires,
computers, theories, etc.)[339, 340]

- There was a powerful **interconnection** between the
  employees and the boss since the boss really cares for his
  people.
- "A successful business is not built just on your expertise, it
  needs mastering of all the business pieces and maintaining the
  interconnection among them in a profitable and fruitful

way." -Pooja Agnihotri, *17 Reasons Why Businesses Fail: Unscrew Yourself From Business Failure*[341]

Disjunction

(dis-**juhngk**-sh*uh*n) - (n.) a difference or lack of connection between two things; a broken connection.[342]

If you have a **disjunction**, things are not joined together—there's a disconnect. If you order a pizza and the waiter brings you caviar, that's a **disjunction**.[343]

- There is a **disjunction** between what he says he will do and what he's actually capable of doing.
- "To attempt to write seriously is always, I feel, to fail—the **disjunction** between my beautifully sonorous, accurate, and painfully affecting mental content, and the leaden, halting sentences on the page always seems a dreadful falling short." -Will Self[344]

Articulation

(ahr-tik-y*uh*-**ley**-sh*uh*n) - (n.) the manner in which things come together and a connection is made; in anatomy, the point of connection between two bones or elements of a skeleton (especially if this connection point allows motion); in speech or music, the act of producing a sound or word clearly, in speech or music.[345]

The articulation of an idea or feeling is the expression of it, especially in words.[346]

- The immigrant had to work very hard to improve his articulation of English words.
- "If the tongue had not been framed for articulation, man would still be a beast in the forest." -Ralph Waldo Emerson[347]

Consanguine

(kon-sang-**gwin**) - (adj.) related by blood; having the same ancestry or descent.[348]

Consanguine describes people who are biologically related. People related through marriage or adoption cannot be called **consanguine**. Consanguineous is a similar form of the word, and both come to us from the Latin meaning "of the same blood."[349]

- Jose treats his affinal relatives just as well as he treats the **consanguine** ones.
- Children born out of **consanguineous** marriages often suffer from serious birth defects.

Ancestry

(**an**-ses-tree) - (n.) lineage or descent, especially if ancient, noble, or otherwise distinguished; ancestors, collectively; the history or developmental process of a phenomenon, object, idea, or style.[350]

- He belongs to an important family with a well-established **ancestry**.
- "I'm so proud of my Chinese **ancestry**, but I was born and raised in America, and I really believe in American values, our American system, our freedom, our liberties." -Gary Locke[351]

Affiliation

(*uh*-fil-ee-**ey**-sh*uh*n) - (n.) noun form of verb affiliate; a connection with a political party or religion, or with a larger organization; the relationship between two companies that are officially connected to each other.[352]

If one group has an **affiliation** with another group, it has a close or official connection. If you have an **affiliation** with a group or another person, you have a close or official connection with them.[353]

- The minister made it clear that his party has no **affiliation** with any religious group.
- "Biophilia, if it exists, and I believe it exists, is the innately emotional **affiliation** of human beings to other living organisms." -E.O. Wilson[354]

Acquaintance

(*uh*-**kweyn**-tns) - (n.) a person that you have met but do not know well enough to call a friend; light knowledge of a subject.[355]

- I'm not **acquainted** enough with Russian literature to comment on it.
- "The dividing line [between friends and **acquaintances**] is communication, I think. A friend is someone to whom you can say any jackass thing that enters your mind. With **acquaintances**, you are forever aware of their slightly unreal image of you, and to keep them content, you edit yourself to fit. Many marriages are between **acquaintances**. You can be with a person for three hours of your life and have a friend. Another will remain an **acquaintance** for thirty years." -John D. MacDonald[356]

Alliance

(*uh*-**lahy**-*uh*ns) - (n.) an agreement to work with another person, organization, etc. to try to achieve the same thing; a group of countries, companies, organizations, etc. who have agreed to work together because of shared interests; an association to further the common interests of the members; union by relationship in qualities; affinity.[357, 358, 359]

- During Medieval times there was a powerful **alliance** between the church and the state.
- "In reality, there appears to be no **alliance** that is impossible because of identity differences. If relative power considerations dictate that two groups unite in an **alliance**, then the elites involved will always find some characteristic that they share and construct a justifying narrative around that attribute." -Fotini Christia, *Alliance Formation in Civil Wars*[360]

Unscramble the following words.

1. UECNSANNGIO
2. CCNTNNTNOOIEREI
3. RNTAOITCLAUI
4. GCOPNUIL
5. EQCANANCTUAI
6. NNDTOCIISUJ
7. ANSLOII
8. EALCLAIN
9. NNJTONCCIOU
10. YACSTNRE
11. SNUEX
12. ANTFAF ILIIO

Practice Section 4: Matching

Match each word with its correct definition.

1. Interconnection	a. At the middle of something
2. Coupling	b. A broken connection
3. Articulation	c. Officially connected to someone or something
4. Consanguine	d. Clearly expressing yourself in words
5. Ancestry	e. A word that joins two words, clauses, or phrases together
6. Nexus	f. Lineage
7. Liaison	g. Copulating
8. Acquaintance	h. Blood-related
9. Conjunction	i. Mutual connection between two or more things
10. Disjunction	j. Illicit romantic or sexual relationship
11. Alliance	k. Someone you know but not too well
12. Affiliation	l. Working together to achieve common goals or shared interests

Perfect Section 5: Pronunciation

Match each word with its correct phonetic pronunciation.

1. Coupling   a. kuhn-**juhngk**-shuhn

2. Disjunction   b. ahr-tik-yuh-**ley**-shuhn

3. Nexus   c. in-ter-kuh-**nekt**-zhuhn

4. Ancestry   d. kon-sang-**gwin**

5. Liaison   e. uh-**lahy**-uhns

6. Consanguine   f. uh-**kweyn**-tns

7. Articulation   g. **an**-ses-tree

8. Affiliation   h. lee-ey-**zawn**

9. Conjunction   i. dis-**juhngk**-shuhn

10. Interconnection   j. **nek**-suhs

11. Alliance   k. uh-fil-ee-ey-**shuhn**

12. Acquaintance   l. **kuhp**-ling

Perfect Section 6: Test Your Knowledge

Has the word been used correctly?

1. There can be a disjunction between what is theoretically taught and what is actually practiced.
   ▢ Yes ▢ No

2. Conjunctions are an essential part of English grammar.
   ▢ Yes ▢ No

3. To be affiliated to an organization implies you are not connected to it.
   ▢ Yes ▢ No

4. You can use gesticulation to improve your articulation.
   ▢ Yes ▢ No

5. You can use the word ancestry only when referring to an aristocratic lineage.
   ▢ Yes ▢ No

6. Telepathy happens when there is some form of interconnection.
   ▢ Yes ▢ No

7. A sacred platonic relationship between two people can be described as a liaison.
   ▢ Yes ▢ No

8. You can use a coupling to separate two parts of equipment from each other.
   ▢ Yes ▢ No

9. The kitchen can be the nexus of all our family activities.
   ▢ Yes ▢ No

10. Sanguinary is a synonym of consanguine.
    ▢ Yes ▢ No

11. Association and alliance can be described as synonyms.
    ▢ Yes ▢ No

12. You can describe your best friend as an acquaintance.
    ▢ Yes ▢ No

Section 3

1. Consanguine; 2. Interconnection; 3. Articulation; 4. Coupling; 5. Acquaintance; 6. Disjunction; 7. Liaison; 8. Alliance 9. Conjunction; 10. Ancestry 11. Nexus; 12. Affiliation

Section 4

1. i; 2. g; 3. d; 4. h; 5. f; 6. a; 7. j; 8. k; 9. e; 10. b; 11. l; 12. c

Section 5

1. l; 2. i; 3. j; 4. g; 5. h; 6. d; 7. b; 8. k; 9. a; 10. c; 11. e; 12. f

Section 6

Yes; 2. Yes; 3. No; 4. Yes; 5. No; 6. Yes; 7. No; 8. No; 9. Yes; 10. No 11. Yes; 12. No

14

FROM MARRIAGE TO DIVORCE

Exposure Section 1: Words in Context

IT WAS A MOMENT TO REMEMBER.

In 2011, Prince William, the heir to the British throne, wed his college girlfriend, Kate Middleton. They were both young and dashing, and the world watched on television as the future King of England and his bride entered into **matrimony**.

Seven years later, his brother, Harry, would wed his fiancee, actress Meghan Markle, in an equally exquisite fashion, with bells ringing outside Windsor Castle. In the years between, their various cousins and relations would marry their respective beaus, like investment bankers, and rugby players, and such. Across the pond, former first daughters Jenna Bush and Chelsea Clinton would also wed their respective beaus. Although untelevised, the curious public would rack up page views to see the photos of the rich and famous in their glamorous **nuptials**.

We have always had a fascination with weddings, and we make them big, grand, elegant, and full of lace and flowers and elaborate cakes, and we learn stuffy etiquette. But underneath the fondant, and place card settings, and carefully chosen playlist, is really just two people, pledging to do life together, pledging to love each other, pledging to be there for each other, till the end.

Except when it's not.

The sad truth is, many couples find "till death" to be too long. They sometimes grow apart and decide on a **dissolution** of the marriage. Other times, one or both partners may find the expectation of **monogamy** too constraining and seek others to fulfill their spouse's roles. This is a practice commonly known as adultery, or more casually, cheating. Other times, they find that the wedding was a mistake and get an **annulment**. Usually done within the first weeks of the marriage, an annulment is like a legal "back" or "delete" button. Rather than going through the divorce process, an annulment can be easier for couples to do.

But since marriage is a union of all things, including finances, couples that get divorces often find themselves in a bit of a predicament. The law has protections such as alimony, requiring a spouse to continue to provide some financial support, usually for some time. These days many couples get **prenuptial agreements** deciding the terms of separations long before the **nuptials** are officiated.

Exposure Section 2: Definitions & Example Sentences

Nuptial

(**nuhp**-sh*uh*l) - (n.) usually used as plural, nuptials, marriage; a wedding; (adj.) of or relating to marriage or the marriage ceremony; in biology, of, relating to, or characteristic of mating or the mating season of animals.[370, 371]

- For a year, the newlyweds lived in perfect **nuptial** bliss.

- "Every year after the first rains, the future kings and queens of fungus-growing termite colonies leave their nest on a **nuptial** flight." -Cecilia Rodriguez, *Forbes*[372]

Matrimony

(**ma**-tr*uh*-moh-nee) - (n.) the state or condition of being married; the ceremony or sacrament of marriage.[373]

Matrimony is just a fancy way of saying "marriage." When a couple ties the knot, they are engaging in **matrimony**. You can describe both the wedding celebration and the state of being married as matrimony.[374]

- On the 13th of March, Sebastian and Ella were united in holy **matrimony**.
- "As a great part of the uneasiness of **matrimony** arises from mere trifles, it would be wise in every young married man to enter into an agreement with his wife, that in all disputes of this kind the party who was most convinced they were right should always surrender the victory. By which means both would be more forward to give up the cause." -Henry Fielding[375]

Espousal

(ih-**spou**-z*uh*l) (n.) - betrothal; engagement to be married; a taking up or adopting of a cause or belief; adoption or advocacy, as of a cause or principle; a marriage ceremony; an engagement or betrothal celebration.[376, 377]

In the old days, an **espousal** was an engagement or a wedding—gaining a spouse, in other words. This literal meaning has fallen out of favor in modern times, replaced with the latter definition today. When you speak up in favor of something or support a cause, that's **espousal**. Your **espousal** of energy conservation can be seen in your electric car and the solar panels on your house.[378]

- Josh eventually started questioning his **espousal** of radical leftist ideologies.
- "The **espousal** of the doctrine of Negro inferiority by the South was primarily because of economic motives and the inter-connected political urge necessary to support slave industry; but to the watching world it sounded like the carefully thought out result of experience and reason; and because of this it was singularly disastrous for modern civilization science and religion, in art and government, as well as in industry." -W.E.B. Du Bois[379]

Monogamy

(m*uh*-**nog**-*uh*-mee) - (n.) marriage with only one person at a time, as compared to bigamy or polygamy; the practice of maintaining a sexual relationship with a single partner, as compared to polyamory; (zoology) the practice of having only one mate.[380]

Monogamy is when you are married to, or in a sexual relationship with, one person at a time. Humans are one of the few species that practice **monogamy**.[381]

- Many pseudo-spiritual cults celebrate promiscuity and vilify **monogamy**.
- "For example, most mammals are either **monogamous** or polygamous. But as every poet or divorce attorney will tell

you, humans are confused. After all, we have **monogamy**, polygamy, polyandry, celibacy, and so on. In terms of the most unique thing we do socially, my vote goes to something we invented alongside cities—we have lots of anonymous interactions with strangers. That has shaped us enormously." - Robert M. Sapolsky[382]

Connubial

(kuh-**noo**-bee-uhl) - (adj.) connected with marriage.[383]

Use the adjective **connubial** to describe something related to marriage or the relationship between spouses, such as **connubial** bliss or a **connubial** argument about who will take out the trash. The Latin prefix con- means "together," and nubilis means "marriageable," where we also find the origin of today's nubile, referring to a young, attractive woman.[384]

- In the aftermath of an ugly breakup, Samantha felt that she would probably never experience **connubial** bliss.
- "The Maldivians have the highest divorce rate in the world, a fact which to my mind uniquely qualifies them to officiate over the interment by water of the **connubial** myth." - Rachel Cusk, *Condé Nast Traveler*[385]

Conjugal

(**kon**-juh-guhl) - (adj.) connected with marriage or the relationship between two married people, especially their sexual relationship.[386]

You've undoubtedly heard of the term "**conjugal** visits" to refer to private meetings between a prisoner and their spouse. But "**conjugal**" can describe anything that happens between married people—such as **conjugal** obligations, which are the things you do to keep a marriage going.[387]

- The inmate was allowed bi-weekly **conjugal** visits from his spouse.
- "If the husband is not in a peaceful state of mind and is deprived of **conjugal** happiness, it would eventually percolate down to everyone else in the family. Hence, if the husband is without bliss, the fate of the wife also remains sunk in gloom." -Nihar Satpathy, *Monologues of Mahalakshmi*[388]

Prenuptial Agreement (prenup)

(pree-**nuhp**-shuhl uh-**gree**-muhnt) - (n.) an official document signed by two people before they get married that says what will happen to their possessions and/or children if they divorce (= officially stop being married).[389]

"**Prenuptial**" means before marriage. Commonly called a **prenup** for short, some couples enter into this legal contract before marriage to specify the division of assets in the event of divorce.[390]

- Jacob asked Ava to sign a **prenuptial agreement** right after they got engaged.
- "We're reviewing all the estate planning work, because some things will have to change now. If they had a partnership agreement, it's contract law, but when you marry you have to adhere to marriage laws, . . . With a marriage, a spouse is entitled to a percentage of your assets, so we're counseling clients about **prenuptial agreements** before they get married, wills that have to be redone, and we're putting money

into budgets for weddings and honeymoons." -John LeBlanc[391]

Annulment

(*uh*-**nuhl**-m*uh*nt) - (n.) an official announcement that something such as a law, agreement, or marriage no longer exists, or the process of making this announcement; a judicial or ecclesiastical pronouncement declaring a marriage invalid; a formal invalidation, especially of a marriage.[392, 393, 394]

- The wife is seeking an **annulment** on the grounds that she was coerced into marriage.
- "Eleanor was estranged from Henry at the time Giraldus was writing, and the king was trying to secure an **annulment** of their marriage from the Pope. It would have been to his advantage to declare her an adulterous wife who had had carnal relations with his father, for that in itself would have rendered their marriage incestuous and would have provided prima facie grounds for its dissolution." -Alison Weir, *Eleanor of Aquitaine: A Life*[395]

Dissolution

(dis-*uh*-**loo**-sh*uh*n) - (n.) the act of breaking up officially an organization or institution, a formal agreement, a marriage or a business partnership; a process by which something becomes weaker and then disappears.[396]

The **dissolution** of a relationship means that it's broken up or ended. The **dissolution** of your band means you better get started on your solo album.[397]

- Increase in depression and stress can be linked to the **dissolution** of traditional family life.
- "I believe that the **dissolution** of a marriage comes about by the breaking down of self-esteem." -Dixie Carter[398]

Alimony

(**al**-*uh*-moh-nee) - (n.) an allowance made to one spouse by the other for support pending or after legal separation or divorce.[399]

- Alicia has been receiving **alimony** from her ex-husband.
- "California has legislatively barred **alimony** payments to a dependent spouse who has attempted to murder the supporting spouse. Cal. Fam. Code § 4324." -D. Kelly Weisberg, *Modern Family Law: Cases and Materials*[400]

Practice Section 3: Pronunciation

Match each word with its phonetic pronunciation.

1. Monogamy	a. **kon**-juh-guhl
2. Matrimony	b. ih-**spou**-zuhl
3. Dissolution	c. pree-**nuhp**-shuhl uh-**gree**-muhnt
4. Conjugal	d. uh-**nuhl**-muhnt
5. Connubial	e. **ma**-truh-moh-nee
6. Alimony	f. dis-uh-**loo**-shuhn
7. Prenuptial Agreement	g. muh-**nog**-uh-mee
8. Nuptial	h. **al**-uh-moh-nee
9. Annulment	i. **nuhp**-shuhl
10. Espousal	j. kuh-**noo**-bee-uhl

Practice Section 4: Fill-in-the-Blank

Fill in the blanks with the correct word.

1. Even though 25 years have passed, their **c** _ _ _ _ _ _ _ _ has only strengthened over time.

2. She has a certain obsession with _ _ _ **r** _ _ _ _ _. Every time she meets even a remotely eligible bachelor, her mind jumps to the idea of being his wife.

3. The bride and groom decided to not get a _ _ _ _ _ _ **t** _ _ _ **a** _ _ _ _ _ _ _ _ as that would be a real romance killer.

4. Playboys don't believe in _ _ _ **o** _ _ _ _.

5. The court ordered the husband to pay a substantial _ _ _ **m** _ _ _ to his wife.

6. The singer filed for _ _ _ _ _ **m** _ _ _ just 24 hours after getting married.

7. Harry and his wife are planning a _ _ _ _ _ _ **a** _ retreat to help revive their marriage.

8. Donald's wife is very happy with his _ _ **p** _ _ _ _ _ of libertarian principles.

9. The scandal led to a _ _ _ _ **o** _ _ _ _ _ _ of Parliament.

10. A day before her _ _ **p** _ _ _ _ _, Cynthia was feeling very nervous and jittery.

Perfect Section 5: True or False

Test your understanding by deciding whether each of these statements is true or false.

1. A conjugal visit is a scheduled time during which a prisoner is allowed to have private time with his spouse.
   ◻ True ◻ False

2. The word marriage and matrimony have the exact same meaning.
   ◻ True ◻ False

3. A monogamous person can have multiple romantic partners.
   ◻ True ◻ False

4. The word dissolution can be used to describe the process of decay.
   ◻ True ◻ False

5. A prenuptial agreement can be created even after the wedding has taken place.
   ◻ True ◻ False

6. You are espousing an idea when you're opposed to it.
   ◻ True ◻ False

7. Husbands can also receive alimony from their ex-wives.
   ◻ True ◻ False

8. Conjugal and connubial are synonyms.
   ◻ True ◻ False

9. Nuptial behavior is a term that can be used for describing mating behavior.
   ◻ True ◻ False

10. Annulment and divorce aren't the same thing.
    ◻ True ◻ False

Perfect Section 6: Drawing Conclusions

Fill in the blanks with the correct word.

1. You are deeply committed to the person you love. You can't imagine thinking of another person as your special someone.
   You are strictly _ _ _ _ g _ _ _ _ _.

2. Your parents have had a beautiful relationship all their life.
   You want to know the secret of their _ _ n _ _ _ _ _ _ happiness.

3. Your friend Josh has gotten married 3 times and is now thinking of getting married one more time.
   Serial _ _ _ _ _ m _ _ _ seems to be Josh's thing.

4. You read about a woman who managed to escape from domestic abuse by running away from her husband's home.
   The woman managed to escape domestic violence by abandoning her _ _ _ _ u _ _ _ abode.

5. Your friend got married on a whim while partying in Vegas. A few hours later, he is shocked to learn that he is married. The marriage needs to be voided since it wasn't exactly intentionally entered into.
   Your friend is going to the court to seek an _ _ _ u _ _ _ _ _.

6. Your friend has separated from her husband. He is paying a certain amount of money to help support her and their kids.
   Your friend is receiving _ _ _ m _ _ _ from her ex-husband.

7. Your friend has hired the best lawyer in town to draft a solid agreement that will help protect her assets in case she and her husband decide to get divorced at some point.
   Your friend has hired the best lawyer in town to draft an ironclad
   _ _ _ u _ _ _ _ _ a _ _ _ _ _ _ _ _.

8. Your neighbors went to court to seek an annulment so that their marriage can be ended.
   Your neighbors went to court to seek an annulment that would lead to the
   _ _ s _ _ _ _ _ _ _ _ of their marriage.

9. You're getting married. You would like the wedding ceremonies to be performed at the local church.
   You would like your _ _ p _ _ _ _ _ to be officiated at the local church.

10. Other people don't like your liberal ideas.
    Your _ s _ _ _ _ _ _ of liberal ideologies has made you quite unpopular amongst your peers.

Section 3

1. g; 2. e; 3. f; 4. a; 5. j; 6. h; 7. c; 8. i; 9. d; 10. b

Section 4

1. Connubial; 2. Matrimony; 3. Prenuptial agreement; 4. Monogamy; 5. Alimony; 6. Annulment; 7. Conjugal; 8. Espousal; 9. Dissolution; 10. Nuptials

Section 5

1. True; 2. True; 3. False; 4. True; 5. False; 6. False; 7. True; 8. True; 9. True; 10. True

Section 6

1. Monogamous; 2. Connubial; 3. Matrimony; 4. Conjugal; 5. Annulment; 6. Alimony; 7. Prenuptial Agreement; 8. Dissolution; 9. Nuptials; 10. Espousal

15

THE FAMILIAL UNIT

Exposure Section 1: Words in Context

FAMILY. You can't live with them, and you can't live without them. Well, depending on who you are, the second part might not be accurate.

But there's nothing quite like family, the ups and downs, the in-laws and outlaws, and yet, you stick together. Like glue, the really annoying kind that you can't get off your fingers for days.

With family comes a lot of responsibilities and a lot of roles, and unspoken expectations. Some families are more hierarchical and formal than others. Some families have a very traditional structure. The father is the head of the family, called a **patriarch**. Although in some families, the mother, or **matriarch**, may be the head.

If the family comes from another place, particularly another country, the original immigrants might be called **progenitors**. They were the original ones, sort of like when you have a large family of rabbits, and you go back and identify the original rabbits.

The children, grandchildren, and so on of the progenitors can be called **progeny**. However, that's a pretty formal word, and most people just say, descendants. Progeny and descendants are the same thing. The opposite of a descendant is an **antecedent**. This means, if you go down the family tree, they are progeny or descendants. If you go up the family tree, they are antecedents or ancestors.

Most people would love to be able to leave their progeny a **patrimony** to be taken care of in their life. Patrimony, or inheritance, is traditionally paid or collected upon the death of the antecedent. However, in recent times, the living will has become vogue, meaning people don't have to wait for their parents to die to inherit their money or assets. They can collect on it, often in smaller increments, at specified points in their lives.

Children must also fully embrace all their **filial** responsibilities making sure that their parents are well cared for, especially after they have retired. It shouldn't matter whether they will eventually receive any **patrimony** or not when parents have already made so many sacrifices to bring up their children. If the kids belong to the **gentry**, they can obviously expect to receive large inheritances. The word gentry is where we get the term "gentleman" in the old money aristocratic sense.

Exposure Section 2: Definitions & Example Sentences

Progenitor

(proh-**jen**-i-ter) - (n.) the parent or direct ancestor of a person, animal, or plant; a person who first thinks of something and causes it to exist; something from which another thing develops or that causes something else to happen or exist.[401]

While any ancestor can be a **progenitor** or previous member of a family line, the word is usually applied to someone who was an originator of or significant contributor to the characteristics of that line.[402]

- Thanks to having a common **progenitor**, the two friends were also third cousins.
- "The more audacious move was to declare herself a moral **progenitor**, to walk with her head high so that Denzel Washington might become a man on fire and Viola Davis could learn how to get away with murder." -*New York Times*[403]

Progeny

(**proj**-*uh*-nee) - (n.) the immediate descendants of a person; the result or outcome of something.

Progeny refers to offspring or children. You and your brothers are the **progeny** of your parents, and your cat's new litter of kittens is her **progeny**.[404]

- Since the wealthy man didn't have a **progeny**, his estate went to a local charity after his death.
- "Nature favors those organisms which leave the environment in better shape for their **progeny** to survive." -James Lovelock[405]

Patriarch

(**pey**-tree-ahrk) - (n.) the male head of family or tribe; a man who is older and higher in rank than yourself.

A **patriarch** is a male leader. Your father might be the **patriarch** of your family, but your kid brother could be the **patriarch** of his clubhouse.[406]

- Upon our arrival, we were greeted by the **patriarch** of the house.
- "It's a terrible thing being a **patriarch**. I don't even have a gray beard. But people keep calling me up for advice." -Pete Seeger[407]

Filial

(**fil**-ee-*uhl*) - (adj.) of, resembling, or suitable to a son or daughter.

You can use **filial** to describe the duties, feelings, or relationships between a son or daughter and his or her parents. Your **filial** duties might include taking out the trash, washing dishes, or ruling empires, depending on who your parents are.[408, 409]

- Richard is a good son who takes all his **filial** duties very seriously.
- "There are three degrees of **filial** piety. The highest is being a credit to our parents, the second is not disgracing them; the lowest is being able simply to support them." -Confucius[410]

Antecedent

(an-t*uh*-**seed**-nt) - (n.) a preceding occurrence, cause, or event; someone from whom you are descended more remotely than a grandparent; (adj.) preceding in time or order.

An **antecedent** is a thing that comes before something else. You might think rap music has no historical **antecedent**, but earlier forms of African-American spoken verse go back for centuries.[411]

- The author wrote a prequel as the **antecedent** to his original novel.

- "The physician must be able to tell the **antecedents**, know the present, and foretell the future—must mediate these things, and have two special objects in view with regard to disease, namely, to do good or to do no harm." -Hippocrates[412]

Patrimony

(**pa**-tr*uh*-moh-nee) - (n.) an inheritance from one's father or other ancestor; the endowment of a church.[413]

If your great-great-grandfather built the house you live in, it is your **patrimony**. The Latin origin of the word patrimony is pater, or "father," plus mōnium, "state or condition."[414]

- Jacob received high-quality antique furniture as part of his **patrimony**.
- "A nation's character is the sum of its splendid deeds; they constitute one common **patrimony**, the nation's inheritance. " -Henry Clay[415]

Nubile

(**noo**-bahyl) - (adj.) of marriageable condition or age; sexually attractive, especially of a young woman.[416]

- The **nubile** intern caused quite a stir at the office.
- "There's also something sexual about watching the **nubile** girl in terror. But you do take on her fear as your own." - Christopher Bollen[417]

Gentry

(**jen**-tree) - (n.) wellborn and well-bred people; those who are not members of the nobility but are entitled to a coat of arms, esp. those owning large tracts of land; the state or condition of being a gentleman.[418]

- The life of the **gentry** has always been starkly different from that of commoners.
- "Please, I do not wish to be rescued by a gentleman. Could you find a farmer or a shopkeep—anyone not of the **gentry**— and then do me a great favor of forgetting you saw me?" - Cindy Anstey, *Love, Lies, and Spies*[419]

Eugenics

(yoo-**jen**-iks) - (n.) the practice or advocacy of controlled selective breeding of human populations (as by sterilization) to improve the population's genetic composition; the idea that it is possible to improve humans by allowing only some people to produce children.[420, 421]

- The dystopian novel portrayed a society in which **eugenics** was glorified.
- "I'm really amused by the people advocating **eugenics**. As if they would make the cut." -Fuad Alakbarov[422]

Miscegenation

(mi-sej-*uh*-**ney**-sh*uh*n) - (n.) reproduction by parents of different races (especially by white and non-white persons); marriage or cohabitation between two people of different races; interbreeding between members of different races; the mixing or a mixture of races by interbreeding.[423, 434]

- **Miscegenation** is very common in today's globalized society.
- "We are all descendants of Adam, and we are all products of racial **miscegenation**." -Lester B. Pearson[425]

Practice Section 3: Matching

Match each word with its definition.

1. Antecedent	a. Of, resembling, or suitable to a son or daughter
2. Patriarch	b. Aristocracy
3. Nubile	c. An inheritance from one's father or other ancestor
4. Progeny	d. Controlled selective breeding of human populations (as by sterilization) to improve the population's genetic composition
5. Miscegenation	e. Forefather
6. Filial	f. Descendants
7. Eugenics	g. Describing a young, sexy woman of marriageable age
8. Progenitor	h. Preceding in time or order
9. Gentry	i. Male head of the family of tribe
10. Patrimony	j. Racial interbreeding

Fill in the blanks with the correct word.

1. There was to be an _____ that led the two nations to war.

2. The _____ had a commanding presence with a ferocious face and a thick _____ mane.

3. Since Adam's deceased father didn't have a will, the _____ will be equally distributed by the court amongst the three brothers.

4. There was a time when the US had anti-_____ laws in place to prevent people of different races from marrying each other.

5. Genetic abnormalities can be passed on to one's _____.

6. The actress enjoyed playing the role of a _____ femme-fatale who can seduce any man she desires.

7. Many people consider _____ to be a diabolical pseudoscience.

8. Jimmy understands that his greatest _____ responsibility is to love, honor, and respect his parents.

9. As a member of the landed _____, the young man was entitled to a life of financial security.

10. Nikola Tesla's _____ belonged to a region of Western Serbia.

Perfect Section 5: True or False

Test your understanding by deciding whether each of these statements is true or false.

1. If patrimony implies inheritance from one's father, matrimony implies inheritance from one's mother.
   ☐ True ☐ False

2. A woman can also be called a patriarch.
   ☐ True ☐ False

3. You can call your ancestor your antecedent.
   ☐ True ☐ False

4. A person's ancestors can be referred to as his progeny.
   ☐ True ☐ False

5. A eugenicist is someone who advocates the practice of eugenics.
   ☐ True ☐ False

6. A person who loves his wife but ignores his parents can be described as having filial affection.
   ☐ True ☐ False

7. The life of the gentry is exactly the same as the life of the bourgeoisie.
   ☐ True ☐ False

8. You won't use the word nubile to describe a woman you find unattractive.
   ☐ True ☐ False

9. A person who practices or advocates the concept of 'racial purity' is definitely in favor of miscegenation.
   ☐ True ☐ False

10. A primogenitor is also a progenitor.
   ☐ True ☐ False

Perfect Section 6: Drawing Conclusions

Fill in the blanks with the correct word.

1. Your friend's father dies and now he must lead the family.
   Your friend is now the _____ of his family.

2. Jack was raised by his uncle whom he regards as his father.
   Jack has _____ love for his uncle.

3. Patrick is generally a peaceful man but the other day he somehow lost his temper.
   There must have been an _____ that caused Patrick to lose his temper.

4. Your friend has just inherited a large estate from his deceased father.
   The estate is his _____.

5. You have recently learned that your ancestors were aristocrats.
   You come from a lineage of the landed _____.

6. Your Caucasian friend has fallen in love with a beautiful African-American woman.
   You approve of their relationship based on _____.

7. Forced sterilization is practiced in many countries as a means for reducing and controlling population.
   There are serious ethical issues surrounding the practice of _____.

8. Your friend's father is worried that none of his kids will be able to handle the business he has built after his death.
   Your friend's father is worried that his _____ won't be able to run the business he has built.

9. Jessica is still very young and inexperienced but she's definitely of a marriageable age and extremely attractive.
   Jessica is a _____ young woman.

10. Modern day dogs are descendants of wolves.
    Wolves are the _____ of modern day dogs.

Section 3

1. h; 2. i; 3. g; 4. f; 5. j; 6. a; 7. d; 8. e; 9. b; 10. c

Section 4

1. Antecedent; 2. Patriarch, Leonine; 3. Patrimony; 4. Miscegenation; 5. Progeny; 6. Nubile; 7. Eugenics; 8. Filial; 9. Gentry; 10. Progenitor

Section 5

1. False; 2. False; 3. True; 4. False; 5. True; 6. False; 7. False; 8. True; 9. False; 10. True

Section 6

1. Patriarch; 2. Filial; 3. Antecedent; 4. Patrimony; 5. Gentry; 6. Miscegenation; 7. Eugenics; 8. Progeny; 9. Nubile; 10. Progenitor

CHAPTERS 11-15 REVIEW

Review Section 1: Synonyms

Choose the word that is synonymous with the word on the left hand side.

1. Patrimony	a. design	b. adoration	c. inheritance	d. fatherhood
2. Gentry	a. peasantry	b. nobility	c. a mob	d. commoners
3. Annulment	a. avoidance	b. legislation	c. legalization	d. ratification
4. Alliance	a. an accord	b. a breakup	c. disaffiliation	d. dissociation
5. Consanguine	a. natural	b. adopted	c. nonbiological	d. adoptive
6. Promiscuous	a. discriminate	b. indiscriminate	c. homogenous	d. distinctive
7. Loathe	a. detest	b. adore	c. admire	d. a fondness
8. Voluptuous	a. crass	b. intensive	c. displease	d. sensual
9. Antecedent	a. later	b. previous	c. succeeding	d. ensuing
10. Alimony	a. bankruptcy	b. debts	c. allowance	d. a tax

Review Section 2: Antonyms

Choose the word that is the antonym of the word on the left hand side.

11. Progenitor a. ancestor b. father c. grandfather d. descendant

12. Miscegenation a. divorce b. intermarriage c. remarriage d. wedlock

13. Matrimony a. marriage b. annulment c. match d. wedlock

14. Affiliation a. alliance b. partnership c. disassociation d. relation

15. Articulation a. comatose b. utterance c. verbalism d. formulation

16. Conjunction a. confluence b. divergence c. meeting d. convergence

17. Salacious a. modest b. lustful c. obscene d. indecent

18. Misogynist a. misanthrope b. sexist c. male chauvinist d. egalitarian

19. Abhor a. adore b. hate c. loathe d. detest

20. Liaison a. affinity b. kinship c. disaffiliation d. confederation

Review Section 3: Split Up

There are twenty words split up below. The boldface represents the stressed part of the word. By recombining both parts of a word, you will know to stress the boldface portion as illustrated by [ab] and [**hor**]. Once the 20 words have been recombined, you will use them to complete review section 4. Note: only ten words will be used.

vo	**spou**sal	**pre**	**ta**lia
arcticu	**bot**	us	**ce**dent
sa	ante	triarch	**la**tion
a	**gen**	**nnul**ment	**so**gynist
ation	**lup**tuous	**mo**ny	**lli**ance
mi	**mis**cuous	try	**pa**
hor	e	a	nup
lacious	**li**	ab	affili
geni	aison	matri	pro
an	net	**nex**	**ti**pathy

Review Section 4: Fill-in-the-Blank

Fill in the blanks with the correct words from review section 3.

1. One can make the assumption that two people who are well known as highly _____ may face a somewhat challenging pursuit of monogamy.

2. It is far better to get in front of the _____ details before the media gets a hold of it, Mr. President.

3. The tragic downfall of my existence is not my _____ cravings; it is how to find an adequate stream of income to sustain these.

4. I am intersex, for I possess both female and male _____, but there is much more to me than my anatomy.

5. Linda is an incredibly poor communicator. I am shocked management chose her to be the _____ at this juncture.

6. A few sessions in speech therapy have the potential to dramatically improve his _____.

7. If Sarah is that concerned about this issue, she should take a genealogy course to learn about _____ and patriarchal boundaries.

8. If you want to decrease the chances of developing diabetes, consider the _____ eating habits most conducive to lowering your sugar intake.

9. It is unfortunate that one's political _____ can break apart even the strongest bonds people share.

10. It is difficult to express our true culture, for the _____ seized our labor sectors, stole our lands, and eradicated much of our social practices.

Review Section 5: Crossword Puzzle

Complete the crossword puzzle based on your acquired knowledge of the vocabulary terms.

Across

4. A disunion

6. Connected to each other

7. People that couple

9. Showing hatred and distrust of men

10. Due to religion or morality, holding off on intercourse

13. Relating to ceremony of marriage

14. Lustful

16. Intense aversion; abhorrence

19. A way to link

20. To arouse sexually in a suggestive manner

21. Pertaining to marriage

22. Lewd; obscene

23. A lascivious man

Down

1. Someone you know, but not closely enough to call them a friend

2. Hatred for humankind

3. The breaking down of a union

5. A marriage of wedlock

8. To detest wholeheartedly

12. The inclination of having lustful thoughts

13. A marriageable young woman

15. Relating to son or daughter

17. Beliefs of improving human population by encouraging reproduction by individuals with desirable genetic traits

18. Exclusive marriage with one individual at a time

Review Section 1

1. c; 2. b; 3. a; 4. a; 5. a; 6. b; 7. a; 8. d; 9. b; 10. c

Review Section 2

11. d; 12. a; 13. b; 14. c; 15. a; 16. b; 17. a; 18. d; 19. a; 20. c

Review Section 4

1. Promiscuous 2. Salacious 3. Voluptuous 4. Genitalia 5. Liaison 6. Articulation 7. consanguine 8. Antecedent 9. Affiliation 10. Gentry

Review Section 5

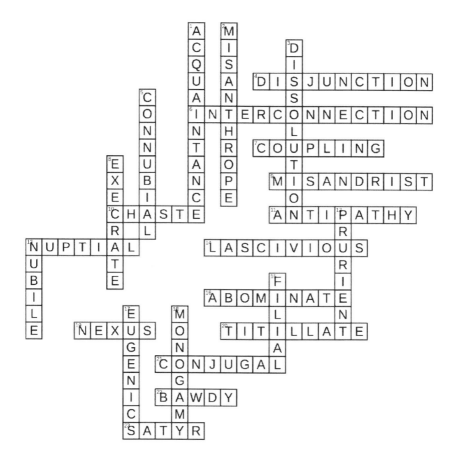

THE TECHNOLOGICAL REVOLUTION

Exposure Section 1: Words in Context

I HAVE TO ADMIT, I'm a bit of an Apple snob.

I have always had a fascination with the **Silicon Valley** wars between Steve Jobs and Bill Gates. But, I didn't join it until about a year after Jobs' death.

I was with a group of friends on a cross-country road trip to San Francisco. We stopped at all the usual places. Of course, there were photo stops on either side of the Golden Gate bridge. It would have been cool, except I had a pooping pigeon **photobomb** my Golden Gate photo.

Actually, I think it's a great photo, one of the funniest I have.

We went to Pier 39 and checked out the eateries and shops along the ocean. After that, we went for coffee at an indie coffee shop, of which there are many. That's a tip for northern California—if you want to be cool, never, ever go to any shop or eatery that's a big box name, like Starbucks. Always shop indie or local.

One of the guys was a graphic designer, and he wanted to travel somewhere down the coast to "The Holy Grail," as he called it. We all knew what he meant. He wanted to visit the Apple headquarters in Cupertino. We took the drive, and saw the building, and took photos in front of it. Then we stopped at the gift shop and looked at expensive computers that none of us could afford. I bought a book, Steve Jobs' biography.

After going to the headquarters and reading the biography, I felt drawn to this cult of **innovative** personality. I was about ready for a technology upgrade, and instead of buying another so-called "Billy Box," as they say, I invested in my first MacBook. I was hooked, and I never looked back.

Technology has revolutionized the way we experience life, and with it comes its own set of lingo. Now that the pandemic has required everyone to update their technology skills, **encryption** is even more important than ever. We are sending our most sensitive information out into the air with just a tap of a finger. So our credit card numbers and personal information should be hidden or scrambled, making it impossible for hackers to steal.

"EXCLUSIVE: Scientists Have Uncovered An Ancient Time Machine, and You Won't Believe What They Found Inside." **Clickbait.**

It's one of the most annoying aspects of digital life. I used to work for clickbait websites, and here's how it works. The internet is paid for by advertising. Advertising rates are based on two things--how many times an ad is clicked and how many times an ad is shown. There are rates for each of these things, usually a fraction of a cent. The ad client produces an ad and then pays an agreed-upon amount upfront that is kept in the client's user account. The ad runs on the page until the client's account runs out of money or they put more money in it.

Knowing that, it is in the website's best monetary interest to get users to their pages. The more views, the more money the advertisers have to pay. How do you get people to your page? You put interesting content on it. Hence, clickbait. Please don't fall for it; it's a scam. **Facepalm**.

Exposure Section 2: Definitions & Example Sentences

Silicon Valley

(**sil**-i-k*uh*n **val**-ee) - (n.) literally, a region in the southern part of the San Francisco Bay Area in Northern California that serves as a global center for high technology and innovation; figuratively, any area in which industries associated with information technology are concentrated.[426, 427]

- Some of the smartest and most talented people can be found in **Silicon Valley**.
- "**Silicon Valley** is a mindset, not a location." -Reid Hoffman[428]

Innovation

(in-*uh*-**vey**-sh*uh*n) - (n.) the practical implementation of ideas that result in the introduction of new goods or services or improvement in offering goods or services.[429]

- Without constant **innovation**, a company can't remain profitable in the long-run.
- "**Innovation** is the unrelenting drive to break the status quo and develop anew where few have dared to go." -Steven Jeffes, marketing & business expert[430]

Encryption

(en-**kript**-sh*uh*n) - (n.) any system for security and fraud prevention that automatically breaks up and reorders information before it is sent via telephone lines or the Internet; the process of encoding information; the process of changing electronic information or signals into a secret code (= system of letters, numbers, or symbols) that people cannot understand or use without special equipment.[431, 432]

- I can tell that the website is quite safe since it obviously uses **encryption** to protect user data.
- "There are two types of **encryption**: one that will prevent your sister from reading your diary and one that will prevent your government." -Bruce Schneier[433]

Net Neutrality

(net noo-**tral**-i-tee) - (n.) the concept that all data on the internet should be treated equally by corporations, such as internet service providers (ISPs) and governments, regardless of content, user, platform, application, or device.[434]

Put simply, net neutrality stipulates that service providers should not slow down nor block content from users.[434]

- Many telecom and cable companies oppose the concept of **net neutrality**.
- "**Net Neutrality** is what makes the Internet so great—and so vital for innovation and creativity." -Justine Bateman[435]

Clickbait

(**klik**-beyt) - (n.) articles, photographs, etc. on the internet that are intended to attract attention and encourage people to click on links to particular websites.[436]

- We all know the feeling when we watch an entire YouTube video only to realize that it has no link with its **clickbait** thumbnail image or catchy title.
- "Newton wouldn't last long as a 'public intellectual' in modern American culture. Sooner or later, he would say 'offensive' things that get reported to Harvard and that get picked up by mainstream media as moral-outrage **clickbait**." -Geoffrey Miller[437]

Ping

(**ping**) - (v.) to send a message from one computer to another to check whether it is reachable and active; to contact, usually in order to remind of something; to make a short high-pitched sound.[438]

Colloquially, to "**ping**" a colleague is to send them a short message, typically a reminder or follow-up regarding a topic already discussed.

- I'll **ping** the marketing team tomorrow to get their input on the project.
- "Based on something called a '**ping**,' where you literally **ping** a cell phone using an electronic signal that then reflects the location of where that cell phone is." -Jeanine Pirro[439]

Botnet

(**bot**-net) - (n.) a network of computers infected by a program that communicates with its creator in order to send unsolicited emails, attack websites, etc.; a number of Internet-connected devices, each of which is running one or more bots.[440, 441]

- Network security companies offer software that can counter **botnet** attacks.
- "Why are experts so polite, patient, and forgiving when talking about cybersecurity and National Security? The drama of each script kiddie **botnet** attack and Nation State pilfering of our IP has been turned into a soap opera through press releases, sound bites, and enforced absurdity of mainstream media." -James Scott, Senior Fellow, Institute for Critical Infrastructure Technology[442]

Open-source

(**oh**-p*uh*n-**sawrs**) - (adj.) pertaining to or denoting software whose source code is available free of charge to the public to use, copy, modify, sublicense, or distribute.[443]

Open-source software (OSS) is computer software released under a license in which the copyright holder grants users the rights to use, study, change, and distribute the software and its source code to anyone and for any purpose.[444]

- The software is now available in the public domain under an **open-source** license.
- "Empowerment of individuals is a key part of what makes **open source** work, since in the end, innovations tend to come from small groups, not from large, structured efforts." - Tim O'Reilly[445]

Photobomb

(**foh**-toh-bom) - (v.) to ruin a photograph by appearing in the image without the photographer's knowledge, often in some dramatic or comical way.[446]

If you photobomb someone, you spoil a photograph of them by stepping in front of them as the picture is taken, often doing something silly such as making a funny face.

- Jacob's sister tried her best to **photobomb** his pictures but didn't succeed.
- "**Photobomb** me at your own risk!" -Ken Poirot[447]

Facepalm

(**feys**-pahm) - (v.) to cover one's face with the hand as an expression of embarrassment, dismay, or exasperation. [448]

The term "**facepalm**" or the emoji depicting such an action is often used on social networking sites to show that you are embarrassed, annoyed, or disappointed.[449]

- I had to **facepalm** when she asked me to explain everything all over again.
- He did a **facepalm** after reading the comments section of his latest YouTube video.

Unscramble the following words.

1. TKCBICLAI

2. OTTNEB

3. EENPRSCOOU

4. BHOMOTBPO

5. MAFPCAEL

6. NNTYLATUTEERI

7. NCNRPTYOIE

8. NONVTAIINO

9. GINP

10. YCSNOIVALLLIE

Practice Section 4: Matching

Match each word with its correct definition.

1. Encryption	a. Treating all data on the internet with equality
2. Botnet	b. Cover one's face with one's hands
3. Ping	c. Online devices being used by bots for attacks
4. Open-source	e. Implementing new ideas to improve goods and services
5. Facepalm	f. Ruin a picture by doing something silly while the photo is being taken
6. Silicon Valley	g. Send a text message through the computer or phone
7. Clickbait	h. Software that can be modified and redistributed by anyone
8. Photobomb	i. Converting electronic information into secret code
9. Innovation	j. Sensationalized picture or headline meant to lure you into clicking on the content
10. Net neutrality	k. An area that is designated as a Technological hub

Practice Section 5: Pronunciation

Match each word with its correct phonetic pronunciation.

1. Clickbait	a. **ping**
2. Net neutrality	b. **sil**-i-k*uhn* **val**-ee
3. Innovation	c. **bot**-net
4. Facepalm	d. en-**kript**-sh*uhn*
5. Open-source	e. **klik**-beyt
6. Silicon Valley	f. **foh**-toh-bom
7. Botnet	g. in-*uh*-**vey**-sh*uhn*
8. Photobomb	h. **feys**-pahm
9. Encryption	i. **oh**-p*uhn*-**sawrs**
10. Ping	j. net noo-**tral**-i-tee

Practice Section 6: Test Your Knowledge

Has the word been used correctly?

1. Using encryption is essential for protecting your digital data.
   ☐ Yes ☐ No

2. A botnet can protect an online device.
   ☐ Yes ☐ No

3. Open-source software is at the core of technological innovation.
   ☐ Yes ☐ No

4. An innovator can innovate anything.
   ☐ Yes ☐ No

5. This is the age of alluring clickbaits and viral headlines.
   ☐ Yes ☐ No

6. Net neutrality is an online extension of gender equality.
   ☐ Yes ☐ No

7. You facepalm to express happiness and delight.
   ☐ Yes ☐ No

8. The microwave pinged when the cake was ready.
   ☐ Yes ☐ No

9. Photobombing implies physically destroying a printed picture that you don't like.
   ☐ Yes ☐ No

10. In the last few months, several Silicon Valley CEOs have resigned.
    ☐ Yes ☐ No

Section 3

1. Clickbait; 2. Botnet; 3. Open-source; 4. Photobomb; 5. Facepalm; 6. Net neutrality; 7. Encryption; 8. Innovation; 9. Ping ; 10. Silicon Valley

Section 4

1. h; 2. c; 3. f; 4. g; 5. b; 6. j; 7. i; 8. e; 9. d; 10. a

Section 5

1. e; 2. j; 3. g; 4. h; 5. i; 6. b; 7. c; 8. f; 9. d; 10. a

Section 6

1. Yes; 2. No; 3. Yes; 4. Yes; 5. Yes; 6. No; 7. No; 8. Yes; 9. No; 10. Yes

17

COMPLIMENTING ONE'S INTELLIGENCE

Exposure Section 1: Words in Context

ONCE, in a psychology class I took, after studying the true meaning of IQ and how it was calculated, the professor passed out an actual IQ test. Not those silly clickbait ones you can find online. But a real one, used in psychology offices.

We all took it, and we learned our official IQ. I don't know how it happened, but someone got hold of the actual score sheet with everyone's IQ on it, and it got passed around. Suddenly, we were confronted with what we already knew, who was the smartest, who was, well, not the smartest, and how everyone fell in between. I was somewhere in the middle, but I remember one girl named Erin, who scored well more than twice of any of us, at over 220. We all looked at her as if she had gone to the moon.

Erin just shrugged as if it didn't matter to her. But, it did matter. It mattered a lot. Her social life was never the same after that.

It's funny how we rank one another as valuable or invaluable based on what we perceive their intelligence to be.

Most highly intelligent and successful people are **voracious** readers. Many of them read 50 or more books in a year. Constant learning and continuous growth are the cornerstones of success.

However, knowledge alone doesn't help in becoming wise. You can become **erudite** by reading and studying a lot, but you may not necessarily be wise.

You become **sagacious** by thinking about what you are reading and learning. You must assimilate the knowledge by understanding it in the context of your own life experiences and personal beliefs.

Intuition also plays an essential role in success as you have to be **percipient** enough to see through people and circumstances to get the best out of them. Many people think that it is something that only the **precocious** few have from an early age, but that's not really true. Even if you weren't unusually wise and insightful as a child, you can work on becoming like that as an adult.

The more you work on yourself, the more **astute** you will become. You will develop the ability to understand any situation and make the most out of it.

Exposure Section 2: Definitions & Example Sentences

Astute

(*uh*-**stoot**) - (adj.) able to understand a situation quickly and see how to take advantage of it; having or showing shrewdness and an ability to notice and understand things clearly; mentally sharp or clever; marked by practical hardheaded intelligence; someone who is astute is clever and has good judgment.[450, 451, 452]

- He's an **astute** judge of human nature.

- "One of the funny things about the stock market is that every time one person buys, another sells, and both think they are **astute**." -William Feather[453]

Canny

(**kan**-ee) - (adj.) showing self-interest and shrewdness in dealing with others.[454]

If you're a **canny** investor, you know how to spend money to make money—that is, you're prudent, farsighted, and capable of protecting your own interests, particularly in matters of finance or business.[454]

- The **canny** man outsmarted the salesman by saying that he wouldn't finalize the deal until the car had been inspected by his mechanic.
- "His **canny** placement of the camera for long shots and use of chiaroscuro lighting in close-ups make just about every scene, all of them filmed in widescreen, a cinematic study." - David Mermelstein, *Wall Street Journal*[455]

Precocious

(pri-**koh**-sh*uh*s) - (adj.) (especially of children) showing mental development or achievement much earlier than usual.

A precocious child behaves as if they are much older than they are.[456]

- The parents found it hard to tolerate their child's **precocious** behavior.
- "When I was still a rather **precocious** young man, I already realized most vividly the futility of the hopes and aspirations

that most men pursue throughout their lives." -Albert Einstein[457]

Adroit

(*uh*-**droyt**) - (adj.) very skillful and quick in thought or movement; having or showing skill, cleverness, or resourcefulness in handling situations.[458, 459]

An **adroit** leader will be able to persuade people to go with his ideas. An **adroit** sculptor can turn a lump of clay into an object of great beauty.[460]

- He has been an **adroit** pianist from a very early age.
- "The law is an **adroit** mixture of customs that are beneficial to society, and could be followed even if no law existed, and others that are of advantage to a ruling minority, but harmful to the masses of men, and can be enforced on them only by terror." -Peter Kropotkin[461]

Sagacious

(*suh*-**gey**-sh*uhs*) - (adj.) having or showing keen mental discernment and good judgement; wise or shrewd; acutely insightful and wise; skillful in statecraft or management.[462, 463]

Someone like an inspirational leader or an expert in a field who seeks knowledge and has foresight can be described as **sagacious**. If you comment on something at a deeper level, you are making a **sagacious** observation.[463]

- He's **sagacious** enough to not get into arguments he can't win.
- "Water is **sagacious** because it carries inside of itself the bottomless profundity of oceans, the cosmic looks of the clouds, subtle wits of the rivers, the inquisitive character of the rains and the silent meditation of the little lakes!" - Mehmet Murat İldan[464]

Erudite

(**er**-yoo-dahyt) - (adj.) having or showing knowledge that is gained by studying; possessing or displaying erudition; characteristic of scholars or scholarship.[465, 466]

- Mr. Smith is an **erudite** scholar who seems to know the answer to every question you can possibly ask him.
- "He was an **erudite** man and began our conversation with a history of slave religion, telling me about the Africans who, newly landed on hostile shores, had sat circled around a fire mixing newfound myths with ancient rhythms, their songs becoming a vessel for those most radical of ideas—survival, and freedom, and hope." -Barack Obama, *Dreams from My Father: A Story of Race and Inheritance*[467]

Virtuoso

(vur-choo-**oh**-soh) - (n.) one who excels in the technique of an art, especially a highly skilled musical performer; a person who has exceptional skill, expertise, or talent at some endeavor; (adj.) having or revealing supreme mastery or skill.[468, 469]

A baseball player who hits a lot of home runs is a slugging **virtuoso**. Usually, this word applies to music. It's very common for a talented pianist or guitarist to be called a **virtuoso**. Whatever your talent, it's a huge compliment to be called a **virtuoso**.[469]

- As a pianist, he is nothing less than a **virtuoso**.
- "All tyrannies are **virtuoso** displays, over many years, of cunning, risk-taking, terror, delusion, narcissism, showmanship, and charm, distilled into a spectacle of total personal control." -Simon Sebag Montefiore[470]

Percipient

(per-**sip**-ee-*uh*nt) - (n.) one that perceives; a person on whose mind a telepathic impulse or message is held to fall; a person who becomes aware (of things or events) through the senses; characterized by ease and quickness in perceiving; good at noticing and understanding things.[471, 472, 473]

- Jessica is so **percipient** that she only needs to look at Jerry's face to know what he's thinking.
- Quentin is extremely **percipient**—he can anticipate the next move of the opposing team in a baseball game.

Ambidextrous

(am-bi-**dek**-str*uh*s) - (adj.) equally expert with each hand; highly skilled or adept; underhanded; deceitful.[474]

Someone who is **ambidextrous** can use both their right hand and their left hand equally skilfully.[474]

238

- Since he is **ambidextrous**, it's no big deal for him to write with his left hand.
- "The real secret to my success was I could shoot with either hand. Ironically, I became ambidextrous as a direct result of breaking my right hand." -Dolph Schayes[475]

Voracious

(vaw-**rey**-sh*uhs*) - (adj.) devouring or craving food in great quantities; very eager or unremitting in some activity, voracious reading.[476]

If you describe a person, or their appetite for something, as **voracious**, you mean that they want a lot of something.[476]

- The swimming champion is a **voracious** eater who can easily consume two turkeys all by himself.
- "Like most lit nerds, I'm a **voracious** reader. I never got enough poetry under my belt growing up but I do read it— some of my favorites, Gina Franco and Angela Shaw and Cornelius Eady and Kevin Young, remind me daily that unless the words sing and dance, what's the use of putting them down on paper." -Junot Dia[477]

Fill in the blanks with the right words. You may have to recall some words from the previous chapters.

1. The rugby team managed to recruit some of the finest and most _ d _ _ _ _ players.
2. She wanted to love him but there was nothing e _ _ _ _ _ _ _ about the _ _ _ c _ _ _ _ _ _ child.
3. Walter has been regarded as a remarkable _ _ _ t _ _ _ _.
4. As a _ _ n _ _ investor, he seems to have a sixth sense about selling stocks.
5. As a _ _ _ _ c _ _ _ _ reader, I have an insatiable appetite for knowledge.
6. The _ _ g _ _ _ _ _ _ businessman made a fortune within a year of launching his business.
7. It's amazing how the _ m _ _ _ _ _ _ _ _ _ cricketer is able to use both his right and left hand for batting the ball.
8. The two professors enjoyed having _ _ u _ _ _ _ conversations together.
9. Mothers are so _ _ _ c _ _ _ _ _ _ that it's impossible to hide anything from them.
10. He is extremely _ _ t _ _ _ in all finance and business related matters.

Practice Section 4: Matching

Match each word with its correct definition.

1. Ambidextrous	a. Skillful and quick in the way you think or move
2. Precocious	b. A highly skilled performer
3. Voracious	c. Practical hardheaded intelligence
4. Virtuoso	d. Insatiable and ravenous appetite for something
5. Astute	e. Acutely wise and insightful
6. Percipient	f. Shrewd in a self-serving and almost cunning way
7. Adroit	h. Leaned
8. Sagacious	i. Adept at using both hands
9. Canny	j. Someone with a keen ability to perceive
10. Erudite	k. Showing mental development or achievement much earlier than usual

Perfect Section 5: True or False

Test your understanding by deciding whether each of these statements is true or false.

1. If someone is described as precocious, it implies that they are very good at taking precautions.
   ☐ True ☐ False

2. You can call an amateur in any field a virtuoso.
   ☐ True ☐ False

3. Clumsy is the perfect antonym to adroit.
   ☐ True ☐ False

4. An illiterate person can be an erudite.
   ☐ True ☐ False

5. Sages are sagacious.
   ☐ True ☐ False

6. A percipient person can see through people and situations better than most people can.
   ☐ True ☐ False

7. Uncanny is the antonym of canny.
   ☐ True ☐ False

8. It's possible for an omnivore to be a voracious eater.
   ☐ True ☐ False

9. An ambidextrous person is able to use both hands with equal ease and skill.
   ☐ True ☐ False

10. The antonym of astute is stupid.
    ☐ True ☐ False

Perfect Section 6: Drawing Conclusions

1. Even as a child, you wondered about the meaning and purpose of human life.
   You were a _____ child.

2. You have a reputation for being very wise, shrewd, and discerning.
   People hold you in high regard as a _____ person.

3. Your boss has the ability to see through people. He is able to figure out people's weaknesses very quickly.
   Your boss is a _____ man.

4. Your friend brings his cousin over to your house. The lanky looking boy devours two pizzas all by himself.
   Your friend's cousin is a _____ eater.

5. Your wealthy friend has a butler who runs his home very efficiently.
   Your friend has an _____ butler.

6. You are surprised by how your university professor seems to know the answer to everything.
   You are surprised by how _____ your professor really is.

7. You come across a computer mouse that can be used with both the left and the right hand.
   The mouse has an _____ design.

8. Your friend is an expert at telling when a player is bluffing in a card game.
   Your friend is a _____ card player.

9. You go to a football match and are delighted by how well the team you support played that game.
   You are delighted by the _____ performance of your favourite football team.

10. You are an expert at finding great deals and bargains.
    You are very _____ in your shopping.

Section 3

1. Adroit; 2. Endearing, Precocious; 3. Virtuoso; 4. Canny; 5. Voracious; 6. Sagacious; 7. Ambidextrous; 8. Erudite; 9. Percipient; 10. Astute

Section 4

1. h; 2. j; 3. d; 4. b; 5. c; 6. i; 7. a; 8. e; 9. f; 10. g

Section 5

1. False; 2. False; 3. True; 4. False; 5. True; 6. True; 7. False; 8. True; 9. True; 10. True

Section 6

1. Precocious; 2. Sagacious; 3. Percipient; 4. Voracious; 5. Adroit; 6. Erudite; 7. Ambidextrous; 8. Canny; 9. Virtuoso; 10. Astute

18

INSULTS BASED ON INTELLIGENCE

Exposure Section 1: Words in Context

THE OPPOSITE OF SMART IS, you guessed it, dumb. However, there are many different ways to measure intelligence. Our current academic system based on reading and writing is simply the most efficient way to mass-educate an entire generation well enough that they can be the nation's workforce.

This doesn't mean it's the most accurate. Those who have a difficult time in school often excel at other areas, some that are not measured by schools at all. But, the sad part is, that after spending their entire childhoods not feeling good enough or feeling "dumb," they can often graduate and approach life feeling like a **dunce**.

It's a sad state of affairs. So if you struggled in school, take heart and find out where your strengths are.

While some people are geniuses, others are **dimwits**. For them, it is hard to understand even that which may be commonsensical to others. It is also possible that a person could be adroit at one thing and an absolute **nitwit** at doing other things.

Listening to a **dullard** talk about the dullest, most boring thing is enough to put you to sleep. Who likes being around someone like that? We all want to have interesting conversations with witty people. But in social settings, we also come across the **ignoramus** fools who think that they are the most important people in the world while being as ignorant and dumb as a block of wood. The canny conversationalist knows how to excuse themselves from such annoying conversations that leave a sour after-taste in the mouth.

However, as human beings, we also have to be kind toward our fellow humans even when they are complete **dolts** who can't do even the simplest of tasks properly. The next time you come across a **lunkhead** who is testing your patience, try to be compassionate and think of things from their perspective. Maybe what is easy and simple for you is very complex and difficult for that person!

Exposure Section 2: Definitions & Example Sentences

Dunce

(**duhns**) - (n.) a person, especially a child at school, who is stupid or slow to learn; a dull, ignorant person; a person slow at learning.[478, 479]

If you say that someone is a **dunce**, you think they are relatively stupid because they find it difficult or impossible to learn what someone is trying to teach them.

- He has become quite smart compared to the **dunce** he was back in school.
- "We want to believe that we're invulnerable, and that people who get tricked deserve it. Well, they don't. And someday the arrogant types who mock the gullible are likely to get their turn to wear the **dunce** cap." -Walter Kirn[480]

Simpleton

(**sim**-p*uh*l-t*uh*n) - (n.) a person who is stupid or easily deceived; a fool.[481]

- It's very easy to fool a **simpleton**.
- "The most difficult character in comedy is that of the fool, and he must be no **simpleton** that plays that part." -Miguel de Cervantes[482]

Dullard

(**duhl**-erd) - (n.) a boring, unintelligent, and unimaginative person.[483]

If something isn't sharp, it's dull. This can apply to pencils and people —if you're sharp, you're a smarty-pants, but if you're dull, you're a **dullard**.[484]

- Only a **dullard** would have difficulty figuring out the answer to such a simple math problem.
- "The **dullard's** envy of brilliant men is always assuaged by the suspicion that they will come to a bad end." -Max Beerbohm[485]

Ignoramus

(ig-n*uh*-**rey**-m*uh*s) - (n.) a person who knows nothing; an ignorant and stupid person.[486, 487]

If you've ever been afraid to speak up in class, you might be worried that you'll look like an **ignoramus**, or an uneducated, ignorant person.[488]

- The **ignoramus** didn't even know that Russia is a country.
- "A person who knows nothing about literature may be an **ignoramus**, but many people don't mind being that." - Northrop Frye[489]

Dolt

(**dohlt**) - (n.) a stupid or ignorant person.

You might be called a **dolt** if you do something dumb, like stand outside your car complaining that you locked your keys inside—even though the window is wide open.[490]

- He is just a **dolt** in an influential position.
- "There is a genius on one side of every trade and a **dolt** on the other, but which is which does not become clear until much later." -Leon Levy[491]

Nincompoop

(**nin**-k*uh*m-poop) - (n.) (informal) a foolish, silly person.

- I don't understand why he suddenly started behaving like a nincompoop.
- "The man is a nincompoop and a fool. Even worse, he took me for a fool as well." -John Flanagan[492]

Lunkhead

(**luhngk**-hed) - (n.) (informal) a dull or stupid person; a blockhead.[493]

- The **lunkhead** had a stupid answer for even the simplest question you could ask him.
- "With such disappointing **lunkheads** for parents, naturally Petunia must leave home." -Paul Schmid, *A Pet for Petunia*[494]

Nitwit

(**nit**-wit) - (n.) (informal) a stupid incompetent person.

It's not nice to call someone a nitwit, but it's hard to resist when people do things that are outrageously incompetent or ridiculous. It's pretty common to refer to entire groups of people as nitwits, like politicians or fans of a rival sports team. The word comes from nit meaning "nothing" in dialectical Yiddish, and wit, meaning a sense of intelligence.[495]

- The **nitwit** was dumb enough to admit on live television that he was having an affair with another woman.
- "These things get passed around via emails from one gullible and naive **nitwit** to the next." -Tom Margenau, *The Dallas Morning News*[496]

Dimwit

(**dim**-wit) - (n.) (informal) a slow-thinking person.[497]

- The **dimwit** acts like he is still five years old.

- "Years ago, before this estate was generously and unwillingly turned over to the crown, the lord here was a genuine **dimwit**. He had a minister stashed behind his throne to whisper clever things to say." -Shannon Hale[498]

Cretin

(**kreet**-n) - (n.)a person considered to be extremely stupid; literally, a person with cretinism (a condition arising from a congenital deficiency of thyroid hormone, characterized by dwarfism and learning difficulties).[499, 500]

- Every time she opens her mouth, it becomes even more evident that she's a **cretin**.
- "Each of us is sometimes a **cretin**, a fool, a moron, or a lunatic. A normal person is just a reasonable mix of these components, these four ideal types." -Umberto Eco, *Foucault's Pendulum*[501]

Practice Section 3: Unscramble the Words

Unscramble the following words.

1. TOLD
2. SINGMROUA
3. DNLHAUKE
4. RITECN
5. PCMPNONOIO
6. DULLARD
7. CDNEU
8. TTNIIW
9. MTDIIW
10. NSMTPLOIE

Practice Section 4: Matching

Match each word with its correct definition.

1. Simpleton	a. Completely ignorant
2. Ignoramus	b. Literally, a person suffering from learning difficulties and dwarfism
3. Dullard	c. Stupid or slow to learn
4. Cretin	d. Someone who does outrageously incompetent things
5. Nitwit	e. An ignorant, foolish, or silly person who is easily deceived
6. Dunce	f. A dull, boring, unintelligent, and unimaginative person

Practice Section 5: True or False

Test your understanding by deciding whether each of these statements is true or false.

1. A lunkhead is a blockhead.
   ☐ True ☐ False

2. A genius would be the opposite of a dolt.
   ☐ True ☐ False

3. You can call someone a nincompoop when you find them intelligent and attractive.
   ☐ True ☐ False

4. A dimwit has a very high IQ.
   ☐ True ☐ False

Perfect Section 6: Pronunciation

Match each word with its correct phonetic pronunciation.

1. Lunkhead	a. ig-n*uh*-**rey**-m*uh*s
2. Dullard	b. **duhl**-erd
3. Dimwit	c. **nin**-k*uh*m-poop
4. Dunce	d. **duhl**-erd
5. Cretin	e. **duhns**
6. Ignoramus	f. **dohlt**
7. Nitwit	g. **dim**-wit
8. Dolt	h. **kreet**-n
9. Simpleton	i. **luhngk**-hed
10. Nincompoop	j. **sim**-p*uh*l-t*uh*n

Perfect Section 7: Test Your Knowledge

Has the word been used correctly?

1. An ignoramus is an incredibly ignorant person.
   Yes   No

2. A very simple person is a simpleton.
   Yes   No

3. A nitwit is very witty.
   Yes   No

4. You can't expect a dolt to talk sense.
   Yes   No

5. There is no hope for a lunkhead who refuses to use his brain.
   Yes   No

6. The nincompoop got hired for the job only because of her connections.
   Yes   No

7. A cretin is a perfect role-model for how a person should be.
   Yes   No

8. A dullard is an excellent conversationalist.
   Yes   No

9. The dimwit thought that he could pet a tiger like a dog.
   Yes   No

10. It's really hard for a dunce to learn anything new.
    Yes   No

Section 3

1. Dolt; 2. Ignoramus; 3. Lunkhead; 4. Cretin; 5. Nincompoop; 6. Dullard; 7. Dunce; 8. Nitwit; 9. Dimwit; 10. Simpleton

Section 4

1. e; 2. a; 3. f; 4. b; 5. d; 6. c

Section 5

1. True; 2. True; 3. False; 4. False

Section 6

1. i; 2. d; 3. g; 4. e; 5. h; 6. a; 7. b; 8. f; 9. j; 10. c

Section 7

1. Yes; 2. No; 3. No; 4. Yes; 5. Yes; 6. Yes; 7. No; 8. No; 9. Yes; 10. Yes

19

COMPLIMENTING ONE'S APPEARANCE

Exposure Section 1: Words in Context

YOU SHOULD BE all dressed up for your last lesson because it's on one of the finer points in our culture—our appearance.

When I graduated college, I hit the pavement full-time, looking for that first real job. I found the interview suits and pressed shirts and slacks and everything that went with it to be part of "the system." I was a revolutionary, and the system was everything that was *repulsive* and *abhorrent* on this earth.

One of my career counselors gave me the best advice I have heard regarding appearance. She said, "It doesn't matter if it's right or wrong. The truth is, people judge you by your appearance. It's just the way it is."

That was a shocking comment because I believed that you should only judge people by what's inside, and paying attention to the outward appearance was shallow and prejudiced.

I had never heard someone say that I should just accept that. Welcome to the real world, kid. This is life after graduation. Get with it, or go broke.

No matter what anyone says, the truth is that physical appearance really does matter. We communicate with the world through our style, deportment, and manner of dressing. They speak volumes about who we are even before we have had a chance to open our mouths to speak. I'm sure that the impression you get when you come across a **debonair** young man who is immaculately dressed and incredibly charming is completely different from how you feel about a shabbily dressed *simpleton*.

That's not to say that all shabbily dressed people are *nincompoops*. Of course, not! Many highly intelligent people prefer not to pay attention to their clothes or deportment, but we can't underestimate the importance of these things.

There is something incredibly **bewitching** about beholding a beautiful woman who is well-dressed and has excellent posture. It's as if she casts a spell on everyone who gets a chance to behold her.

You don't need to have too much time to **adorn** yourself with fineries. You just have to make an effort to look put together and neat. In fact, the most **elegant** and **aristocratic**-looking people are often dressed in a straightforward manner. What makes them stand out is their focus on quality and refined simplicity.

Exposure Section 2: Definitions & Example Sentences

Winsome

(**win**-*suh*m) - (adj.) generally pleasing and engaging, often because of a childlike charm and innocence; cheerful; lighthearted.[502]

- Terry has a **winsome** smile that can melt all your resistance away.
- "It is not easy to be crafty and **winsome** at the same time, and few accomplish it after the age of six." -John W. Gardner[503]

Resplendent

(ri-**splen**-d*uh*nt) - (adj.) having a brilliant or splendid appearance; shining brightly; full of splendor; dazzling.[504]

Someone or something **resplendent** has great beauty and is a pleasure to behold. The adjective **resplendent** comes from a Latin word that means "to shine brightly."[505]

- The princess looked **resplendent** in her jewels and gorgeous silk gown.
- "None of the **resplendent** names in history—Egypt, Athens, Rome—can compare in eternal grandeur with Jerusalem. For Israel has given to mankind the category of holiness. Israel alone has known the thirst for social justice, and that inner saintliness which is the source of justice." - Charles Wagner[506]

Pulchritude

(**puhl**-kri-tood) - (n.) (formal or literary) physical beauty (especially of a woman).

Pulchritude is one of those words more often commented upon for its oddness than actually used in its intended meaning. Many people dislike the sound of this word or are surprised to find that it is a synonym of beauty. These days **pulchritude** is considered outdated and is usually only used in highly literary writing or, in more common writing, to achieve a witty effect.[507]

- Evangelina isn't just a woman of great **pulchritude**, she's also incredibly kind and compassionate.
- "The place of beauty in our lives is a profound subject, and Harmon offers a complex understanding that respects the hazardous yet life-enhancing power of physical **pulchritude**." -*Los Angeles Times*[508]

Debonair

(deb-*uh*-**nair**) - (adj.) confident, charming, and well-dressed, particularly of a handsome man; having a sophisticated, gentlemanly charm.[509]

When you're **debonair**, you impress women, other men, and pretty much everyone with your manners, wit, and style. **Debonair** is a little bit of an old-fashioned word. Old movie stars like Cary Grant were often called **debonair**, but not many people are today.[510]

- The actor played the role of the **debonair** young man with ease and perfection.
- "Bow ties always look **debonair** á la James Bond, but Southern men can wear them in every color and pattern under the sun for a little extra flair." -Kaitlyn Yarborough, *Southern Living*[511]

Dapper

(**dap**-er) - (adj.) neat and trim in appearance; alert and lively in movement and manners; very spruce and stylish.[512]

A neatly and stylishly dressed man can be described as **dapper**. Think of the words dashing, jaunty, and spiffy when you think of dapper, as these are all near-synonyms. All of these words are explicitly used to describe men.[513]

- Jacob decided to wear his most **dapper** attire to the Viennese Ball.
- "Just like the NBA, the NFL has guys that can pull off multiple looks, ranging from street style to more **dapper**, buttoned-up looks, and people are starting to notice." -Cam Newton[514]

Adorn

(*uh*-**dawrn**) - (v.) make more attractive by adding ornament, color, etc.; be beautiful to look at; to furnish with power or authority.

Adorn shares some Latin roots with words like ornament and ornate, so it makes sense that some people **adorn** their Christmas trees with tinsel and lights. Others **adorn** their eyelids with glitter.[515]

- The bride's hair was **adorned** with beautiful flowers.
- "Any opportunity to **adorn** oneself is human, and accessories are an easy way to do it." -Marc Jacobs[516]

Comely

(**kuhm**-lee) - (adj.) very pleasing to the eye; according to custom or propriety.

Comely is related to the word becoming, in the sense of something being attractive and appropriate.[517]

- The comely young woman caused a stir wherever she went.
- "A comely sight indeed it is to see a world of blossoms on an apple tree." -John Bunyan[518]

Bewitching

(bih-**wich**-ing) - (adj.) so beautiful or attractive that you cannot think about anything else; enchanting; charming; fascinating; capturing interest as if by a spell.[519, 520, 521]

- His **bewitching** smile was enough to completely disarm the suspicious women.
- "She has a perfect body, and she's supposed to be sexy, but it doesn't turn me on. She has an ethereal sort of look to her, as though I'm looking at a piece of art. There is no carnal desire there—just a **bewitching** beauty." -Hirukuma[522]

Elegant

(**el**-i-g*uh*nt) - (adj.) refined and tasteful in appearance or behavior or style; suggesting taste, ease, and wealth; displaying effortless beauty and simplicity in movement or execution.

The word comes, via Old French, from the same Latin source that gave rise to the English word "elect," and it does seem that especially

elegant people and things are in a select group. Very stylishly dressed men and women are **elegant**, and fine restaurants with distinctive delicacies are elegant. Most ordinary places and people can become **elegant** when dressed up or adorned for special occasions. Even walruses can appear **elegant** when they're swimming.[523]

- The **elegant** woman conducts herself with dignity and refinement at all times.
- "I was trying to make the web more civil. I was trying to make it more **elegant**. I got rid of anonymity. I combined a thousand disparate elements into one unified system. But I didn't picture a world where Circle membership was mandatory, where all government and all life was channeled through one network." -Dave Eggers, *The Circle*[524]

Aristocratic

(*uh*-ris-t*uh*-**krat**-ik) - (adj.) belonging to or characteristic of the nobility or aristocracy.

The word **aristocratic** describes a person at the highest level of society—such as a prince or a duchess—or those people or things that are so distinguished they seem to belong to that group.[525]

- The young man's demeanor is extremely **aristocratic** and refined.
- "My tastes are **aristocratic**, my actions democratic." -Victor Hugo[526]

Practice Section 3: Fill-in-the-Blank

Fill in the blanks with the correct words. You may have to recall some words from the previous chapters.

1. She is the most _ _ _ _ _ _ t woman I have ever met.

2. Everyone was mesmerised when the peacock spread its _ _ s _ _ _ _ _ _ _ feathers.

3. Emma loves to _ _ o _ _ herself with beautiful jewels.

4. A nice suit can make any man look _ _ p _ _ _.

5. The Hollywood actor was looking exceptionally suave and _ _ _ _ n _ _ _.

6. Despite his working class upbringing, James carries himself with _ _ _ s _ _ _ _ _ _ _ _ elegance.

7. Helen of Troy is regarded as a woman of extraordinary _ _ _ c_ _ _ _ _ _ _.

8. Her _ _ _ _ t _ _ _ _ _ beauty drives many men crazy.

9. Victoria's eldest daughter is a w _ _ _ _ _ _ girl with gorgeous blue eyes and a cheerful smile.

10. The singer with the beautiful voice turned out to be a _ _ m _ _ _ young woman.

Practice Section 4: Pronunciation

Match each word with its correct phonetic pronunciation.

1. Adorn	a. **kuhm**-lee
2. Debonair	b. ri-**splen**-duhnt
3. Aristocratic	c. bih-**wich**-ing
4. Winsome	d. **dap**-er
5. Elegant	e. *uh*-ris-t*uh*-**krat**-ik
6. Bewitching	f. **el**-i-g*uh*nt
7. Pulchritude	g. **win**-s*uh*m
8. Comely	h. *uh*-**dawrn**
9. Dapper	i. **puhl**-kri-tood
10. Resplendent	j. deb-*uh*-**nair**

Perfect Section 5: True or False

Test your understanding by deciding whether each of these statements is true or false.

1. Comely and homely mean the same thing.
   ░ True ░ False

2. Only a witch can be bewitching.
   ░ True ░ False

3. You don't have to be born into an aristocratic family to have an aristocratic demeanor and style.
   ░ True ░ False

4. The word adorn can be used to express the idea of beautifying both human beings and inanimate objects.
   ░ True ░ False

5. You can call an unsophisticated man with unkempt hair debonair.
   ░ True ░ False

6. Pulchritude is a synonym for the word pulverize.
   ░ True ░ False

7. Dapper is a word that's used exclusively for describing men.
   ░ True ░ False

8. The Latin root of resplendent quite literally means 'to shine brightly.'
   ░ True ░ False

9. The word elegant can be used only for describing women.
   ░ True ░ False

10. When someone is winsome, they can quite literally win you over.
    ░ True ░ False

Perfect Section 6: Drawing Conclusions

1. Your friend has bought a well-fitted tuxedo to wear to the ball.
   He is determined to look _____ at the ball.

2. You go suit-shopping with your brother. He comes out of the trial room looking incredibly attractive and sharp.
   Your brother is looking _____ in the suit.

3. Your colleague has tried out a new hairstyle and people can't stop complimenting her on it.
   Indeed, it is a _____ hairstyle.

4. Your friend has a very upper class accent and manner of speaking.
   His accent is extremely _____.

5. The moment the beautiful blonde walked into the door, all eyes were transfixed on her as if she had cast a spell on the entire room.
   The entire room was captivated by the blonde's _____ beauty.

6. You go to the grocery store and come face-to-face with an exceptionally beautiful woman.
   You are awe-struck by the _____ of the woman.

7. You meet an old classmate after almost a decade—you are amazed by how graceful and refined she is in every way.
   She is a very _____ woman.

8. Your friend walks in looking absolutely stunning in a beautiful red silk dress.
   Your friend is looking _____ in the red silk dress.

9. You are amazed to enter your hotel room—there are so many beautiful paintings on the wall.
   Beautiful paintings _____ the walls of the hotel room.

10. You come across a salesman who is very charming and innocent-looking. It's hard to say no to him.
    It's hard to say no to the _____ salesman.

Section 3

1. Elegant; 2. Resplendent; 3. Adorn; 4. Dapper; 5. Debonair; 6. Aristocratic; 7. Pulchritude; 8. Bewitching; 9. Winsome; 10. Comely

Section 4

1. h; 2. j; 3. e; 4. g; 5. f; 6. c; 7. i; 8. a; 9. d; 10. b

Section 5

1. False; 2. False; 3. True; 4. True; 5. False; 6. False; 7. True; 8. True; 9. False; 10. True

Section 6

1. Debonair; 2. Dapper; 3. Comely; 4. Aristocratic; 5. Bewitching; 6. Pulchritude; 7. Elegant; 8. Resplendent; 9. Adorn; 10. Winsome

20

INSULTS BASED ON APPEARANCE

Exposure Section 1: Words in Context

WE HAVE REACHED the last lesson in our study of vocabulary. You should be a master of our vocabulary method by now. You can't hear it, but I'm playing Pomp and Circumstance for you and wiping a tear from my eye. You've come so far!

Now we look at the opposite of those *dapper, debonair* lads and ladies. We talk about old shriveled-up **crones** and **beldams**, with their **disagreeable** manner, sitting on their porches, passing gas, and yelling at the neighbor kids.

Yeah, let's not talk about them.

While some things and people are comely, others are **horrid** and **obnoxious**. They horrify you and leave a bad taste in your mouth because of how unpleasant they are.

But other people have strange tastes. They like that which is **grotesque** and ugly. Somehow their heart finds delight in those things that others would deem disfigured and distorted. They like to surround themselves with what in the field of art and architecture is described as 'the grotesque.' The focus is on creating distortions as a piece of artistic marvel.

For most people, such art and architecture would be a **revolting** sight —something that nauseates and disgusts them in the worst possible way. The old adage "one man's meat is another man's poison" really does ring true here. Art and fashion are often a matter of personal taste and preferences.

If you don't believe that, watch the Oscars. Which, now that you're all dressed up for your EPP graduation ceremony, you should fit right in.

Exposure Section 2: Definitions & Example Sentences

Repulsive

(ri-**puhl**-siv) - (adj.) offensive to the mind; so extremely ugly as to be terrifying; possessing the ability to repel.

If something's **repulsive**, it's so disgusting you don't want to go near it. You may find rotting meat **repulsive**, but maggots find it delicious.[527]

- The old man behaved in such a **repulsive** way that no one wanted to sit near him at the dining table.
- "Immodest and attractive is easy. Modest and **repulsive** is easy too. But modest and attractive is an art form." -Douglas Wilson, 5 *Paths to the Love of Your Life: Defining Your Dating Style*[528]

Grotesque

(groh-**tesk**) - (adj.) characterized by distortions or striking incongruities in appearance, shape, or manner; fantastic; bizarre; horrendously ugly.[529]

- Lucy has a strange decorative style—she likes to surround herself with **grotesque** figurines.
- "Sometimes the poor are praised for being thrifty. But to recommend thrift to the poor is both **grotesque** and insulting. It is like advising a man who is starving to eat less." - Oscar Wilde[530]

Horrid

(**hawr**-id, **hor**-id) - (adj.) such as to cause horror; shockingly dreadful; abominable; extremely unpleasant or disagreeable; repulsive or frightening.[531]

Horrid things are absolutely dreadful—they horrify or disgust you. A **horrid** dream can make you wake with a gasp and lie there with your heart pounding. You might cover your eyes during a particularly horrid scene in a scary movie or skip past the **horrid** photos of a war zone in the newspaper. Things are also **horrid** when they're in bad taste: "That wallpaper in your bedroom is absolutely horrid."[532]

- I wanted her to spare me the **horrid** details of the train wreck she had witnessed a few days ago.
- "For, if a good speaker, never so eloquent, does not see into the fact, and is not speaking the truth of that—is there a more **horrid** kind of object in creation?" -Thomas Carlyle[533]

Abhorrent

(ab-**hawr**-*uh*nt, ab-**hor**-*uh*nt) - (adj.) morally very bad; causing or deserving strong dislike or hatred; being so repugnant as to stir up positive antagonism; not agreeable; contrary; feeling or showing strong dislike or hatred.[534, 535]

- Jacob couldn't imagine living in such a filthy and **abhorrent** environment.
- "It is **abhorrent** to me when a fine intelligence is paired with an unsavory character." -Albert Einstein[536]

Disagreeable

(dis-*uh*-**gree**-*uh*-b*uh*l) - (adj.) not to one's taste; unpleasant; offensive; hard to get along with; quarrelsome; not likable, esp. bad-tempered, offensive, or disobliging.[537]

If something is **disagreeable**, it's unpleasant, like the **disagreeable** smell of your wet sneakers. And if a person is **disagreeable**, they're rude or irritable, like your **disagreeable** upstairs neighbor.[538]

- The **disagreeable** weather completely ruined our plans for a picnic.
- "You can disagree without being **disagreeable**." -Ruth Bader Ginsburg[539]

Obnoxious

(*uh*b-**nok**-sh*uh*s) - (adj.) extremely unpleasant; highly objectionable or offensive; odious; annoying or objectionable due to being a showoff or attracting undue attention to oneself.[540]

If something is **obnoxious**, it's annoying and unpleasant. Generally, people like to avoid **obnoxious** folks. Any time someone is **obnoxious**, someone else probably wants them to stop it.[541]

- The little brat behaves in the most **obnoxious** way you can imagine.
- "I am free, no matter what rules surround me. If I find them tolerable, I tolerate them; if I find them too **obnoxious**, I break them. I am free because I know that I alone am morally responsible for everything I do." -Robert A. Heinlein[542]

Crone

(**krohn**) - (n.) an ugly, withered old woman; hag; a withered, witchlike old woman.[543]

The haggard old woman who lives down the street in a dilapidated house, shaking her fist while chasing children out of her yard? You might call her a **crone**. Since the late fourteenth century, the word **crone** has been a term of abuse describing old and bad-tempered women. It traces back to the Anglo-French word charoine, meaning "dead flesh."[544]

- The **crone** down the street has a very disagreeable temper.
- "In art and mythology, the Goddess appears in three forms. White represents the virgin, red the mother, and black, the **crone**, or the death-goddess." -Erin O'Riordan, *Cut*[545]

Beldam

(**bel**-d*u*hm, **bel**-dam) - (n.) an old woman, esp. an ugly or malicious one; a hag.[546]

- You can't help but wonder if that **beldam** has ever smiled in her entire life.
- Who wants to go near that obnoxious **beldam**!

Grisly

(**griz**-lee) - (adj.) extremely unpleasant, especially because death or blood is involved; extremely unpleasant or disgusting, and usually causing fear; causing a shudder or feeling of horror; horrible; gruesome; formidable; grim.[547, 548]

Grisly means disgusting and bloody, absolutely repulsive and horrible. There's a wonderfully creepy movie about a man who suffers a **grisly** death at the hands of the grizzly bears he was studying.[549]

- The senator suffered a **grisly** death at the hands of the psychopath.
- "Ever and again, our mind may become befuddled when we have to find out what is heads or tails. Ever and again, bewilderment may strike our brain when we have to interpret the contrasts between the dark and the bright sides of things when we have got to read complex cases and assess the divergences between the iridescent outward appearances and the **grisly** undercurrents of particular characters." -Erik Pevernagie[550]

Revolting

(ri-**vohl**-ting) - (adj.) causing revulsion; nauseating, disgusting, or repulsive.[551]

If you say that something or someone is **revolting**, you mean you think they are horrible and disgusting.

- The sight of animals being slaughtered in the field was too **revolting** for her sensitive heart.
- "There is just a lot of spitting; a dugout after a game is truly **revolting**."[552]

Practice Section 3: Unscramble the Words

Unscramble the following words.

1. RECNO

2. DRHIOR

3. OENHRABRT

4. EEEARASDILGB

5. EDM – LABMED

6. BOSOOUIXN

7. GLONVITER

8. LPERSEUIV

9. IGYSLR

10. QRTSGEEUO

Practice Section 4: Matching

Match each word with its correct definition.

1. Horrid	a. So disgusting that you wouldn't want to go near it
2. Disagreeable	b. Extremely unpleasant, especially because death or blood is involved
3. Repulsive	c. Not agreeing with your tastes or expectations
4. Grisly	d. An ugly, evil-looking old woman
5. Crone	e. Horrifyingly dreadful and bad

Practice Section 5: Fill-in-the-Blank

Fill in the blanks with the correct word.

1. There is nothing more **a** _ _ _ _ _ _ _ than racism.

2. The _ _ _ **d** _ _ hated having any visitors coming over to her house.

3. Layla couldn't stand the _ _ **r** _ _ **d** and **r** _ _ _ _ _ _ _ stench of rotten cabbage any longer.

4. Emilia showed up at the business meeting wearing a _ _ **r** _ _ _ fluorescent dress.

5. Everyone in the room was discussing how loud and _ _ **n** _ _ _ _ _ the new candidate is.

6. The gargoyle was so _ _ _ **t** _ _ _ _ _ that I was afraid to go inside the building.

7. I couldn't stand the _ _ **p** _ _ _ _ _ smell any longer.

Perfect Section 6: Pronunciation

Match each word with its correct phonetic pronunciation.

1. Crone	a. **bel**-dam
2. Horrid	b. **griz**-lee
3. Revolting	c. **groh**-tesk
4. Obnoxious	d. dis-*uh*-**gree**-*uh*-buhl
5. Repulsive	e. ri-**vohl**-ting
6. Beldam	f. ab-**hawr**-*uh*nt
7. Disagreeable	g. **krohn**
8. Grisly	h. *uh*b-**nok**-sh*uh*s
9. Grotesque	i. ri-**puhl**-siv
10. Abhorrent	j. **hawr**-id

Perfect Section 7: Test Your Knowledge

Has the word been used correctly?

1. Anyone who is closely related to the crone family can be called a crone.
   ▢ Yes ▢ No

2. You can call something revolting only when people are vociferously revolting against it.
   ▢ Yes ▢ No

3. When you agree with something, you call it disagreeable.
   ▢ Yes ▢ No

4. You won't call an old woman a beldam when you love and respect her.
   ▢ Yes ▢ No

5. A cold-blooded murder can be described as a grisly crime.
   ▢ Yes ▢ No

6. Horrid is a word that can be used only for describing people's behavior.
   ▢ Yes ▢ No

7. You enjoy being in the presence of an obnoxious person.
   ▢ Yes ▢ No

8. When you abhor something, you can call it abhorrent.
   ▢ Yes ▢ No

9. The artist produced some of the finest grotesques of his times.
   ▢ Yes ▢ No

10. Delightful would be a perfect antonym to obnoxious.
    ▢ Yes ▢ No

11. When something is repulsive, it repels you because of how disgusting it is.
    ▢ Yes ▢ No

Section 3

1. Crone; 2. Horrid; 3. Abhorrent; 4. Disagreeable; 5. Beldam; 6. Obnoxious; 7. Revolting ; 8. Repulsive; 9. Grisly; 10. Grotesque

Section 4

1. e; 2. c; 3. a; 4. b; 5. d

Section 5

1. Abhorrent; 2. Beldam; 3. Horrid, Revolting; 4. Horrid; 5. Obnoxious; 6. Grotesque; 7. Repulsive

Section 6

1. g; 2. j; 3. e; 4. h; 5. i; 6. a; 7. d; 8. b; 9. c; 10. f

Section 7

1. No; 2. No; 3. No; 4. Yes; 5. Yes; 6. No; 7. No; 8. Yes; 9. Yes; 10. Yes; 11. Yes

CHAPTERS 16-20 REVIEW

Each of the twenty words below is split by one stressed syllable, the boldfaced text. By combining them, you can more easily pronounce the word correctly and further reinforce the retention of the word. List the words on the lines below, and then choose the most appropriate word from the twenty you have combined to fill out the ten sentences in section 2. This provides you yet another way to perfect your knowledge of how the word is used in a sentence.

vations	**pul**	per	y
greeable	er	debo	**co**cious
acious	ambi	**horr**	**sim**
pre	pleton	**dorn**	be
cratic	sa	inno	head
cipient	**come**	er	ly
udite	**lunk**	id	disa
cann	**dextrous**	chritude	aristo
nair	**dapp**	a	**witch**ing
palm	**win**	**face**	some

1. _____ 11. _____

2. _____ 12. _____

3. _____ 13. _____

4. _____ 14. _____

5. _____ 15. _____

6. _____ 16. _____

7. _____ 17. _____

8. _____ 18. _____

9. _____ 19. _____

10. _____ 20. _____

Review Section 2: Fill-in-the-Blank

1. The very technological   that facilitate our world may end it in the not too distant future unless we intervene in some manner.

2. By 12 years of age, my   son was already fluent in 6 languages.

3. The murderer had a disturbingly   upbringing of abuse and torture.

4. Ever since my brother and I were very young, my brother always got by based on his   looks and I remained in his shadow.

5. My father is the most wise and   person I have ever known. As a businessman, he has never failed.

6. Your uncle was always the type of person who needed to look   with a new suit and hat regardless of the occasion. His appearance was his first priority.

7. The only element of certainty one can ever attribute to your unpredictable aunt is when she does not get what she wants, she becomes   and intolerable.

8. Many say that looking beneath the   on the outside permits one to see the very essence of an individual on the inside.

9. The only reason I   myself with expensive designer clothing is because I don't pay for it.

10. The dapper gentleman was from an   family with a sense of entitlement filled with self-centeredness and arrogance.

Review Section 3: Crossword Puzzle

Complete the crossword puzzle based on your acquired knowledge of the vocabulary terms.

Across

2. A mean or ugly woman

4. To cover face in embarrassment

6. A dumb person

7. Placing oneself in a photo when it is being taken

10. Highly upsetting to one's aesthetic sense

13. Demonstrating an insightful application of knowledge

14. Neat in appearance and style

16. Using either hand with proficiency

18. Attractiveness, sexiness

20. Designed to attract those on the Internet to visit particular content

21. Mentally sharp and shrewd

24. Dull-witted person

25. Coding data for security

Down

1. A highly skilled person in the arts

3. Arousing disgust; to repel from disgust

5. Being clever and resourceful

9. Shining brilliantly

11. Insatiable

12. Generally pleasing and engaging

15. A person who has telepathic perception

17. Intensely alluring or charming

19. A crass, insensitive person

22. Possessing cleverness

23. A signal sent from computer to computer via network

Section 1

Innovations, Precocious, Aristocratic, Erudite, Disagreeable, Horrid, Lunkhead. Comely, Canny, Sagacious, Simpleton, Percipient, Ambidextrous, Pulchritude, Debonair, Dapper, Adorn, Bewitching

Section 2

1. Innovations, 2. Erudite, 3. Horrid, 4. Comely, 5. Sagacious, 6. Dapper, 7. Disagreeable, 8. Pulchritude, 9. Adorn, 10. Aristocratic

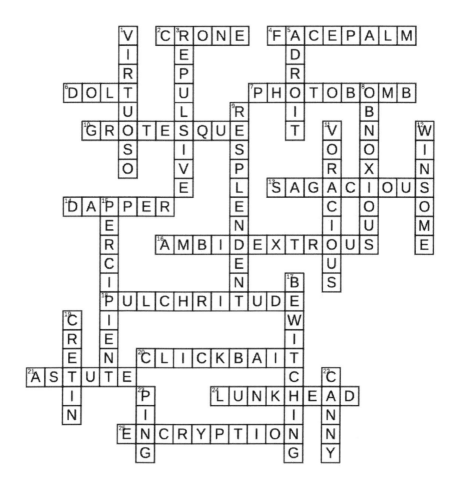

APPENDIX: PREFIXES, ROOT WORDS, AND SUFFIXES

ALONGSIDE ACQUIRING AND RETAINING VOCABULARY, a helpful way to tackle unknown words you will inevitably encounter along your professional, academic, and personal path is by deepening your knowledge of how English words are assembled, known as morphological awareness. By learning these prefixes, roots, and suffixes, you can deconstruct the composition of a word and decipher its meaning within a given context or when there is no context with which to work.

While studies seem to vary on the precise numbers, about 45 to 55 percent of English words are based on Latin and Greek. The former being the most influential of the two. When considering words related to technology and science, upwards of 75-85% of them are based on Latin and Greek. In fact, in the tables below, I included 28 prefixes, 46 roots, and 31 suffixes, while the amount that exists is much greater, these essential parts can generate 1,000s of words to add to your lexical inventory. By mastering these components, you will gain a substantial advantage in discovering thousands of words. Imagine how many of them you may very well run across, be it on an exam or in a working environment.

Below are a few helpful hints to keep in mind when learning how to examine different parts of words:

1. Words can have more than one prefix, root, and/or suffix, as in:

- in-sub-ordinate, which contains the prefixes in and sub
- matri-cide, which contains the root matri (mother) and cide (kill); the killing one's mother
- lust-ful-ly, which contains the suffixes ful and ly

2. Typically, most words have at least one root.

3. Prefixes don't typically change the spelling of a word when added to a root though hyphens may be used in certain circumstances; however, suffixes do sometimes change the spelling.

- A hyphen is used with the following prefixes: all-, cross-, ex-, & self-, e.g., all-encompassing, cross-reference, ex-girlfriend, self-administering
- Use a hyphen for all prefixes before proper nouns, numbers, or abbreviations: e.g., trans-Atlantic pathway, late-1500s, or non-binding peptides
- Use a hyphen for prefixes that have the same vowel the root starts with: e.g., intra-arterial, co-obligation, anti-immunity
- Use a hyphen to avoid ambiguities of the accurate meaning of the word: e.g., re-sign, re-create

4. Some root words may change in meaning depending upon whether they are from Greek or Latin.

- Homo erectus: homo is a Latin root that means man
- Homogeneity: homo is a Greek root that refers to make the same

Exposure Section 2: Prefixes Table

Prefixes attach themselves to the front of a word. While they alter meaning, they do not typically change the spelling of a word. As mentioned above, the use of hyphens does occur to avoid clashing vowels.

Origin: **G** Greek, **L** Latin, **OE** Old English

Prefix	Origin	Meaning	Example Words
a/an-	G	lacking	asexual, asymmetry
ab-	L	from, away	absent, abduct, abhor
ad-	L	at, near, toward	admit, advertise
ben-	L	well, good	benefit, benediction
be-	OE	cause to be, about, easy, to notice	bewitch, bedevil
bi-	L	double	bisexual, bigender
cis	L	on this side of	cisgender
com/con/co-	L	together	combine, convivial , co-chair
di-	L	two	dilute
dis-	G	apart	dishonorable
ect/ecto-	G	outside of, external	ectoplasm
ex-	L	out of, former	exult, excommunicate
en-	L	put into cover up with	encapsulate
eu-	G	well, good	eulogy
giga-	G	billion	gigabyte
im/in-	L	not, without	improbable, immature
ne/neo-	G	new	neon
mis-	G	ill, unfortunate	misconstrue
mal-	L	badly	maltreatment, malicious
pan/pano-	G	all, entire	pandemic, panspermia
peri-	G	all around, about	periscope
pre/pro-	L	before, forward	prenup, project, provision
re-	L	back, again	regain, reject, rescind
sub-	L	under, lower	subservient
tri-	L	three, every third	tripod, trimester
un-	OE	not	untampered, unfinished
uni-	L	one	universal, uniform

Practice Section 3: Prefixes Matching

Match each prefix with its correct definition and origin.

1. pre-	a. single (L)
2. ect/ecto-	b. all/around/about (G)
3. ab-	c. billion (G)
4. mal-	d. well/good (G)
5. a-	e. good (L)
6. sub-	f. put into/cover up (L)
7. uni-	g. all/entire (G)
8. peri-	h. end (L)
9. fin-	i. before/in front of (L)
10. ey-	j. under (L)
11. be-	k. cause to be/about (OE)
12. ben-	l. badly (L)
13. en-	m. outside/external (G)
14. pan-	n. lacking (G)
15. giga-	o. depart from/outside of (L)

Practice Section 4: Prefixes Fill-in-the-Blank

Complete each sentence by selecting the appropriate prefix.

cis-	con-	mal-	un-	en-
in-	de-	be-	sub-	dis-
pre-	bi-	re-	ne-	im-

1. To ▢bel against authority often comes with significant consequences.

2. You always ▢little my most cherished accomplishments.

3. It is ▢probable that the accused could have committed the crime given there wasn't enough time to cover up the evidence.

4. One can easily ▢capsulate the whole presentation in one word: unproductive.

5. The patient experienced such extreme ▢treatment it is a miracle the person survived during the torturous stay at the convalescent home.

6. ▢contracting smaller companies by large companies is a rather common practice, and it is a way to save money.

7. It is essential as a leader to ▢gender feelings of loyalty and trust in those who look up to you.

8. Just because John's family comes from immense wealth, he thinks it is normal to ▢ride those who come from little means.

9. The ▢passionate judge calmly, yet sternly sentenced the murderer to the stiffest of possible sentences; life with no possibility of parole.

10. The 18 foot tsunami ▢gulfed everything and anything in its path.

11. Philp defines himself as ▢gender. While he dresses in conventional male attire, his gestures are effeminate.

12. Even with the rescue workers ___ reletenting dedication, they were unable to reach those buried by wreckage of the collapsed building in time.

13. While I was adopted, my ___ sanguineous siblings don't even think of the fact that we are not related by blood.

14. Right before frank slipped into a coma, he uttered a ___ bulous statement as to where he hid all of the cash.

15. Most people may not even be aware that they are ___ gender, for typically no conflict arises from the anatomy they are born with and how they identify themselves.

Prefixes and suffixes bind themselves to the root word. The roots that derive from Latin and Greek typically do not stand on their own as words. These can be seen as parts of words that become meaningful words once bound with either Latin or Greek affixes.

The word 'incredible' consists of a prefix and suffix bound to the root **cred**, which means *believe* in Latin. While **cred** is the foundation of the word incredible, once detached from the prefix and suffix, the meaningfulness of a word in English no longer carries.

---

in + **cred** + ible = incredible

cred = a word part

By studying the root **cred**, regardless of whether or not it stands alone as its own word, the advantages become quite evident. As you see below, a plethora of words in English are built from it.

---

in**cred**ible**cred**it

credible **cred**itor

in**cred**ibly **cred**ibility

credulous **cred**ential

credulity ac**cred**it

in**cred**ulity dis**cred**it

credoac**cred**it

There are, however, those root words that do stand as meaningful words without the binding of a prefix or suffix.

In the word **form**, which means shape, it cannot be separated. Not only is it meaningful as its own word, but it is also a root that can be built upon. By adding prefixes and/or suffixes, you find these words

de**form**ity

re**form**

formulate

re**form**ation

con**form**

Origin: **G** Greek, **L** Latin, **OE** Old English

Root	Origin	Meaning	Example
archaeo	G	ancient	archeology
aster/astro	L	star	astrobiology
ambi	L	both sides	ambivalent
anthro	G	anthropomorphic	human-like
adu/audit	L	hear	audio
bene	L	good/well	beneficial
bell	L	war & fighting	belligerent
bio	G	life	biology
chron	G	time	chronology
circum	L	around	circumspect
cide/cise	L	kill	insecticide
corp	L	body	corpus
cred	L	believe	credibility
dict/dic	L	tell/say	dictation
dem	G	people	democracy
e/ec/ef	L	out	elaborate/eccentric/effervesce
eco	G	earth	ecology
fic/fect	L	to do/to make	amplification/defective
fid	L	faith	fidelity
fer	L	carry	transfer
inter	L	between	interwoven, internet
gene	G	race	genocide
graph	G	write/recording	telegraph
logy	G	study	sociology
hetero	G	different	heterogenous
homos/homo	G/L	same/man	homogeneous/homicidal
mit/miss	L	send	permit/dismiss
mort/mor	L	die	mortal

Root	Origin	Meaning	Example
nom	L	name	nominate
path/patho	G	disease	pathology
pend	L	to hang	impending
phono	G	sound	telephone
photo	G	light	photosensitivity
port	L	carry	transport
quisit/quir	L	seek	requisite
sang/sangui	L	blood	sanguineous
scrib/script	L	write	inscribe
sen/sent	L	feel	insensitivity
spect/spic/spect	L	look	retrospect
techno	G	craft/skill	technology
temp	L	time	temporary
terr/terre	L	land	terrestrial
tort	L	twist	tortuous
theo	G	God	theology
ven/vent	L	come	convention
ver	L	truth	verify
vis/vid	L	see	visible
voc	L	call	vocation

Practice Section 7: Root Words Fill-in-the-Blank

Combine two root words based on each corresponding number below. Each sentence provides enough contextual clues to decipher the most appropriate word to complete the sentence.

graph	spect	bene	dict
phobia	matri	retro	xeno
cide	terra	(o)logy	form
demo	bio	sphere	cracy
manu	drama	melo	script

1. I have been studying _____ for two years. Studying the character of someone by the way in which they sign their name is quite fascinating.

2. The technology to _____ Mars is already said to be theoretically possible. If humans are successful in changing the atmospheric conditions on Mars, I certainly hope I am still alive to witness it.

3. That gentleman, Charlie, was a bachelor for over a decade before marrying Rose. To see the _____ settle down with such a beautiful bride is heartwarming.

4. In _____, I wish I had changed careers 20 years ago when I had the motivation and discipline required to become a medical doctor.

5. A _____ is a form of government where the power to govern comes from the very people as opposed to a dictatorship, for instance, where an individual possesses all the power.

6. To date we have not found any evidence of life outside of our own _____.

7. As the borders of nations shrink, _____ expands. This disdain or fear of people from other cultures is counterproductive to the progress of a nation.

8. Committing _____, the killing of one's own maternal figure is abhorrently and utterly abominable.

9. Living with my roommate is such a _____. Something so trivial as a fork left in the sink becomes an exaggerated emotional upheaval of how utterly vile the kitchen is, or the bathroom light left on becomes a tear jerking episode of complete emotional meltdown that the earth is being destroyed.

10. The book's original _____ is by far more thorough and informative than the final version.

Exposure Section 8: Suffixes Table

Suffixes are a type of affix that bind themselves to the end of the root or attach onto another suffix. They are important not only because they alter the meaning of the root but also change its part of speech.

L Latin, **OE** Old English, **F** French, **GER** German, **G** Greek

Suffix	Origin	Meaning	Example
-ate	L	become	eradicate
-able/-ible	L	capable of	reliable/tangible
-acy	L	state or quality	fallacy
-al	L	Process of	rebuttal
-ance	L	state or quality	assurance
-ary	L	reference to	primary
-ant	L	one who	participant
-dom	L	place or state of being	boredom
-en	OE	become	weaken
-ence	L	state or quality	reference
-er/-or	F	someone who	barber/traitor
-eer	F	someone who	engineer
-hood	OE	reference to	adulthood
-ic/-ical	L/G	to pertain to	comic/magical
-ify	L	make or become	justify
-ish	F	quality	sheepish
-ism	G	belief	nepotism
-ist	L	someone who	narcissist
-ive	L	nature of	divisive
-ize	G	to become	jeopardize
-ity	L	quality of	veracity
-less	OE	without	penniless
-ful	OE	notable	fruitful
-ment	L	condition	achievement
-ness	GER	ful	gleefulness
-ous/-ious	L	characterization of	nervous/obvious
-ship	OE	position held	stewardship
-tion/-sion	L	state of being	communication/tension
-y	G	characterization	racy
-ward	OE	reference to	homeward

Combine a word on the left with its appropriate suffix on the right to complete the sentences below.

insurgent	ventriloquist	-cy	-some
obliterate	loquacious	-ism	-ly
fastidious	maleficence	-ness	-ent
loathe	fortitudinous	-tion	-ible
infallibility	morbid	-tude	-ity

1. The _____ with which Marie examines every detail of the painting makes her one of the most respected and sought after appraisers of valuable art.

2. I am forever haunted by that repulsively _____ odor in the basement and by that horrid painting of that beast in my nightmare.

3. Destined for utter _____, the small village on the coast line was in the direct path of a category five hurricane.

4. Amazement filled the room as the guest _____ carried on about a topic she really had no clue about.

5. As your daughter is already vulnerable in her state, keeping her away from _____ characters would be a prudent piece of advice.

6. As the oppressed grew tired of such abominable treatment by their own government, the _____ executed plans to bring down the political heads of state from within.

7. Since Samuel was young, he had an exquisite ability to mimic every sound he heard. Naturally, when he began studying _____, he mastered throwing his voice to perfection.

8. The young woman's _____ permitted her to face her brutal assailant and forgive him for the brutal murder of her entire family.

9. Just because the _____ rates of a particular disease may be high, does not necessarily mean the mortality rate will also be high. For instance, COVID-19 has a lower rate of mortality.

10. Not one person who has ever existed has been _____, for we are human.

Perfect Section 10: Cumulative Review of Prefixes, Roots, and Suffixes

In concluding our lexical journey, for now, apply what you have learned utilizing all prefixes, roots, and suffixes. Reconstruct a word from its constituent parts and focus on the sentence that provides context for this word. You will know you have built the correct word if it makes sense when you complete the sentence. While you may encounter more than one possible word for each number, only one will be the most appropriate to complete the sentence. This exercise focuses on the almighty coupling of practicing and perfecting through cumulative understanding.

1. While my family was shocked and saddened when they found out my cousin was born with a mental disability, I was the only person unencumbered by denial, for it was a direct consequence of my aunt and uncle being a   couple.

sanguine   ous   con
   ness   en   tion

2. The glass of wine I had at dinner last night had a   after taste. I find myself struggling to understand the reason behind my finishing that bottle 10 minutes later.

ly   dis   able
agree   re   come

3. My wife and I have a great marriage and have so much fun when we have sex. Imagine for a moment how exciting it could be if your wife was also the world's best ▓▓▓▓▓▓. You would be exploring positions you didn't even know were humanly possible.

tion	able	tor
un	con	ist

4. As soon as Jeff was old enough to rationalize what he believed, he immediately began questioning the notion of ▓▓▓▓▓. He was never comfortable with the idea that billions of people have a close relationship with only one God. Making an appointment to speak with such a God would be rather difficult.

theo	ism	mono
ed	tion	cis

5. The nature of nuclear power is such that it can be used in the production of ▓▓▓▓▓.

electric	thermo	dis
un	tude	lty

6. As a character trait, ▓▓▓▓▓ can be exciting; however, there is a cost associated with this danger. Foresight is something that can never be taken for granted.

bel	ism	able
un	cide	terror
ness	dict	pre

7. Rosa is wholeheartedly convinced that her marriage ended in tragic, stomach-turning, abhorrently distasteful bloodshed because the priest had never delivered the _____ during the wedding.

tion	hood	bene
logy	dic	fic

8. Superficially, it may appear as if those who _____ their feelings have mastered a way of not permitting emotion to interfere. In all practicality, the only thing mastered is the sheer velocity and thickness of the dog poo erupting exposively toward the fan's inevitable annihilation.

e	tion	ize
al	ment	ly
compart	dis	ful

9. During my four years of graduate school, I _____ myself within the NYU library with a coffee in one hand and a stylus in the other. It wasn't the most fun I have ever had, but it paid off in spades years later.

il	ly	mur
dict	leg	mono
un	in (im)	ed

10. The extent to which _____ exists in a given society is correlated to the inevitable and undeniable varying levels of exploitation and corruption an individual experiences.

ism	dis	ment
arian	anti	cide
con	establish	ist
pre	ped	or

Section 3

1. i, 2. m, 3. o, 4. l, 5. n, 6. j, 7. a, 8. b, 9. h, 10. d, 11. k, 12. e, 13. f, 14. g, 15. c

Section 4

1. Rebel, 2. Belittle, 3. Improbable, 4. Incapsulate, 5. Maltreatment, 6. Subcontracting, 7. Engender, 8. Deride, 9. Impassionate, 10. Engulfed, 11. Bigender, 12. Supernatural, Unrelenting, 13. Consanguineous, 14. Nebulous, 15. Cisgender

Section 7

1. Graphology, 2. Terraform, 3. Benedict, 4. Retrospect, 5. Democracy, 6. Biosphere, 7. Xenophobia, 8. Matricide, 9. Melodrama, 10. Manuscript

Section 10

1. Consanguineous, 2. Disagreeable, 3. Contortionist, 4. Monotheism, 5. Thermoelectricity, 6. Unpredictableness, 7. Benediction, 8. Compartmentalization, 9. Immured, 10. Anti-establishmentarianism

REFERENCES

Chapter 1

[1] "Cisgender." *Wikipedia,* (2021, May 31) https://en.wikipedia.org/wiki/Cisgender accessed 6/26/2021

[2] *Cambridge Dictionary*, s.v. "cisgender," https://dictionary.cambridge.org/dictionary/english/cisgender accessed 6/26/2021

[3] Ryan, Hugh, "It's Time to Take Cisgender Seriously." *Slate,* (2016, May 2) https://slate.com/human-interest/2016/05/cisgender-identity-is-a-crucial-part-of-trans-awareness.html accessed 6/20/2021

[4] Nazario, Brunilda, "When You Don't Feel at Home With Your Assigned Gender." *WebMD,* (2021, May 20) https://www.webmd.com/sex/gender-dysphoria accessed 6/26/2021

[5] "Chaz Bono Quotes." *AZQuotes*, (n.d.), https://www.azquotes.com/author/1648-Chaz_Bono accessed 6/20/2021

[6] "What is Fluid?" *WebMD*, (n.d.), https://www.webmd.com/sex/what-is-fluid accessed 6/26/2021

[7] "Mvxx. Amillivn Quotes." *Goodreads* (n.d.), https://www.goodreads.com/author/quotes/13851179.Mvxx_Amillivn accessed 6/20/2021

[8] Dictionary.com, s.v. "bigender," https://www.dictionary.com/e/gender-sexuality/bigender/ accessed 6/26/2021

[9] "About." *RBLemberg.net,* (n.d.), http://rblemberg.net/?page_id=16 accessed 6/26/2021

[10] "Pansexuality: What it Means." *WebMD* (n.d.), https://www.webmd.com/sex/pansexuality-what-it-means accessed 6/26/2021

[11] Bruner, Raisa, "Miley Cyrus Opens Up About Sobriety, Liam Hemsworth, and Being 'Pansexual'." *Time*, (2017, May 4) https://time.com/4766858/miley-cyrus-interview-on-sobriety/ accessed 6/20/2021

[12] "What is Asexual?" *WebMD*, (n.d.), https://www.webmd.com/sex/what-is-asexual accessed 6/26/2021

[13] "Julie Sondra Decker Quotes." *Goodreads*, (n.d.), https://www.goodreads.com/author/quotes/7710164.Julie_Sondra_Decker accessed 6/20/2021

[14] "What is Intersex?" *Planned Parenthood*, (n.d.), https://www.plannedparenthood.org/learn/gender-identity/sex-gender-identity/whats-intersex accessed 6/26/2021

[15] "Christina Engela Quotes." *Goodreads*, (n.d.), https://www.goodreads.com/author/quotes/3358833.Christina_Engela accessed 6/20/2021

[16] "What Does Aromantic Mean?" *WebMD*, (n.d.), https://www.webmd.com/sex/what-does-aromantic-mean accessed 6/26/2021

[17] "What It Means to Be Aromantic." Healthline, (2019, January 7), https://www.healthline.com/health/aromantic accessed 6/26/2021

Chapter 2

[18] *Collins Dictionary*, s.v. "anthropoid," https://www.collinsdictionary.com/dictionary/english/anthropoid accessed 6/26/2021

[19] *Vocabulary.com*, s.v. "anthropoid," https://www.vocabulary.com/dictionary/anthropoid accessed 6/26/2021

[20] "Henry Fairfield Osborn Quotes." *Goodreads,* (n.d.), https://www.goodreads.com/author/quotes/251773.Henry_Fairfield_Osborn accessed 6/26/2021

[21] *Collins Dictionary*, s.v. "bestial," https://www.collinsdictionary.com/dictionary/english/bestial accessed 6/26/2021

[22] *Vocabulary.com*, s.v. "bestial," https://www.vocabulary.com/dictionary/bestial accessed 6/26/2021

[23] "Oscar Wilde Quotes." *AZQuotes* (n.d.), https://www.azquotes.com/author/15644-Oscar_Wilde accessed 6/26/2021

[24] *Collins Dictionary*, s.v. "castrate," https://www.collinsdictionary.com/dictionary/english/castrate accessed 6/26/2021

[25] *Vocabulary.com*, s.v. "castrate," https://www.vocabulary.com/dictionary/castrate accessed 6/26/2021

[26] "Friedrich Nietzsche Quotes." *AZQuotes,* (n.d.), https://www.azquotes.com/author/10823-Friedrich_Nietzsche accessed 6/26/2021

[27] *Lexico.com*, s.v. "dorsal," https://www.lexico.com/definition/dorsal accessed 6/26/2021

[28] *Dictionary.com*, s.v. "dorsal," https://www.dictionary.com/browse/dorsal accessed 6/26/2021

[29] "Rick Riordan Quotes." *Goodreads,* (n.d.), https://www.goodreads.com/author/quotes/15872.Rick_Riordan accessed 6/26/2021

[30] *Mirriam-Webster Dictionary*, s.v. "equine," https://www.merriam-webster.com/dictionary/equine accessed 6/26/2021

[31] *Vocabulary.com*, s.v. "equine," https://www.vocabulary.com/dictionary/equine accessed 6/26/2021

[32] *Dictionary.com*, s.v. "fodder," https://www.dictionary.com/browse/fodder accessed 6/27/2021

[33] "Fodder Quotes." *Goodreads,* (n.d.), https://www.goodreads.com/quotes/tag/fodder accessed 6/27/2021

[34] *Collins Dictionary*, s.v. "granary," https://www.collinsdictionary.com/dictionary/english/granary accessed 6/27/2021

[35] *Vocabulary.com*, s.v. "granary," https://www.vocabulary.com/dictionary/granary accessed 6/27/2021

[36] "Prêt à Penser Quotes." *Goodreads,* (n.d.), https://www.goodreads.com/quotes/tag/pr%C3%AAt-%C3%A0-penser accessed 6/27/2021

[37] *Dictionary.com*, s.v. "husbandry," https://www.dictionary.com/browse/husbandry accessed 6/27/2021

[38] *Vocabulary.com*, s.v. "husbandry," https://www.vocabulary.com/dictionary/husbandry accessed 6/27/2021

[39] "Aldo Leopold Quotes." *AZQuotes,* (n.d.), https://www.azquotes.com/author/8737-Aldo_Leopold accessed 6/27/2021

[40] *Collins Dictionary*, s.v. "leonine," https://www.collinsdictionary.com/dictionary/english/leonine accessed 6/27/2021

[41] *Lexico.com*, s.v. "leonine," https://www.lexico.com/definition/leonine accessed 6/27/2021

[42] "Rumi Quotes." *Goodreads,* (n.d.), https://www.goodreads.com/author/quotes/875661.Rumi accessed 6/27/2021

[43] *Collins Dictionary*, s.v. "phylum," https://www.collinsdictionary.com/dictionary/english/phylum accessed 6/27/2021

[44] *Miriam-Webster Dictionary*, s.v. "phylum," https://www.merriam-webster.com/dictionary/phylum accessed 6/27/2021

[45] *Vocabulary.com*, s.v. "phylum," https://www.vocabulary.com/dictionary/phylum accessed 6/27/2021

[46] "Irradiating small animals used as fish food makes them bigger." *The Economist*, (2021, January 21), https://www.economist.com/science-and-technology/2021/01/21/irradiating-small-animals-used-as-fish-food-makes-them-bigger accessed 6/27/2021

[47] *Collins Dictionary*, s.v. "ursine," https://www.collinsdictionary.com/dictionary/english/ursine accessed 6/27/2021

[48] *Vocabulary.com*, s.v. "ursine," https://www.vocabulary.com/dictionary/ursine accessed 6/27/2021

[49] "Kiss Quotes." *Goodreads*, (n.d.), https://www.goodreads.com/quotes/tag?id=kiss+&page=36&utf8=%E2%9C%93 accessed 6/27/2021

Chapter 3

[50] *Miriam-Webster Dictionary*, s.v. "comatose," https://www.merriam-webster.com/dictionary/comatose accessed 6/27/2021

[51] *Cambridge Dictionary*, s.v. "comatose," https://dictionary.cambridge.org/dictionary/english/comatose accessed 6/27/2021

[52] *Vocabulary.com*, s.v. "comatose," https://www.vocabulary.com/dictionary/comatose accessed 6/27/2021

[53] "James Alan Gardner Quotes." *Goodreads*, (n.d.), https://www.azquotes.com/author/28676-James_Alan_Gardner accessed 6/27/2021

[54] *Cambridge Dictionary*, s.v. "doze," https://dictionary.cambridge.org/dictionary/english/doze accessed 6/27/2021

55 "Lao Tzu Quotes." *BrainyQuote*, (n.d.), https://www.brainyquote.com/quotes/lao_tzu_120030 accessed 6/27/2021

56 *Miriam-Webster Dictionary*, s.v. "forty winks," https://www.google.com/url?q=https://www.merriam-webster.com/dictionary/forty%2520winks accessed 6/27/2021

57 *Cambridge Dictionary*, s.v. "forty winks," https://dictionary.cambridge.org/dictionary/english/forty-winks accessed 6/27/2021

58 "Forty Winks." *TheIdioms.com*, (n.d.), https://www.theidioms.com/forty-winks/ accessed 6/27/2021

59 Ratina, Malinda in WebMD, (2020, January 4), "Insomnia." https://www.webmd.com/sleep-disorders/insomnia-symptoms-and-causes accessed 6/27/2021

60 "Banana Yoshimoto Quotes." *Goodreads*, (n.d.), https://www.goodreads.com/author/quotes/28229.Banana_Yoshimoto accessed 6/27/2021

61 *Collins Dictionary*, s.v. "reverie," https://www.collinsdictionary.com/dictionary/english/reverie accessed 6/27/2021

62 *Vocabulary.com*, s.v. "reverie," https://www.vocabulary.com/dictionary/reverie accessed 6/27/2021

63 "John Locke Quotes." *Goodreads*, (n.d.), https://www.goodreads.com/author/quotes/51746.John_Locke accessed 6/27/2021

64 *Cambridge Dictionary*, s.v. "somnambulist," https://dictionary.cambridge.org/dictionary/english/somnambulist accessed 6/27/2021

65 *Wiktionary.com*, s.v. "somnambulist," https://en.wiktionary.org/wiki/somnambulist accessed 6/27/2021

66 "Somnambulist Quotes." *Goodreads*, (n.d.), https://www.goodreads.com/quotes/tag/somnambulist accessed 6/27/2021

67 *Vocabulary.com*, s.v. "somnolent," https://www.vocabulary.com/dictionary/somnolent accessed 6/27/2021

68 "Joseph Conrad Quotes." *Goodreads*, (n.d.), https://www.goodreads.com/author/quotes/3345.Joseph_Conrad accessed 6/27/2021

69 *Vocabulary.com*, s.v. "soporific," https://www.vocabulary.com/dictionary/soporific accessed 6/27/2021

70 "Aaron Copland Quotes." *Goodreads*, (n.d.), https://www.goodreads.com/author/quotes/40015.Aaron_Copland accessed 6/27/2021

71 *TheFreeDictionary.com*, s.v. "herbetudinous," https://www.thefreedictionary.com/hebetudinous accessed 6/27/2021

72 Walker, Ruth, "Shaking off late-summer hebetude." The Christian Science Monitor, (2017, September 7), https://www.csmonitor.com/The-Culture/Verbal-Energy/2017/0907/Shaking-off-late-summer-hebetude accessed 6/27/2021

Chapter 4

73 Bhargava, Hansa D in *WebMD*, (2020, September 16), "Aphasia." https://www.webmd.com/brain/aphasia-causes-symptoms-types-treatments accessed 6/27/2021

74 "Debra Meyerson Quotes." *Goodreads*, (n.d.), https://www.goodreads.com/author/quotes/516811.Debra_Meyerson accessed 6/27/2021

75 *Cambridge Dictionary*, s.v. "hypochondria," https://dictionary.cambridge.org/dictionary/english/hypochondria accessed 6/27/2021

76 *Miriam-Webster Dictionary*, s.v. "hypochondria," https://www.merriam-webster.com/dictionary/hypochondria accessed 6/27/2021

77 "Stephen Colbert Quotes." *QuotePark.com*, (n.d.), https://quotepark.com/authors/stephen-colbert/ accessed 6/27/2021

[78]   *Safeopedia*,   s.v.   "laceration,"   https://www.safeopedia.com/ definition/178/laceration accessed 6/27/2021

[79] *Collins Dictionary*, s.v. "laceration," https://www.collinsdictionary. com/dictionary/english/laceration accessed 6/27/2021

[80] "Mason Cooley Quotes." *AZQuotes*, (n.d.), https://www.azquotes. com/author/3230-Mason_Cooley accessed 6/27/2021

[81] *Collins Dictionary*, s.v. "palliate," https://www.collinsdictionary. com/dictionary/english/palliate accessed 6/27/2021

[82] *Vocabulary.com*, s.v. "palliate," https://www.vocabulary.com/ dictionary/palliate accessed 6/27/2021

[83] "Anaïs Nin Quotes." *Goodreads*, (n.d.), https://www.goodreads.com/ author/quotes/7190.Ana_s_Nin accessed 6/27/2021

[84] *Collins Dictionary*, s.v. "pell-mell," https://www.collinsdictionary. com/dictionary/english/pell-mell accessed 6/27/2021

[85] *Vocabulary.com*, s.v. "pell-mell," https://www.vocabulary.com/ dictionary/pell-mell accessed 6/27/2021

[86] "William Shakespeare Quotes." *Goodreads*, (n.d.), https://www. goodreads.com/author/quotes/947.William_Shakespeare accessed 6/27/2021

[87] *Collins Dictionary*, s.v. "prophylactic," https://www. collinsdictionary.com/dictionary/english/prophylactic accessed 6/27/2021

[88] *Vocabulary.com*, s.v. "prophylactic," https://www.vocabulary.com/ dictionary/prophylactic accessed 6/27/2021

[90] *Cambridge Dictionary*, s.v. "resuscitate," https://dictionary. cambridge.org/dictionary/english/resuscitate accessed 6/27/2021

[91] *Collins Dictionary*, s.v. "resuscitate," https://www.collinsdictionary. com/dictionary/english/resuscitate accessed 6/27/2021

[92] "Anatole Broyard Quotes." *AZQuotes*, (n.d.), https://www.azquotes.com/author/2058-Anatole_Broyard accessed 6/27/2021

[93] *Collins Dictionary*, s.v. "salubrious," https://www.collinsdictionary.com/dictionary/english/salubrious accessed 6/27/2021

[94] *Oxford Learners Dictionary*, s.v. "salubrious," https://www.oxfordlearnersdictionaries.com/definition/english/salubrious accessed 6/27/2021

[95] "Andie MacDowell Quotes." *BrainyQuote*, (n.d.), https://www.brainyquote.com/quotes/andie_macdowell_673375 accessed 6/27/2021

[96] *Vocabulary.com*, s.v. "unguent," https://www.vocabulary.com/dictionary/unguent accessed 6/27/2021

[97] *Mariam-Webster Dictionary*, s.v. "unguent," https://www.merriam-webster.com/dictionary/unguent accessed 6/27/2021

[98] *QuotesLife.com*, (n.d.), https://www.quoteslyfe.com/quote/Each-night-when-she-prepared-for-bed-184484 accessed 6/27/2021

[99] *Cambridge Dictionary*, s.v. "vertigo," https://dictionary.cambridge.org/dictionary/english/vertigo accessed 6/27/2021

[100] *Collins Dictionary*, s.v. "vertigo," https://www.collinsdictionary.com/dictionary/english/vertigo accessed 6/27/2021

[101] "Ramez Naan Quotes." *BrainyQuote*, (n.d.), https://www.brainyquote.com/authors/ramez-naam-quotes accessed 6/27/2021

Chapter 5

[102] *Cambridge Dictionary*, s.v. "decimate," https://dictionary.cambridge.org/dictionary/english/decimate accessed 6/27/2021

[103] *Dictionary.com*, s.v. "decimate," https://www.dictionary.com/browse/decimate accessed 6/27/2021

[104] "Adam Lashinsky Quotes." *BrainyQuote*, (n.d.), https://www.brainyquote.com/authors/adam-lashinsky-quotes accessed 6/27/2021

[105] *Merriam-Webster Dictionary*, s.v. "dirge," https://www.merriam-webster.com/dictionary/dirge accessed 6/27/2021

[106] *Oxford Learners Dictionary*, s.v. "dirge," https://www.oxfordlearnersdictionaries.com/definition/english/dirge accessed 6/27/2021

[107] "Maya Angelou Quotes." *Goodreads*, (n.d.), https://www.goodreads.com/author/quotes/3503.Maya_Angelou accessed 6/27/2021

[108] *Collins Dictionary*, s.v. "epitaph," https://www.collinsdictionary.com/dictionary/english/epitaph accessed 6/27/2021

[109] "Epitaph." *Wikipedia* (2021, May 15), https://en.wikipedia.org/wiki/Epitaph accessed 6/27/2021

[110] "J.K. Rowling Quotes." *Goodreads*, (n.d.), https://www.goodreads.com/author/quotes/1077326.J_K_Rowling accessed 6/27/2021

[111] *Cambridge Dictionary*, s.v. "lurid," https://dictionary.cambridge.org/dictionary/english/lurid accessed 6/27/2021

[112] *Vocabulary.com*, s.v. "lurid," https://www.vocabulary.com/dictionary/lurid accessed 6/27/2021

[113] "Joseph Conrad Quotes." *Goodreads*, (n.d.), https://www.goodreads.com/author/quotes/3345.Joseph_Conrad accessed 6/17/2021

[114] *Cambridge Dictionary*, s.v. "macabre," https://dictionary.cambridge.org/dictionary/english/macabre accessed 6/27/2021

[115] *Vocabulary.com*, s.v. "macabre," https://www.vocabulary.com/dictionary/macabre accessed 6/27/2021

[116] "Effots Quotes." *Goodreads*, (n.d.), https://www.goodreads.com/quotes/tag/effots accessed 6/27/2021

[117] *Merriam-Webster Dictionary*, s.v. "martyr," https://www.merriam-webster.com/dictionary/martyr accessed 6/27/2021

[118] *Oxford Learners Dictionary*, s.v. "martyr," https://www.oxfordlearnersdictionaries.com/definition/english/martyr_1 accessed 6/27/2021

[119] *Cambridge Dictionary*, s.v. "martyr," https://dictionary.cambridge.org/dictionary/english/martyr accessed 6/27/2021

[120] "Mahatma Gandhi Quotes." *BrainyQuote*, (n.d.), https://www.brainyquote.com/authors/mahatma-gandhi-quotes accessed 6/27/2021

[121] *Lexico.com*, s.v. "sepulchre," https://www.lexico.com/definition/sepulchre accessed 6/27/2021

[122] *Vocabulary.com*, s.v. "sepulchre," https://www.vocabulary.com/dictionary/sepulchre accessed 6/27/2021

[123] *Cambridge Dictionary*, s.v. "necromancy," https://dictionary.cambridge.org/dictionary/english/necromancy accessed 6/27/2021

[124] *Vocabulary.com*, s.v. "necromancy," https://www.vocabulary.com/dictionary/necromancy accessed 6/27/2021

[125] "Beth Revis Quotes." *Goodreads*, (n.d.), https://www.goodreads.com/author/quotes/4018722.Beth_Revis accessed 6/27/2021

[126] *Cambridge Dictionary*, s.v. "inter," https://dictionary.cambridge.org/dictionary/english/inter accessed 6/27/2021

[127] *Vocabulary.com*, s.v. "inter," https://www.vocabulary.com/dictionary/inter accessed 6/27/2021

[128] *Vocabulary.com*, s.v. "regicide," https://www.vocabulary.com/dictionary/regicide accessed 6/27/2021

[129] "Bill Willingham Quotes." *Goodreads*, (n.d.), https://www.goodreads.com/author/quotes/12444.Bill_Willingham accessed 6/27/2021

Chapter 6

[130] *Vocabulary.com*, s.v. "matricide," https://www.vocabulary.com/dictionary/matricide accessed 6/27/2021

[132] *Vocabulary.com*, s.v. "uxoricide," https://www.vocabulary.com/dictionary/uxoricide accessed 6/27/2021

[133] *Merriam-Webster Dictionary*, s.v. "cruentation," https://www.merriam-webster.com/dictionary/cruentation accessed 6/27/2021

[134] "Cruentation." *Wikipedia* (2021, June 15), https://en.wikipedia.org/wiki/Cruentation accessed 6/27/2021

[135] *Wiktionary.com*, s.v. "manqueller," https://en.wiktionary.org/wiki/manqueller accessed 6/27/2021

[136] *Merriam-Webster Dictionary*, s.v. "obliterate," https://www.merriam-webster.com/dictionary/obliterate accessed 6/27/2021

[137] "Yayoi Kusama Quotes." *BrainyQuote*, (n.d.), https://www.brainyquote.com/authors/yayoi-kusama-quotes accessed 6/27/2021

[138] *Vocabulary.com*, s.v. "eradicate," https://www.vocabulary.com/dictionary/eradicate accessed 6/27/2021

[139] *"The Mountain of Ignorance* Quotes." *Goodreads*, (n.d.), https://www.goodreads.com/work/quotes/55481990-the-mountain-of-ignorance?page=9 accessed 6/27/2021

[140] *Vocabulary.com*, s.v. "slain," https://www.vocabulary.com/dictionary/slain accessed 6/27/2021

[141] "Tacitus Quotes." *BrainyQuote*, (n.d.), https://www.brainyquote.com/authors/tacitus-quotes accessed 6/27/2021

[142] *Cambridge Dictionary*, s.v. "asphyxiate," https://dictionary.cambridge.org/dictionary/english/asphyxiate accessed 6/27/2021

[143] *Vocabulary.com*, s.v. "asphyxiate," https://www.vocabulary.com/dictionary/asphyxiate accessed 6/27/2021

[144] "Horace Fletcher Quotes." *QuoteFancy*, (n.d.) https://quotefancy.com/horace-fletcher-quotes accessed 6/27/2021

[145] *Cambridge Dictionary*, s.v. "mutilate," https://dictionary.cambridge.org/dictionary/english/mutilate accessed 6/27/2021

[146] *Vocabulary.com*, s.v. "mutilate," https://www.vocabulary.com/dictionary/mutilate accessed 6/27/2021

[147] "Herman Hesse Quotes." *Goodreads*, (n.d.) https://www.goodreads.com/author/quotes/1113469.Hermann_Hesse accessed 6/27/2021

[148] *Cambridge Dictionary*, s.v. "decapitate," https://dictionary.cambridge.org/dictionary/english/decapitate accessed 6/27/2021

[149] *Oxford Learners Dictionary*, s.v. "decapitate," https://www.oxfordlearnersdictionaries.com/definition/english/decapitate accessed 6/27/2021

[150] Roth, Annie, "Meet the Sea Slugs That Chop Off Their Heads and Grow New Bodies." *The New York Times*, (2021, March 8), https://www.nytimes.com/2021/03/08/science/decapitated-sea-slugs.html accessed 6/27/2021

Chapter 7

[151] *Merriam-Webster Dictionary*, s.v. "yore," https://www.merriam-webster.com/dictionary/yore accessed 6/27/2021

[152] *Vocabulary.com*, s.v. "yore," https://www.vocabulary.com/dictionary/yore accessed 6/27/2021

[153] Silva, Horacio, "Why the Pandemic Turned Miami Into the New Monaco." *Town and Country*, (2021, June 3) https://www.townandcountrymag.com/society/money-and-power/a36502002/miami-tech-utopia-post-pandemic/ accessed 6/27/2021

[154] *Vocabulary.com*, s.v. "ephemeral," https://www.vocabulary.com/dictionary/ephemeral accessed 6/27/2021

[155] "Ephemeral Quotes." *AZQuotes*, (n.d.), https://www.azquotes.com/quotes/topics/ephemeral.html accessed 6/27/2021

[156] *Cambridge Dictionary*, s.v. "supersede," https://dictionary.cambridge.org/us/dictionary/english/supersede accessed 6/27/2021

[157] "Henry David Thoreau Quotes." *Goodreads*, (n.d.), https://www.goodreads.com/author/quotes/10264.Henry_David_Thoreau accessed 6/27/2021

[158] *Vocabulary.com*, s.v. "prognosticate," https://www.vocabulary.com/dictionary/prognosticate accessed 6/27/2021

[159] "Donald Trump Quotes." *AZQuotes*, (n.d.), https://www.azquotes.com/author/14823-Donald_Trump accessed 6/27/2021

[160] *Vocabulary.com*, s.v. "preternatural," https://www.vocabulary.com/dictionary/preternatural accessed 6/27/2021

[161] "*Prince Lestat* Quotes." *Goodreads*, (n.d.), https://www.goodreads.com/work/quotes/40713679-prince-lestat accessed 6/27/2021

[162] *Vocabulary.com*, s.v. "perennial," https://www.vocabulary.com/dictionary/perennial accessed 6/27/2021

[163] Kinsley, Michael, "Be a Patriot. Don't Hoard Cipro!" *Time Magazine*, (2001, October 29), http://content.time.com/time/subscriber/article/0,33009,1001073,00.html accessed 6/27/2021

[164] *Dictionary.com*, s.v. "marred," https://www.dictionary.com/browse/marred accessed 6/27/2021

165 *Vocabulary.com*, s.v. "marred," https://www.vocabulary.com/dictionary/marred accessed 6/27/2021

166 "Theodore Roosevelt Quotes." *Goodreads*, (n.d.), https://www.goodreads.com/author/quotes/44567.Theodore_Roosevelt accessed 6/27/2021

167 *Vocabulary.com*, s.v. "hoary," https://www.vocabulary.com/dictionary/hoary accessed 6/27/2021

168 "James Fallows Quotes." *BrainyQuotes*, (n.d.), https://www.brainyquote.com/authors/james-fallows-quotes accessed 6/27/2021

169 *Collins Dictionary*, s.v. "epoch," https://www.collinsdictionary.com/dictionary/english/epoch accessed 6/27/2021

170 "Ludwig Mies van der Rohe Quotes." *BrainyQuote*, (n.d.), https://www.brainyquote.com/authors/ludwig-mies-van-der-rohe-quotes accessed 6/27/2021

171 *Vocabulary.com*, s.v. "biennial," https://www.vocabulary.com/dictionary/biennial accessed 6/27/2021

172 *Merriam-Webster Dictionary*, s.v. "antediluvian," https://www.merriam-webster.com/dictionary/antediluvian accessed 6/27/2021

173 *Vocabulary.com*, s.v. "antediluvian," https://www.vocabulary.com/dictionary/antediluvian accessed 6/27/2021

174 "Antediluvian Quotes." *Goodreads*, (n.d.), https://www.goodreads.com/quotes/tag/antediluvian accessed 6/27/2021

Chapter 8

175 *Collins Dictionary*, s.v. "acrophobia," https://www.collinsdictionary.com/dictionary/english/acrophobia accessed 6/28/2021

176 *Vocabulary.com*, s.v. "acrophobia," https://www.vocabulary.com/dictionary/acrophobia accessed 6/28/2021

[177] *Collins Dictionary*, s.v. "hydrophobia," https://www.collinsdictionary.com/dictionary/english/hydrophobia accessed 6/28/2021

[178] *Vocabulary.com*, s.v. "hydrophobia," https://www.vocabulary.com/dictionary/hydrophobia accessed 6/28/2021

[179] *Merriam-Webster Dictionary*, s.v. "xenophobia," https://www.google.com/url?q=https://www.merriam-webster.com/dictionary/xenophobia accessed 6/28/2021

[180] "Ted Lieu Quotes." *BrainyQuote*, (n.d.), https://www.brainyquote.com/authors/ted-lieu-quotes accessed 6/28/2021

[181] *Collins Dictionary*, s.v. "trepidation," https://www.collinsdictionary.com/dictionary/english/trepidation accessed 6/28/2021

[182] "Michael Bassey Johnson Quotes." *Goodreads*, (n.d.), https://www.goodreads.com/author/quotes/7189272.Michael_Bassey_Johnson accessed 6/28/2021

[183] *Oxford Learners Dictionary*, s.v. "timorous," https://www.oxfordlearnersdictionaries.com/definition/english/timorous accessed 6/28/2021

[184] *Vocabulary.com*, s.v. "timorous," https://www.vocabulary.com/dictionary/timorous accessed 6/28/2021

[185] *Vocabulary.com*, s.v. "pusillanimous," https://www.vocabulary.com/dictionary/pusillanimous accessed 6/28/2021

[186] "Tom Robbins Quotes." *Goodreads*, (n.d.), https://www.goodreads.com/author/quotes/197.Tom_Robbins accessed 6/28/2021

[187] *Cambridge Dictionary*, s.v. "timidity," https://dictionary.cambridge.org/dictionary/english/timidity accessed 6/28/2021

[188] *Vocabulary.com*, s.v. "timidity," https://www.vocabulary.com/dictionary/timidity accessed 6/28/2021

[189] "Walter de la Mare Quotes." *Goodreads*, (n.d.), https://www. goodreads.com/author/quotes/1126.Walter_de_la_Mare accessed 6/28/2021

[190] *Vocabulary.com*, s.v. "eerie," https://www.vocabulary.com/ dictionary/eerie accessed 6/28/2021

[191] "Eerie Quotes." *Goodreads*, (n.d.), https://www.goodreads.com/ quotes/tag/eerie accessed 6/28/2021

[192] *Cambridge Dictionary*, s.v. "titter," https://dictionary.cambridge. org/dictionary/english/titter accessed 6/28/2021

[193] *Collins Dictionary*, s.v. "titter," https://www.collinsdictionary.com/ dictionary/english/titter accessed 6/28/2021

[194] *Merriam-Webster Dictionary*, s.v. "titter," https://www.merriam-webster.com/dictionary/titter accessed 6/28/2021

[195] *Merriam-Webster Dictionary*, s.v. "bugaboo," https://www.google.-com/url?q=https://www.merriam-webster.com/dictionary/bugaboo accessed 6/28/2021

[196] "Robert A. Heinlein Quotes." *Goodreads*, (n.d.), https://www. goodreads.com/author/quotes/205.Robert_A_Heinlein accessed 6/28/2021

Chapter 9

[197] "Battalion." Wikipedia (2021, April 21), https://en.wikipcdia.org/ wiki/Battalion accessed 6/28/2021

[198] *Collins Dictionary*, s.v. "battalion," https://www.collinsdictionary. com/dictionary/english/battalion accessed 6/28/2021

[199] "Voltaire Quotes." *BrainyQuotes*, (n.d.), https://www.brainyquote. com/authors/voltaire-quotes accessed 6/28/2021

200 *Cambridge Dictionary*, s.v. "convalescent," https://dictionary. cambridge.org/dictionary/english/convalescent accessed 6/28/2021

201 "Aldous Huxley Quotes." *BrainyQuote*, (n.d.), https://www. azquotes.com/author/7118-Aldous_Huxley accessed 6/28/2021

202 *Merriam-Webster Dictionary*, s.v. "coxswain," https://www. merriam-webster.com/dictionary/coxswain accessed 6/28/2021

203 *Oxford Learners Dictionary*, s.v. "coxswain," https://www.merriam-webster.com/dictionary/coxswain accessed 6/28/2021

204 "Daniel James Brown Quotes." *Goodreads*, (n.d.), https://www. goodreads.com/author/quotes/486329.Daniel_James_Brown accessed 6/28/2021

206 *Cambridge Dictionary*, s.v. "bivouac," https://dictionary.cambridge. org/dictionary/english/bivouac accessed 6/28/2021

207 *Merriam-Webster Dictionary*, s.v. "bivouac," https://www.merriam-webster.com/dictionary/bivouac accessed 6/28/2021

208 *Vocabulary.com*, s.v. "bivouac," https://www.vocabulary.com/ dictionary/bivouac accessed 6/28/2021

209 "Peter Sagal Quotes." *AZQuotes*, (n.d.), https://www.azquotes.com/ author/58886-Peter_Sagal accessed 6/28/2021

210 *Collins Dictionary*, s.v. "stockade," https://www.collinsdictionary. com/dictionary/english/stockade accessed 6/28/2021

211 *Vocabulary.com*, s.v. "stockade," https://www.vocabulary.com/ dictionary/stockade accessed 6/28/2021

212 Schuessler, Jennifer, "Brooklyn's Muslim Presence Goes Back Centuries. Here's Proof From 1643." *New York Times*, (2019, December 3) https://www.nytimes.com/2019/12/03/arts/design/ Brooklyn-Historical-Society-deed-muslim.html accessed 6/28/2021

213 *Cambridge Dictionary*, s.v. "insurgent," https://dictionary. cambridge.org/dictionary/english/insurgent accessed 6/28/2021

214 "Insurgent Quotes." *AZQuotes*, (n.d.), https://www.azquotes.com/ quotes/topics/insurgent.html accessed 6/28/2021

215 *Collins Dictionary*, s.v. "blitzkrieg," https://www.collinsdictionary. com/dictionary/english/blitzkrieg accessed 6/28/2021

216 *Merriam-Webster Dictionary*, s.v. "blitzkrieg," https://www. merriam-webster.com/dictionary/blitzkrieg accessed 6/28/2021

217 *Collins Dictionary*, s.v. "blitzkrieg," https://www.collinsdictionary. com/dictionary/english/blitzkrieg accessed 6/28/2021

218 "Blitzkrieg." *History.com*, (2019, November 14) https://www. history.com/topics/world-war-ii/blitzkrieg accessed 6/28/2021

219 Seabrook, John, "The E-Scooters Loved by Silicon Valley Roll Into New York." *The New Yorker*, (2021, May 3) https://www.newyorker. com/magazine/2021/04/26/the-e-scooters-loved-by-silicon-valley-roll-into-new-york accessed 6/28/2021

220 *Merriam-Webster Dictionary*, s.v. "espionage," https://www. merriam-webster.com/dictionary/espionage accessed 6/28/2021

221 *Cambridge Dictionary*, s.v. "espionage," https://dictionary. cambridge.org/dictionary/english/espionage accessed 6/28/2021

222 "Espionage Quotes." *AZQuotes*, (n.d.) https://www.azquotes.com/ quotes/topics/espionage.html accessed 6/28/2021

223 *Merriam-Webster Dictionary*, s.v. "furlough," https://www.merriam-webster.com/dictionary/furlough accessed 6/28/2021

224 "Furlough Quotes." *Goodreads*, (n.d.) https://www.goodreads.com/ quotes/tag/furlough accessed 6/28/2021

225 *Cambridge Dictionary*, s.v. "regiment," https://dictionary.cambridge. org/dictionary/english/regiment accessed 6/28/2021

[226] *Oxford Learners Dictionary*, s.v. "regiment," https://www.oxfordlearnersdictionaries.com/definition/english/regiment accessed 6/28/2021

[227] *Dictionary.com*, s.v. "regiment," https://www.dictionary.com/browse/regiment accessed 6/28/2021

[288] "Regiment Quotes." *BrainyQuote*, (n.d.) https://www.brainyquote.com/topics/regiment-quotes accessed 6/28/2021

[229] *Cambridge Dictionary*, s.v. "bellicosity," https://dictionary.cambridge.org/dictionary/english/bellicosity accessed 6/28/2021

[230] *Oxford Learners Dictionary*, s.v. "bellicosity," https://www.oxfordlearnersdictionaries.com/definition/english/bellicosity accessed 6/28/2021

[231] "Joe Klein Quotes." *BrainyQuote*, (n.d.) https://www.brainyquote.com/authors/joe-klein-quotes accessed 6/28/2021

[232] *Cambridge Dictionary*, s.v. "belligerence," https://dictionary.cambridge.org/dictionary/english/belligerence accessed 6/28/2021

[233] *Merriam-Webster Dictionary*, s.v. "belligerence," ttps://www.merriam-webster.com/dictionary/belligerence accessed 6/28/2021

[234] Cohen, Ariel, "To Deter Russia, Hit Them Where It Hurts." *Forbes*, (2021, April 27) https://www.forbes.com/sites/arielcohen/2021/04/27/to-deter-russia-hit-them-where-it-hurts/?sh=239ef7f26c2d accessed 6/28/2021

Chapter 10

[235] *Collins Dictionary*, s.v. "fervency," https://www.collinsdictionary.com/dictionary/english/fervency accessed 6/28/2021

[236] *Cambridge Dictionary*, s.v. "fervent," https://dictionary.cambridge.org/dictionary/english/fervent accessed 6/28/2021

[237] *Vocabulary.com*, s.v. "fervency," https://www.vocabulary.com/dictionary/fervency accessed 6/28/2021

[238] "Fervent Quotes." *AZQuotes*, (n.d.) https://www.azquotes.com/quotes/topics/fervent.html accessed 6/28/2021

[239] *Merriam-Webster Dictionary*, s.v. "infatuation," http://www.merriam-webster.com/dictionary/infatuation accessed 6/28/2021

[240] *Cambridge Dictionary*, s.v. "infatuation," https://dictionary.cambridge.org/dictionary/english/infatuation accessed 6/28/2021

[241] "Infatuation Quotes." *AZQuotes*, (n.d.) https://www.azquotes.com/quotes/topics/infatuation.html accessed 6/28/2021

[242] *Merriam-Webster Dictionary*, s.v. "endearing," https://www.merriam-webster.com/dictionary/endearing accessed 6/28/2021

[243] *Collins Dictionary*, s.v. "endearing," https://www.collinsdictionary.com/dictionary/english/endearing accessed 6/28/2021

[244] "Endearing Quotes." *Goodreads*, (n.d.) https://www.goodreads.com/quotes/tag/endearing accessed 6/28/2021

[245] *Cambridge Dictionary*, s.v. "amorous," https://dictionary.cambridge.org/dictionary/english/amorous accessed 6/28/2021

[246] *Collins Dictionary*, s.v. "amorous," https://dictionary.cambridge.org/dictionary/english/amorous accessed 6/28/2021

[247] "Amorous Quotes." *Goodreads*, (n.d.) https://www.azquotes.com/quotes/topics/amorous.html accessed 6/28/2021

[248] *Merriam-Webster Dictionary*, s.v. "tenderhearted," https://www.merriam-webster.com/dictionary/tenderhearted accessed 6/28/2021

[249] *Cambridge Dictionary*, s.v. "tenderhearted," https://dictionary.cambridge.org/dictionary/english/tender-hearted accessed 6/28/2021

[250] "Tenderhearted Quotes." *YourDictionary.com*, (n.d.), https://quotes.yourdictionary.com/tenderhearted accessed 6/28/2021

[251] *Merriam-Webster Dictionary*, s.v. "oversexed," https://www.merriam-webster.com/dictionary/oversexed accessed 6/28/2021

[252] *Cambridge Dictionary*, s.v. "oversexed," https://dictionary.cambridge.org/dictionary/english/oversexed accessed 6/28/2021

[253] *Collins Dictionary*, s.v. "oversexed," https://www.collinsdictionary.com/dictionary/english/oversexed accessed 6/28/2021

[254] "Oversexed Quotes." *YourDictionary.com*, (n.d.) https://quotes.yourdictionary.com/oversexed accessed 6/28/2021

[255] *Collins Dictionary*, s.v. "amatory," https://www.collinsdictionary.com/dictionary/english/amatory accessed 6/28/2021

[256] *Dictionary.com*, s.v. "affianced," https://www.dictionary.com/browse/affiance accessed 6/28/2021

[257] Trepany, Charles, "Emma Stone and Dave McCary are engaged! They announce it by flashing her ring on Instagram." *USA Today*, (2019, December 4) https://www.usatoday.com/story/entertainment/celebrities/2019/12/04/emma-stone-and-dave-mccary-engaged-you-need-see-ring/2614888001/ accessed 6/28/2021

[258] *Cambridge Dictionary*, s.v. "betrothed," https://dictionary.cambridge.org/dictionary/english/betrothed accessed 6/28/2021

[259] *Merriam-Webster Dictionary*, s.v. "betrothed," https://www.merriam-webster.com/dictionary/betrothed accessed 6/28/2021

[260] *Collins Dictionary*, s.v. "betrothed," https://www.collinsdictionary.com/dictionary/english/betrothed accessed 6/28/2021

[261] "Betrothed Quotes." *Goodreads*, (n.d.) https://www.goodreads.com/quotes/tag/betrothed accessed 6/28/2021

[262] *Cambridge Dictionary*, s.v. "paramour," https://dictionary.cambridge.org/dictionary/english/paramour accessed 6/28/2021

[263] *Merriam-Webster Dictionary*, s.v. "paramour," https://www.merriam-webster.com/dictionary/paramour accessed 6/28/2021

Chapter 11

[264] *Cambridge Dictionary*, s.v. "abominate," https://dictionary.cambridge.org/dictionary/english/abominate accessed 6/29/2021

[265] *Collins Dictionary*, s.v. "abominate," https://www.collinsdictionary.com/dictionary/english/abominate accessed 6/29/2021

[266] "Abomination Quotes." *AZQuotes*, (n.d.) https://www.azquotes.com/quotes/topics/abomination.html accessed 6/29/2021

[267] *Cambridge Dictionary*, s.v. "abhor," https://dictionary.cambridge.org/dictionary/english/abhor accessed 6/29/2021

[268] *Merriam-Webster Dictionary*, s.v. "abhor," https://www.merriam-webster.com/dictionary/abhor accessed 6/29/2021

[269] *Collins Dictionary*, s.v. "abhor," https://www.collinsdictionary.com/dictionary/english/abhor accessed 6/29/2021

[270] "Abhor Quotes." *Goodreads*, (n.d.) https://www.goodreads.com/quotes/tag/abhor accessed 6/29/2021

[271] *Cambridge Dictionary*, s.v. "despise," https://dictionary.cambridge.org/dictionary/english/despise accessed 6/29/2021

[272] *Merriam-Webster Dictionary*, s.v. "despise," https://www.merriam-webster.com/dictionary/despise accessed 6/29/2021

[273] *Collins Dictionary*, s.v. "despise," https://www.collinsdictionary.com/dictionary/english/despise accessed 6/29/2021

[274] "Despise Quotes." *Goodreads*, (n.d.) https://www.azquotes.com/quotes/topics/despise.html accessed 6/29/2021

[275] *Merriam-Webster Dictionary*, s.v. "detest," https://www.merriam-webster.com/dictionary/detest accessed 6/29/2021

[276] *Cambridge Dictionary*, s.v. "detest," https://www.merriam-webster.com/dictionary/detest accessed 6/29/2021

[277] "Detest Quotes." *BrainyQuote*, (n.d.) https://www.brainyquote.com/topics/detest-quotes accessed 6/29/2021

[278] *Merriam-Webster Dictionary*, s.v. "execrate," https://www.merriam-webster.com/dictionary/execrate accessed 6/29/2021

[279] *Collins Dictionary*, s.v. "execrate," https://www.collinsdictionary.com/dictionary/english/execrate accessed 6/29/2021

[280] Will, George, "How can presidential candidates be so silly?" The Dispatch, (2019, July 7) https://www.dispatch.com/opinion/20190707/will-how-can-presidential-candidates-be-so-silly accessed 6/29/2021

[281] *Cambridge Dictionary*, s.v. "loathe," https://dictionary.cambridge.org/dictionary/english/loathe accessed 6/29/2021

[282] *Merriam-Webster Dictionary*, s.v. "loathe," https://www.merriam-webster.com/dictionary/loathe accessed 6/29/2021

[283] "Loathe Quotes." *BrainyQuote*, (n.d.) https://www.brainyquote.com/topics/loathe-quotes accessed 6/29/2021

[284] *Lexico.com*, s.v. "misandrist," https://www.lexico.com/definition/misandrist accessed 6/29/2021

[285] *Dictionary.com*, s.v. "misandrist," https://www.dictionary.com/browse/misandrist accessed 6/29/2021

[286] *Cambridge Dictionary*, s.v. "misandrist," https://dictionary.cambridge.org/dictionary/english/misandrist accessed 6/29/2021

[287] "Misandrist Rhymes." *RhymeZone.com*, (n.d.) https://www.rhymezone.com/r/rhyme.cgi?typeofrhyme=wke&loc=thesql&Word=misandrist accessed 6/29/2021

288 *Dictionary.com*, s.v. "misogynist," https://www.dictionary.com/browse/misogynist accessed 6/29/2021

289 *Merriam-Webster Dictionary*, s.v. "misogynist," https://www.merriam-webster.com/dictionary/misogynist accessed 6/29/2021

290 "Quotes About Misogyny." *Soapboxie.com*, (n.d.) https://soapboxie.com/social-issues/Quotes-about-Misogyny accessed 6/29/2021

291 *Merriam-Webster Dictionary*, s.v. "misanthrope," https://www.merriam-webster.com/dictionary/misanthrope accessed 6/29/2021

292 *Cambridge Dictionary*, s.v. "misanthrope," https://dictionary.cambridge.org/dictionary/english/misanthropy accessed 6/29/2021

293 "Misanthropy Quotes." *AZQuotes*, (n.d.) https://www.azquotes.com/quotes/topics/misanthropy.html accessed 6/29/2021

294 *Dictionary.com*, s.v. "antipathy," https://www.dictionary.com/browse/antipathy accessed 6/29/2021

295 "Antipathy Quotes." *Goodreads*, (n.d.) https://www.goodreads.com/quotes/tag/antipathy accessed 6/29/2021

Chapter 12

296 *Cambridge Dictionary*, s.v. "bawdy," https://dictionary.cambridge.org/dictionary/english/bawdy accessed 6/29/2021

297 *Merriam-Webster Dictionary*, s.v. "bawdy," https://www.merriam-webster.com/dictionary/bawdy accessed 6/29/2021

298 *Vocabulary.com*, s.v. "bawdy," https://www.vocabulary.com/dictionary/bawdy accessed 6/29/2021

299 Carroll, Elle, "Every Cher Movie Performance Ranked." *Vulture*, (2021, May 20) https://www.vulture.com/article/best-cher-movies-ranked.html accessed 6/29/2021

[300] *Cambridge Dictionary*, s.v. "chaste," https://dictionary.cambridge.org/dictionary/english/chaste accessed 6/29/2021

[301] *Merriam-Webster Dictionary*, s.v. "chaste," https://www.merriam-webster.com/dictionary/chaste accessed 6/29/2021

[302] "Chaste Quotes." *Goodreads*, (n.d.) https://www.goodreads.com/quotes/tag/chaste accessed 6/29/2021

[303] *Cambridge Dictionary*, s.v. "lascivious," https://dictionary.cambridge.org/dictionary/english/lascivious accessed 6/29/2021

[304] *Dictionary.com*, s.v. "lascivious," https://www.dictionary.com/browse/lascivious accessed 6/29/2021

[305] *Collins Dictionary*, s.v. "lascivious," https://www.collinsdictionary.com/dictionary/english/lascivious accessed 6/29/2021

[306] *Merriam-Webster Dictionary*, s.v. "lascivious," https://www.merriam-webster.com/dictionary/lascivious accessed 6/29/2021

[307] *Merriam-Webster Dictionary*, s.v. "promiscuous," https://www.merriam-webster.com/dictionary/promiscuous accessed 6/29/2021

[308] *Vocabulary.com*, s.v. "promiscuous," https://www.merriam-webster.com/dictionary/promiscuous accessed 6/29/2021

[309] "Promiscuity Quotes." *AZQuotes*, (n.d.) https://www.azquotes.com/quotes/topics/promiscuity.html accessed 6/29/2021

[310] *Collins Dictionary*, s.v. "satyr," https://www.collinsdictionary.com/dictionary/english/satyr accessed 6/29/2021

[311] Green, Jesse, "Review: 'The Lightning Thief,' a Far Cry From Olympus." *New York Times*, (2019, October 16) https://www.nytimes.com/2019/10/16/theater/review-the-lightning-thief-broadway.html accessed 6/29/2021

[312] *Merriam-Webster Dictionary*, s.v. "salacious," https://www.merriam-webster.com/dictionary/salacious accessed 7/1/2021

[313] *Vocabulary.com*, s.v. "salacious," https://www.vocabulary.com/dictionary/salacious accessed 7/1/2021

[314] Williams, Jason, "Our System Criminalizes Black Pregnancy. As a District Attorney, I Refuse to Prosecute These Cases." *Time*, (2021, May 21) https://time.com/6049587/pregnancy-criminalization/ accessed 7/1/2021

[315] *Collins Dictionary*, s.v. "titillate," https://www.collinsdictionary.com/us/dictionary/english/titillate accessed 7/1/2021

[316] *Vocabulary.com*, s.v. "titillate," https://www.vocabulary.com/dictionary/titillate accessed 7/1/2021

[317] "Tamannaah Quotes." *BrainyQuote*, (n.d.) https://www.brainyquote.com/quotes/tamannaah_971310 accessed 7/1/2021

[318] *Cambridge Dictionary*, s.v. "voluptuous," https://dictionary.cambridge.org/dictionary/english/voluptuous accessed 7/1/2021

[319] *Collins Dictionary*, s.v. "voluptuous," https://www.collinsdictionary.com/dictionary/english/voluptuous accessed 7/1/2021

[320] *Vocabulary.com*, s.v. "voluptuous," https://www.vocabulary.com/dictionary/voluptuous accessed 7/1/2021

[321] "Voluptuous Quotes." *AZQuotes*, (n.d.) https://www.azquotes.com/quotes/topics/voluptuous.html accessed 7/1/2021

[322] *Collins Dictionary*, s.v. "prurient," https://www.collinsdictionary.com/dictionary/english/prurient accessed 7/1/2021

[323] *Vocabulary.com*, s.v. "prurient," https://www.collinsdictionary.com/dictionary/english/prurient accessed 7/1/2021

[324] "Oscar Wilde Quotes." *Goodreads*, (n.d.) https://www.goodreads.com/quotes/266335-when-the-prurient-and-the-impotent-attack-you-be-sure accessed 7/1/2021

[325] *Collins Dictionary*, s.v. "genitals," https://www.collinsdictionary.com/dictionary/english/genitals accessed 7/1/2021

[326] "Genitalia Quotes." *Goodreads*, (n.d.) https://www.goodreads.com/quotes/tag/genitalia accessed 7/1/2021

Chapter 13

[327] *Cambridge Dictionary*, s.v. "nexus," https://dictionary.cambridge.org/dictionary/english/nexus accessed 7/1/2021

[328] *Vocabulary.com*, s.v. "nexus," https://www.vocabulary.com/dictionary/nexus accessed 7/1/2021

[329] "Nexus Quotes." *AZQuotes*, (n.d.) https://www.azquotes.com/quotes/topics/nexus.html accessed 7/1/2021

[330] *Collins Dictionary*, s.v. "conjunction," https://www.collinsdictionary.com/dictionary/english/conjunction accessed 7/1/2021

[331] *Cambridge Dictionary*, s.v. "conjunction," https://dictionary.cambridge.org/dictionary/english/conjunction accessed 7/1/2021

[332] *Merriam-Webster Dictionary*, s.v. "conjunction," https://www.merriam-webster.com/dictionary/conjunction accessed 7/1/2021

[333] "Conjunctions Quotes." *AZQuotes*, (n.d.) https://www.azquotes.com/quotes/topics/conjunctions.html accessed 7/1/2021

[334] *Merriam-Webster Dictionary*, s.v. "coupling," https://www.merriam-webster.com/dictionary/coupling accessed 7/1/2021

[335] "Coupling Quotes." *AZQuotes*, (n.d.) https://www.azquotes.com/quotes/topics/coupling.html accessed 7/1/2021

[336] *Merriam-Webster Dictionary*, s.v. "liaison," https://www.merriam-webster.com/dictionary/liaison accessed 7/1/2021

[337] *Collins Dictionary*, s.v. "liaison," https://www.collinsdictionary. com/dictionary/english/liaison accessed 7/1/2021

[338] "Liaison Quotes." *AZQuotes*, (n.d.) https://www.azquotes.com/ quotes/topics/liaison.html accessed 7/1/2021

[339] *Lexico.com*, s.v. "interconnection," https://www.lexico.com/ definition/interconnection accessed 7/1/2021

[340] *Vocabulary.com*, s.v. "interconnection," https://www.vocabulary. com/dictionary/interconnection accessed 7/1/2021

[341] "Interconnection Quotes." *Goodreads*, (n.d.) https://www. goodreads.com/quotes/tag/interconnection accessed 7/1/2021

[342] *Cambridge Dictionary*, s.v. "disjunction," https://dictionary. cambridge.org/dictionary/english/disjunction accessed 7/1/2021

[343] *Vocabulary.com*, s.v. "disjunction," https://www.vocabulary.com/ dictionary/disjunction accessed 7/1/2021

[344] "Disjunction Quotes." *QuoteStats.com*, (n.d.) https://quotestats. com/topic/disjunction-quotes/ accessed 7/1/2021

[345] *Vocabulary.com*, s.v. "articulation," https://www.vocabulary.com/ dictionary/articulation accessed 7/1/2021

[346] *Collins Dictionary*, s.v. "articulation," https://www. collinsdictionary.com/dictionary/english/articulation accessed 7/1/2021

[347] "Articulation Quotes." *AZQuotes*, (n.d.) https://www.azquotes. com/quotes/topics/articulation.html accessed 7/3/2021

[348] *Collins Dictionary*, s.v. "consanguineous," https://www. collinsdictionary.com/dictionary/english/consanguineous accessed 7/3/2021

[349] *Vocabulary.com*, s.v. "consanguine," https://www.vocabulary.com/ dictionary/consanguine accessed 7/3/2021

[350] *Collins Dictionary*, s.v. "ancestry," https://www.collinsdictionary.com/dictionary/english/ancestry accessed 7/3/2021

[351] "Ancestry Quotes." *BrainyQuote*, (n.d.) https://www.brainyquote.com/topics/ancestry-quotes accessed 7/3/2021

[352] *Cambridge Dictionary*, s.v. "affiliation," https://dictionary.cambridge.org/dictionary/english/affiliation accessed 7/3/2021

[353] *Collins Dictionary*, s.v. "affiliation," https://www.collinsdictionary.com/dictionary/english/affiliation accessed 7/3/2021

[354] "Affiliation Quotes." *AZQuotes*, (n.d.) https://www.azquotes.com/quotes/topics/affiliation.html accessed 7/3/2021

[355] *Cambridge Dictionary*, s.v. "acquaintance," https://dictionary.cambridge.org/dictionary/english/acquaintance accessed 7/3/2021

[356] "Acquaintance Quotes." *AZQuotes*, (n.d.) https://www.azquotes.com/quotes/topics/acquaintance.html accessed 7/3/2021

[357] *Cambridge Dictionary*, s.v. "alliance," https://dictionary.cambridge.org/dictionary/english/alliance accessed 7/3/2021

[358] *Merriam-Webster Dictionary*, s.v. "alliance," https://www.merriam-webster.com/dictionary/alliance accessed 7/3/2021

[359] *Dictionary.com*, s.v. "alliance" https://www.dictionary.com/browse/alliance accessed 7/3/2021

[360] "Alliances Quotes." *Goodreads*, (n.d.) https://www.goodreads.com/quotes/tag/alliances accessed 7/3/2021

Chapter 14

[370] *Merriam-Webster Dictionary*, s.v. "nuptial," https://www.merriam-webster.com/dictionary/nuptial accessed 7/3/2021

[371] *Dictionary.com*, s.v. "nuptial," https://www.dictionary.com/browse/nuptial accessed 7/3/2021

372 Rodriguez, Cecilia, "20 Great Wildlife Photo Winners Of Nature TTL Photographer Of The Year." *Forbes*, (2021, June 6) https://www.forbes.com/sites/ceciliarodriguez/2021/06/06/20-great-wildlife-photo-winners-of-nature-ttl-photographer-of-the-year/?sh=751bc5683fac accessed 7/3/2021

373 *Collins Dictionary*, s.v. "matrimony," https://www.collinsdictionary.com/dictionary/english/matrimony accessed 7/3/2021

374 *Vocabulary.com*, s.v. "matrimony," https://www.vocabulary.com/dictionary/matrimony accessed 7/3/2021

375 "Matrimony Quotes." *AZQuotes*, (n.d.) https://www.azquotes.com/quotes/topics/matrimony.html accessed 7/3/2021

376 *Merriam-Webster Dictionary*, s.v. "espousal," https://www.merriam-webster.com/dictionary/espousal accessed 7/3/2021

377 *Collins Dictionary*, s.v. "espousal," https://www.collinsdictionary.com/dictionary/english/espousal accessed 7/3/2021

378 *Vocabulary.com*, s.v. "espousal," https://www.vocabulary.com/dictionary/espousal accessed 7/3/2021

379 "W.E.B. Du Bois Quotes." *Goodreads*, (n.d.) https://www.goodreads.com/author/quotes/10710.W_E_B_Du_Bois accessed 7/3/2021

380 *Dictionary.com*, s.v. "monogamy," https://www.dictionary.com/browse/monogamy accessed 7/3/2021

381 *Vocabulary.com*, s.v. "monogamy," https://www.vocabulary.com/dictionary/monogamy accessed 7/3/2021

382 "Monogamy Quotes." *AZQuotes*, (n.d.) https://www.azquotes.com/quotes/topics/monogamy.html accessed 7/3/2021

383 *Cambridge Dictionary*, s.v. "connubial," https://dictionary.cambridge.org/dictionary/english/connubial accessed 7/3/2021

[384] *Vocabulary.com*, s.v. "Connubial," https://www.vocabulary.com/dictionary/connubial accessed 7/3/2021

[385] Cusk, Rachel, "Novelist Rachel Cusk on the Complicated Romance of the Maldives." *Condé Nast Traveler*, (2017, February 2), https://www.cntraveler.com/story/novelist-rachel-cusk-on-the-complicated-romance-of-the-maldives accessed 7/3/2021

[386] *Cambridge Dictionary*, s.v. "conjugal," https://dictionary.cambridge.org/dictionary/english/conjugal accessed 7/3/2021

[387] *Vocabulary.com*, s.v. "conjugal," https://www.vocabulary.com/dictionary/conjugal accessed 7/3/2021

[388] "Conjugal Life Quotes." *Goodreads*, (n.d.) https://www.goodreads.com/quotes/tag/conjugal-life accessed 7/3/2021

[389] *Cambridge Dictionary*, s.v. "prenuptial agreement," https://dictionary.cambridge.org/dictionary/english/prenuptial-agreement accessed 7/3/2021

[390] *Dictionary.com*, s.v. "prenuptial," https://www.dictionary.com/browse/prenuptial accessed 7/3/2021

[391] "Quotes About Prenuptial." *InspirationalStories.com*, (n.d.) https://www.inspirationalstories.com/quotes/t/about-prenuptial/ accessed 7/3/2021

[392] *Cambridge Dictionary*, s.v. "annulment," https://dictionary.cambridge.org/dictionary/english/annulment accessed 7/3/2021

[393] *Merriam-Webster Dictionary*, s.v. "annulment," https://www.merriam-webster.com/dictionary/annulment accessed 7/3/2021

[394] *Collins Dictionary*, s.v. "annulment," https://www.collinsdictionary.com/dictionary/english/annulment accessed 7/3/2021

[395] "Annulment Quotes." *Goodreads*, (n.d.) https://www.goodreads.com/quotes/tag/annulment accessed 7/3/2021

[396] *Collins Dictionary*, s.v. "dissolution," https://www.collinsdictionary.com/dictionary/english/dissolution accessed 7/3/2021

[397] *Vocabulary.com*, s.v. "dissolution," https://www.vocabulary.com/dictionary/dissolution accessed 7/3/2021

[398] "Dissolution Quotes." *BrainyQuote*, (n.d.) https://www.brainyquote.com/topics/dissolution-quotes accessed 7/3/2021

[399] *Merriam-Webster Dictionary*, s.v. "alimony," https://www.merriam-webster.com/dictionary/alimony accessed 7/3/2021

[400] "Alimony Quotes." *Goodreads*, (n.d.) https://www.goodreads.com/quotes/tag/alimony accessed 7/3/2021

Chapter 15

[401] *Cambridge Dictionary*, s.v. "progenitor," https://dictionary.cambridge.org/dictionary/english/progenitor accessed 7/3/2021

[402] *Vocabulary.com*, s.v. "progenitor," https://www.vocabulary.com/dictionary/progenitor accessed 7/3/2021

[403] "Cicely Tyson Kept It Together So We Didn't Fall Apart." *New York Times*, (2021, January 29) https://www.nytimes.com/2021/01/29/arts/cicely-tyson.html accessed 7/3/2021

[404] *Vocabulary.com*, s.v. "progeny," https://www.vocabulary.com/dictionary/progeny accessed 7/3/2021

[405] "James Lovelock Quotes." *SuccessStories.com*, (n.d.) https://www.successories.com/iquote/author/1071/james-lovelock-quotes accessed 7/3/2021

[406] *Vocabulary.com*, s.v. "patriarch," https://www.vocabulary.com/dictionary/patriarch accessed 7/3/2021

[407] "Patriarch Quotes." *AZQuotes*, (n.d.) https://www.azquotes.com/quotes/topics/patriarch.html accessed 7/3/2021

408 *Collins Dictionary*, s.v. "filial," https://www.collinsdictionary.com/dictionary/english/filial accessed 7/3/2021

409 *Vocabulary.com*, s.v. "filial," https://www.vocabulary.com/dictionary/filial accessed 7/3/2021

410 "Filial Quotes." *AZQuotes*, (n.d.) https://www.azquotes.com/quotes/topics/filial.html accessed 7/3/2021

411 *Vocabulary.com*, s.v. "antecedent," https://www.vocabulary.com/dictionary/antecedent accessed 7/3/2021

412 "Antecedents Quotes." *Goodreads*, (n.d.) https://www.goodreads.com/quotes/tag/antecedents accessed 7/3/2021

413 *Collins Dictionary*, s.v. "patrimony," https://www.collinsdictionary.com/dictionary/english/patrimony accessed 7/3/2021

414 *Vocabulary.com*, s.v. "patrimony," https://www.vocabulary.com/dictionary/patrimony accessed 7/3/2021

415 "Patrimony Quotes." *AZQuotes*, (n.d.) https://www.azquotes.com/quotes/topics/patrimony.html accessed 7/3/2021

416 *Merriam-Webster Dictionary*, s.v. "nubile," https://www.merriam-webster.com/dictionary/nubile accessed 7/3/2021

417 "Nubile Quotes." *AZQuotes*, (n.d.) https://www.azquotes.com/quote/1038119 accessed 7/3/2021

418 *Collins Dictionary*, s.v. "gentry," https://www.collinsdictionary.com/dictionary/english/gentry accessed 7/3/2021

419 "Gentry Quotes." *Goodreads*, (n.d.) https://www.goodreads.com/quotes/tag/gentry accessed 7/3/2021

420 *Merriam-Webster Dictionary*, s.v. "eugenics," https://www.merriam-webster.com/dictionary/eugenics accessed 7/3/2021

421 *Cambridge Dictionary*, s.v. "eugenics," https://dictionary.cambridge.org/dictionary/english/eugenics accessed 7/3/2021

422 "Eugenics Quotes." *Goodreads*, (n.d.) https://www.goodreads.com/quotes/tag/eugenics accessed 7/3/2021

423 *Vocabulary.com*, s.v. "miscegenation," https://www.vocabulary.com/dictionary/miscegenation accessed 7/3/2021

424 *Collins Dictionary*, s.v. "miscegenation," https://www.collinsdictionary.com/dictionary/english/miscegenation accessed 7/3/2021

425 "Miscegenation Quotes." *AZQuotes*, (n.d.) https://www.azquotes.com/quotes/topics/miscegenation.html accessed 7/3/2021

Chapter 16

426 "Silicon Valley." *Wikipedia*, (2021, July 2) https://en.wikipedia.org/wiki/Silicon_Valley accessed 7/5/2021

427 *Collins Dictionary*, s.v. "Silicon Valley," https://www.collinsdictionary.com/dictionary/english/silicon-valley accessed 7/5/2021

428 "Silicon Valley Quotes." *BrainyQuote*, (n.d.) https://www.brainyquote.com/topics/silicon-valley-quotes accessed 7/5/2021

429 "Innovation." *Wikipedia*, (2021, July 2) https://en.wikipedia.org/wiki/Innovation accessed 7/5/2021

430 "Innovation Quotes." *Viima.com*, (n.d.) https://www.viima.com/blog/innovation-quotes accessed 7/5/2021

431 *Collins Dictionary*, s.v. "encryption," https://www.collinsdictionary.com/dictionary/english/encryption accessed 7/5/2021

432 *Cambridge Dictionary*, s.v. "encryption," https://dictionary.cambridge.org/dictionary/english/encryption accessed 7/5/2021

433 "Encryption Quotes." *AZQuotes*, (n.d.) https://www.azquotes.com/quotes/topics/encryption.html accessed 7/5/2021

434 "Net Neutrality." *Investopedia.com*, (n.d.) https://www.investopedia.com/terms/n/net-neutrality.asp accessed 7/5/2021

435 "Net Neutrality Quotes." *AZQuotes*, (n.d.) https://www.azquotes.com/quotes/topics/net-neutrality.html accessed 7/5/2021

436 *Cambridge Dictionary*, s.v. "clickbait," https://dictionary.cambridge.org/dictionary/english/clickbait accessed 7/5/2021

437 "Clickbait Quotes." *Goodreads.com*, (n.d.) https://www.goodreads.com/quotes/tag/clickbait accessed 7/5/2021

438 *Vocabulary.com*, s.v. "ping," https://www.vocabulary.com/dictionary/ping accessed 7/5/2021

439 "Ping Quotes." *AZQuotes*, (n.d.) https://www.azquotes.com/quotes/topics/ping.html accessed 7/5/2021

440 *Collins Dictionary*, s.v. "botnet," https://www.collinsdictionary.com/dictionary/english/botnet accessed 7/5/2021

441 "Botnet." *Wikipedia*, (2021, July 5) https://en.wikipedia.org/wiki/Botnet accessed 7/5/2021

442 "Botnet Quotes." *Goodreads*, (n.d.) https://www.goodreads.com/quotes/tag/botnet accessed 7/5/2021

443 *Dictionary.com*, s.v. "open-source," https://www.dictionary.com/browse/open-source accessed 7/5/2021

444 "Open-source Software." *Wikipedia*, (2021, July 5) https://en.wikipedia.org/wiki/Open-source_software accessed 7/5/2021

445 "Open-source Quotes." *AZQuotes*, (n.d.) https://www.azquotes.com/quotes/topics/open-source.html accessed 7/5/2021

446 *Dictionary.com*, s.v. "photobomb," https://www.dictionary.com/browse/photobomb# accessed 7/5/2021

447 "Photobomb Quotes." *Goodreads*, (n.d.) https://www.goodreads.com/quotes/tag/photobomb accessed 7/5/2021

[448] *Merriam-Webster Dictionary*, s.v. "face-palm," https://www.merriam-webster.com/dictionary/face-palm accessed 7/5/2021

[449] *Cambridge Dictionary*, s.v. "facepalm," https://dictionary.cambridge.org/dictionary/english/facepalm accessed 7/5/2021

Chapter 17

[450] *Cambridge Dictionary*, s.v. "astute," https://dictionary.cambridge.org/dictionary/english/astute accessed 7/9/2021

[451] *Merriam-Webster Dictionary*, s.v. "astute," https://www.merriam-webster.com/dictionary/astute accessed 7/9/2021

[452] *Vocabulary.com*, s.v. "astute," https://www.vocabulary.com/dictionary/astute accessed 7/9/2021

[453] "Astute Quotes." *BrainyQuote*, (n.d.) https://www.brainyquote.com/topics/astute-quotes accessed 7/9/2021

[454] *Vocabulary.com*, s.v. "uncanny," https://www.vocabulary.com/dictionary/canny accessed 7/9/2021

[455] Mermelstein, David, "'The Human Condition' Review: A Japanese Epic in High-Def." Wall Street Journal, (2021, June 8) https://www.wsj.com/articles/the-human-condition-review-a-japanese-epic-in-high-def-11623187343 accessed 7/9/2021

[456] *Cambridge Dictionary*, s.v. "precocious," https://dictionary.cambridge.org/dictionary/english/precocious accessed 7/9/2021

[457] "Precocious Quotes." *AZQuotes*, (n.d.) https://www.azquotes.com/quotes/topics/precocious.html accessed 7/9/2021

[458] *Cambridge Dictionary*, s.v. "adroit," https://dictionary.cambridge.org/dictionary/english/adroit accessed 7/9/2021

[459] *Merriam-Webster Dictionary*, s.v. "adroit," https://www.merriam-webster.com/dictionary/adroit accessed 7/9/2021

460 *Vocabulary.com*, s.v. "adroit," https://www.vocabulary.com/dictionary/adroit accessed 7/9/2021

461 "Adroit Quotes." *BrainyQuote*, (n.d.) https://www.brainyquote.com/quotes/peter_kropotkin_106274 accessed 7/9/2021

462 *Lexico.com*, s.v. "sagacious," https://www.lexico.com/definition/sagacious accessed 7/9/2021

463 *Vocabulary.com*, s.v. "sagacious," https://www.vocabulary.com/dictionary/sagacious accessed 7/9/2021

464 "Sagacious Quotes." *Goodreads*, (n.d.) https://www.goodreads.com/quotes/tag/sagacious accessed 7/9/2021

465 *Merriam-Webster Dictionary*, s.v. "erudite," https://www.merriam-webster.com/dictionary/erudite accessed 7/9/2021

466 *Vocabulary.com*, s.v. "erudite," https://www.vocabulary.com/dictionary/erudite accessed 7/9/2021

467 "Erudite Quotes." *Goodreads.com*, (n.d.) https://www.goodreads.com/quotes/tag/erudite accessed 7/9/2021

468 *Merriam-Webster Dictionary*, s.v. "virtuoso," https://www.merriam-webster.com/dictionary/virtuoso accessed 7/9/2021

469 *Vocabulary.com*, s.v. "virtuoso," https://www.vocabulary.com/dictionary/virtuoso accessed 7/9/2021

470 "Virtuoso Quotes." *BrainyQuote*, (n.d.) https://www.brainyquote.com/topics/virtuoso-quotes accessed 7/9/2021

471 *Merriam-Webster Dictionary*, s.v. "percipient," https://www.merriam-webster.com/dictionary/percipient accessed 7/9/2021

472 *Vocabulary.com*, s.v. "percipient," https://www.vocabulary.com/dictionary/percipient accessed 7/9/2021

473 *Cambridge Dictionary*, s.v. "percipient," https://dictionary.cambridge.org/dictionary/english/percipient accessed 7/9/2021

474 *Collins Dictionary*, s.v. "ambidextrous," https://www.collinsdictionary.com/dictionary/english/ambidextrous accessed 7/9/2021

475 "Ambidextrous Quotes." *AZQuotes*, (n.d.) https://www.azquotes.com/quotes/topics/ambidextrous.html accessed 7/9/2021

476 *Collins Dictionary*, s.v. "voracious," https://www.collinsdictionary.com/dictionary/english/voracious accessed 7/9/2021

477 "Voracious Quotes." *BrainyQuote*, (n.d.) https://www.brainyquote.com/topics/voracious-quotes accessed 7/9/2021

Chapter 18

478 *Oxford Learners Dictionary*, s.v. "dunce," https://www.oxfordlearnersdictionaries.com/definition/english/dunce accessed 7/9/2021

479 *Collins Dictionary*, s.v. "dunce," https://www.collinsdictionary.com/dictionary/english/dunce accessed 7/9/2021

480 "Dunce Quotes." *BrainyQuotes*, (n.d.) https://www.brainyquote.com/topics/dunce-quotes accessed 7/9/2021

481 *Collins Dictionary*, s.v. "simpleton," https://www.collinsdictionary.com/dictionary/english/simpleton accessed 7/9/2021

482 "Simpleton Quotes." *BrainyQuote*, (n.d.) https://www.brainyquote.com/quotes/miguel de_cervantes_157060 acccssed 7/9/2021

483 *Collins Dictionary*, s.v. "dullard," https://www.collinsdictionary.com/dictionary/english/dullard accessed 7/9/2021

484 *Vocabulary.com*, s.v. "dullard," https://www.vocabulary.com/dictionary/dullard accessed 7/9/2021

485 "Quotes About Dullard." *WiseFamousQuotes.com*, (n.d.) https://www.wisefamousquotes.com/quotes-about-dullard/ accessed 7/9/2021

486 *Cambridge Dictionary*, s.v. "ignoramus," https://dictionary.cambridge.org/dictionary/english/ignoramus accessed 7/9/2021

487 *Collins Dictionary*, s.v. "ignoramus," https://www.collinsdictionary.com/dictionary/english/ignoramus accessed 7/9/2021

488 *Vocabulary.com*, s.v. "ignoramus," https://www.vocabulary.com/dictionary/ignoramus accessed 7/9/2021

489 "Ignoramus Quotes." *YourDictionary.com*, (n.d.) https://quotes.yourdictionary.com/ignoramus accessed 7/9/2021

490 *Vocabulary.com*, s.v. "dolt," http://vocabulary.com/dictionary/dolt accessed 7/9/2021

491 "Dolt Quotes." *QuoteStats*, (n.d.) https://quotestats.com/topic/dolt-quotes/ accessed 7/9/2021

492 "Quotes About Nincompoop." *WiseFamousQuotes.com*, (n.d.) https://www.wisefamousquotes.com/quotes-about-nincompoop/ accessed 7/9/2021

493 *Collins Dictionary*, s.v. "lunkhead," https://www.collinsdictionary.com/dictionary/english/lunkhead accessed 7/9/2021

494 "Lunkhead Quotes." *Goodreads*, (n.d.) https://www.goodreads.com/quotes/34952-with-such-disappointing-lunkheads-for-parents-naturally-petunia-must-leave accessed 7/9/2021

495 *Vocabulary.com*, s.v. "nitwit," https://www.vocabulary.com/dictionary/nitwit accessed 7/9/2021

496 Margenau, Tom, "Setting the record straight: Internet lies about Social Security never go away." *The Dallas Morning News*, (2020, September 13) https://www.dallasnews.com/sponsored/2020/09/13/

setting-the-record-straight-internet-lies-about-social-security-never-go-away/ accessed 7/9/2021

[497] *Collins Dictionary*, s.v. "dimwit," https://www.collinsdictionary.com/dictionary/english/dimwit accessed 7/9/2021

[498] "Dimwits Quotes." *AZQuotes*, (n.d.) https://www.azquotes.com/quotes/topics/dimwits.html accessed 7/9/2021

[499] *Collins Dictionary*, s.v. "cretin," https://www.collinsdictionary.com/dictionary/english/cretin accessed 7/9/2021

[500] *Collins Dictionary*, s.v. "cretinism," https://www.collinsdictionary.com/dictionary/english/cretinism accessed 7/9/2021

[501] "Cretin Quotes." *Goodreads*, (n.d.) https://www.goodreads.com/quotes/449222-each-of-us-is-sometimes-a-cretin-a-fool-a accessed 7/9/2021

Chapter 19

[502] *Merriam-Webster Dictionary*, s.v. "winsome," https://www.merriam-webster.com/dictionary/winsome accessed 7/9/2021

[503] "Winsome Quotes." *AZQuotes*, (n.d.) https://www.azquotes.com/quotes/topics/winsome.html accessed 7/9/2021

[504] *Collins Dictionary*, s.v. "resplendent," https://www.collinsdictionary.com/dictionary/english/resplendent accessed 7/9/2021

[505] *Vocabulary.com*, s.v. "resplendent," https://www.vocabulary.com/dictionary/resplendent accessed 7/9/2021

[506] "Resplendent Quotes." *YourDictionary.com*, (n.d.) https://quotes.yourdictionary.com/resplendent accessed 7/9/2021

[507] *Vocabulary.com*, s.v. "pulchritude," https://www.vocabulary.com/dictionary/pulchritude accessed 7/9/2021

[508] "Review: Idina Menzel lights up the sexy-neurotic comedy 'Skintight' at the Geffen Playhouse." *Los Angeles Times*, (2019, September 13), https://www.latimes.com/entertainment-arts/story/2019-09-13/idina-menzel-skintight-geffen-playhouse-review accessed 7/9/2021

[509] *Collins Dictionary*, s.v. "debonair," https://www.collinsdictionary.com/dictionary/english/debonair avvessed 7/9/2021

[510] *Vocabulary.com*, s.v. "debonair," https://www.vocabulary.com/dictionary/debonair accessed 7/9/2021

[511] Yarborough, Kaitlyn, "What Does It Really Mean To Have Southern Taste?" *Southern Living*, (n.d.) https://www.southernliving.com/culture/southern-in-taste accessed 7/9/2021

[512] *Merriam-Webster Dictionary*, s.v. "dapper," https://www.merriam-webster.com/dictionary/dapper accessed 7/9/2021

[513] *Vocabulary.com*, s.v. "dapper," https://www.vocabulary.com/dictionary/dapper accessed 7/9/2021

[514] "Dapper Quotes." *AZQuotes*, (n.d.) https://www.azquotes.com/quotes/topics/dapper.html accessed 7/9/2021

[515] *Vocabulary.com*, s.v. "adorn," https://www.azquotes.com/quotes/topics/dapper.html accessed 7/9/2021

[516] "Adorn Quotes." *BrainyQuote*, (n.d.) https://www.brainyquote.com/topics/adorn-quotes accessed 7/9/2021

[517] *Vocabulary.com*, s.v. "comely," https://www.vocabulary.com/dictionary/comely accessed 7/9/2021

[518] "John Bunyan Quotes." *QuoteFancy*, (n.d.) https://quotefancy.com/quote/1113508/John-Bunyan-A-comely-sight-indeed-it-is-to-see-a-world-of-blossoms-on-an-apple-tree accessed 7/9/2021

[519] *Cambridge Dictionary*, s.v. "bewitching," https://dictionary.cambridge.org/dictionary/english/bewitching accessed 7/9/2021

520 *Collins Dictionary*, s.v. "bewitching," https://www.collinsdictionary.com/dictionary/english/bewitching accessed 7/9/2021

521 *Vocabulary.com*, s.v. "bewitching," https://www.vocabulary.com/dictionary/bewitching accessed 7/9/2021

522 "Bewitching Quotes." *Goodreads*, (n.d.) https://www.goodreads.com/quotes/tag/bewitching accessed 7/9/2021

523 *Vocabulary.com*, s.v. "elegant," https://www.vocabulary.com/dictionary/elegant accessed 7/9/2021

524 "Elegant Quotes." *Goodreads*, (n.d.) https://www.goodreads.com/quotes/tag/elegant accessed 7/9/2021

525 *Vocabulary.com*, s.v. "aristocratic," https://www.vocabulary.com/dictionary/aristocratic accessed 7/9/2021

526 "Aristocratic Quotes." *BrainyQuotes*, (n.d.) https://www.brainyquote.com/topics/aristocratic-quotes accessed 7/9/2021

Chapter 11

527 *Vocabulary.com*, s.v. "repulsive," https://www.vocabulary.com/dictionary/repulsive accessed 7/10/2021

528 "Repulsive Quotes." *Goodreads*, (n.d.) https://www.goodreads.com/quotes/tag/repulsive accessed 7/10/2021

529 *Collins Dictionary*, s.v. "grotesque," https://www.collinsdictionary.com/dictionary/english/grotesque accessed 7/10/2021

530 "Grotesque Quotes." *AZQuotes*, (n.d.) https://www.azquotes.com/quotes/topics/grotesque.html accessed 7/10/2021

531 *Collins Dictionary*, s.v. "horrid," https://www.azquotes.com/quotes/topics/grotesque.html accessed 7/10/2021

532 *Vocabulary.com*, s.v. "horrid," https://www.vocabulary.com/dictionary/horrid accessed 7/10/2021

[533] "Horrid Quotes." *BrainyQuote*, (n.d.) https://www.brainyquote.com/topics/horrid-quotes accessed 7/10/2021

[534] *Cambridge Dictionary*, s.v. "abhorrent," https://dictionary.cambridge.org/dictionary/english/abhorrent accessed 7/10/2021

[535] *Merriam-Webster Dictionary*, s.v. "abhorrent," https://www.merriam-webster.com/dictionary/abhorrent accessed 7/10/2021

[536] "Abhorrent Quotes." *AZQuotes*, (n.d.) https://www.azquotes.com/quotes/topics/abhorrent.html accessed 7/10/2021

[537] *Collins Dictionary*, s.v. "disagreeable," https://www.collinsdictionary.com/dictionary/english/disagreeable accessed 7/10/2021

[538] *Vocabulary.com*, s.v. "disagreeable," https://www.vocabulary.com/dictionary/disagreeable accessed 7/10/2021

[539] "Disagreeable Quotes." *BrainyQuote*, (n.d.) https://www.brainyquote.com/topics/disagreeable-quotes accessed 7/10/2021

[540] *Collins Dictionary*, s.v. "obnoxious," https://www.collinsdictionary.com/dictionary/english/obnoxious accessed 7/10/2021

[541] *Vocabulary.com*, s.v. "obnoxious," https://www.vocabulary.com/dictionary/obnoxious accessed 7/10/2021

[542] "Obnoxious Quotes." *AZQuotes*, (n.d.) https://www.azquotes.com/quotes/topics/obnoxious.html accessed 7/10/2021

[543] *Collins Dictionary*, s.v. "crone," https://www.collinsdictionary.com/dictionary/english/crone accessed 7/10/2021

[544] *Vocabulary.com*, s.v. "crone," https://www.vocabulary.com/dictionary/crone accessed 7/10/2021

[545] "Crone Quotes." *Goodreads*, (n.d.) https://www.goodreads.com/quotes/tag/crone accessed 7/10/2021

[546] *Collins Dictionary*, s.v. "beldam," https://www.collinsdictionary.com/dictionary/english/beldam accessed 7/10/2021

[547] *Cambridge Dictionary*, s.v. "grisly," https://dictionary.cambridge.org/dictionary/english/grisly accessed 7/10/2021

[548] *Collins Dictionary*, s.v. "grisly," https://www.collinsdictionary.com/dictionary/english/grisly accessed 7/10/2021

[549] *Vocabulary.com*, s.v. "grisly," https://www.collinsdictionary.com/dictionary/english/grisly accessed 7/10/2021

[550] "Grisly Quotes." *Goodreads*, (n.d.) https://www.goodreads.com/quotes/tag/grisly accessed 7/10/2021

[551] *Dictionary.com*, s.v. "revolting," https://www.dictionary.com/browse/revolting accessed 7/10/2021

[552] *Merriam-Webster Dictionary*, s.v. "revolting," https://www.merriam-webster.com/dictionary/revolting accessed 7/10/2021